IMAGES
of America

WIRT COUNTY

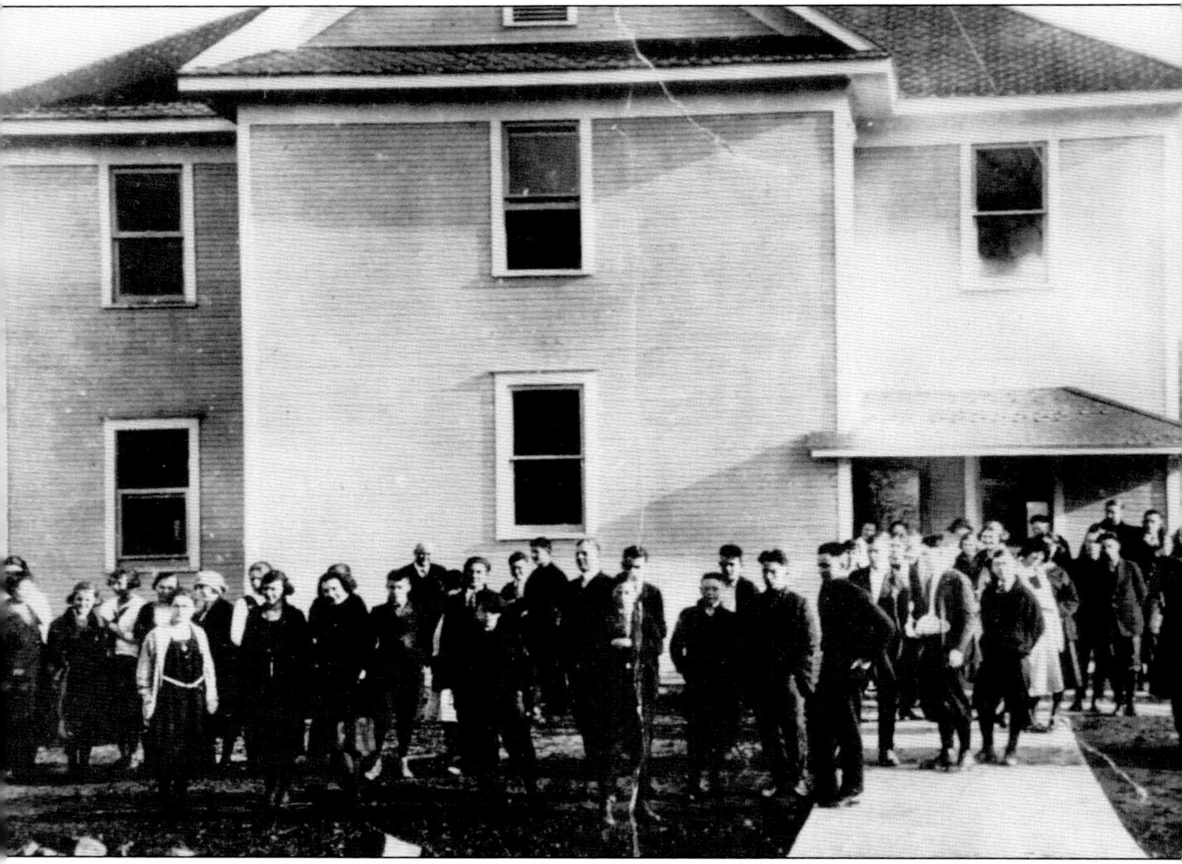

Elizabeth High School was built on Mulberry Street in the summer of 1920. C. H. Snodgrass was the principal during the 1920–1921 school term, when this photograph was taken. (Courtesy of the Ludwig family.)

On the Cover: I. P. Thorn opened this general merchandise store in the Dulin community near Palestine in the early 1900s. This photograph taken in 1908 shows I. P. (right) leaning against the porch post of his general store. The store offered its patrons a wide variety of everyday staples and useful implements necessary for country living. I. P. eventually moved from this location and reopened a store in Elizabeth with his son Van W. Thorn. Together they ran the store until I. P.'s death in 1937. The family grocery business continued from 1946 with Van W. and his son Richard "Dick" Thorn until Van's death in 1958. From that time, Dick continued the business as Dick's Market in Elizabeth until his retirement in the mid-1990s. Today the market is owned and operated by his sons Dean and Greg. (Courtesy of Betty Thorn.)

IMAGES
of America

WIRT COUNTY

Richard T. Lowe

ARCADIA
PUBLISHING

ISBN 978-0-7385-6679-5

Published by Arcadia Publishing
Charleston, South Carolina

Printed in the United States of America

Library of Congress Control Number: 2009934085

For all general information contact Arcadia Publishing at:
Telephone 843-853-2070
Fax 843-853-0044
E-mail sales@arcadiapublishing.com
For customer service and orders:
Toll-Free 1-888-313-2665

Visit us on the Internet at www.arcadiapublishing.com

To my loving parents, Bob and Gayle Lowe. Thanks for always inspiring me to take on projects like this!

Contents

Acknowledgments

It seems like only yesterday that I contacted Arcadia Publishing about developing a history book for Wirt County. Shortly thereafter, I found myself with a new project—Images of America: *Wirt County*. Realizing that this was a major undertaking, I recruited support from my community to gather a collection of photographs and historical information that represents Wirt County's rich history. This project would not have been possible without the help of others. I first want to thank everyone who contributed photographs and information for this book. A special thank-you goes out to the Wirt County Chapter of the Daughters of the American Pioneers (DAP) for sharing rare photographs contained in this book. I especially want to thank Carole Menefee and Susan Kirby for the time they spent helping me scan photographs at the museum—you guys are awesome! Words cannot express my gratitude for all you did to make this history book a reality. Additionally, I would like to thank the following people who supported this project: Marjorie Mayes, Sherry Smith, Russ Snyder, Betty Thorn, Sue Douglas, Linda Sams, Debbie Hennen, Bob and Gayle Lowe, the Ludwig family, Debbie Hartshorn, Waneta Thorn Lawrence, Elizabeth-Wirt Volunteer Fire Department (VFD), Paula Licklider Smith, James Matheny, Ann Cale Boyce, Wirt County Fair Association, Helen Burns, Mildred Kirby, Diane Ludwig, Annabelle Snider, the West Virginia Department of Culture and History, Lori Lee Siers, Randall James, Basil Cline, and Robert Lowe. All photographs are from the author's collection unless otherwise noted.

Introduction

Wirt County, a picturesque community centered in the heart of the Little Kanawha Valley, was named in honor of the famed author and statesman William Wirt by an act of the Virginia General Assembly on January 19, 1848. Wirt was born on November 8, 1772, in Bladensburg, Prince George's County, Maryland, and died at the age of 61 on February 18, 1834, in Washington, D.C. Wirt was admitted to the bar at Culpeper Courthouse, Virginia, after receiving his education from Georgetown. By 1799, Wirt was appointed the clerk of the Virginia House of Delegates, and in 1802, he was appointed chancellor of the eastern judicial district. Wirt gained national attention in 1807, when he was appointed by Pres. Thomas Jefferson to represent the United States in the trial of Vice Pres. Aaron Burr, who was accused of treason. Wirt went on to be appointed the ninth U.S. attorney general under Pres. James Monroe's administration in 1817 and held the office for 12 consecutive years—he holds the record for longest tenure as attorney general.

When formed in 1848, Wirt County was comprised of parts of Wood and Jackson Counties, contained approximately 187,000 acres, and was bordered by the counties of Wood, Ritchie, Calhoun, Roane, and Jackson. Wirt County's first settler was William Beauchamp, who came to the area in 1796. He was born in 1743 and died on October 11, 1808, at 65 years of age. Beauchamp, recognizing the economic potential that the river offered, quickly built a gristmill on the waters of the Little Kanawha River and named it Beauchamp's Mill. His son David married Elizabeth Woodyard and changed the name of the settlement to Elizabeth in her honor. David operated the family's gristmill until it burned to the ground. Afterward, David and Elizabeth took their 17-year-old son Alfred and left the area. Alfred eventually returned to his hometown of Elizabeth around 1835 and built a grand redbrick home near the Little Kanawha River. Alfred was a noted community leader whose service was recognized by the Virginia General Assembly when the county was first formed. The assembly selected the Beauchamp home as the meeting place of the first county court. The home still stands today and has been converted into the Beauchamp-Newman Museum. This was as a result of Alfred's grandson, R. B. Newman, working with community leaders to secure the funding to preserve the home and turn it into a museum that houses heirlooms from the county's rich history.

Although Wirt County is the smallest county in the state of West Virginia, both in terms of population and geographic area, this has not always been the case. When the oil and gas industry boomed here in its infancy around 1859, the county's population soared to record numbers as news of the greatest petroleum-producing region was publicized in headlines across the globe. Thousands of fortune seekers rushed to the Burning Springs area of Wirt County in hopes of striking it rich in the oil business. The number of arrivals to the Burning Springs area was so overwhelming that it was compared to San Francisco, California, during the great California Gold Rush that happened 11 years earlier.

During this period of industrial growth and prosperity in Wirt County, the Little Kanawha River soon became a valued source of trade and survival. Travel from Parkersburg to Wirt County by horse and buggy was extremely difficult. Most people traveling to Wirt County did so by riverboat. This, too, was a slow pilgrimage. To make the rivers more navigable by boat, a series of locks and dams were built in the late 1870s. These efforts made it possible to ship thousands of barrels of oil down the Little Kanawha River to Parkersburg, where they were loaded onto the Baltimore and Ohio Railroad and transported across the country.

As a thriving source for the nation's oil production, Burning Springs attracted the unwanted attention of the Confederate raiding parties. On May 9, 1863, Burning Springs fell to the fate of the Civil War. Gen. William Jones and Gen. John Imboden led 1,500 Confederate soldiers to Burning Springs for the purpose of destroying the oil fields and preventing any tax from being collected on the oil by the U.S. government. Pres. Abraham Lincoln sought to protect the nation's oil investments by supporting West Virginia's admission into the Union. On June 20, 1863, West Virginia was admitted to the Union and became the only state to be born out of the conflict of the Civil War.

A new oil boom started in 1865; however, the county eventually settled back into sleepy obscurity, emerging into the national spotlight again only in 2003, when the miracle recovery of captured U.S. soldier and Wirt County resident Pvt. Jessica Lynch brought over 300 members of the national media into the county.

Wirt County remains a quiet bedroom community with a population approximately 6,000 strong. The majority of the county's working population drives to other counties for employment, returning home at the end of the day to enjoy the quiet, peaceful lifestyle a small community offers. The area is growing again, albeit at a much slower rate than in the past. Many people move here, drawn by the beautiful scenery, affordable housing and land, and award-winning school system.

This book—Images of America: *Wirt County*—was intended to capture the spirit of Wirt County and her people and share the rich history that the tiny county has to offer. I hope you find this book informative and enjoyable.

One

The Early Years

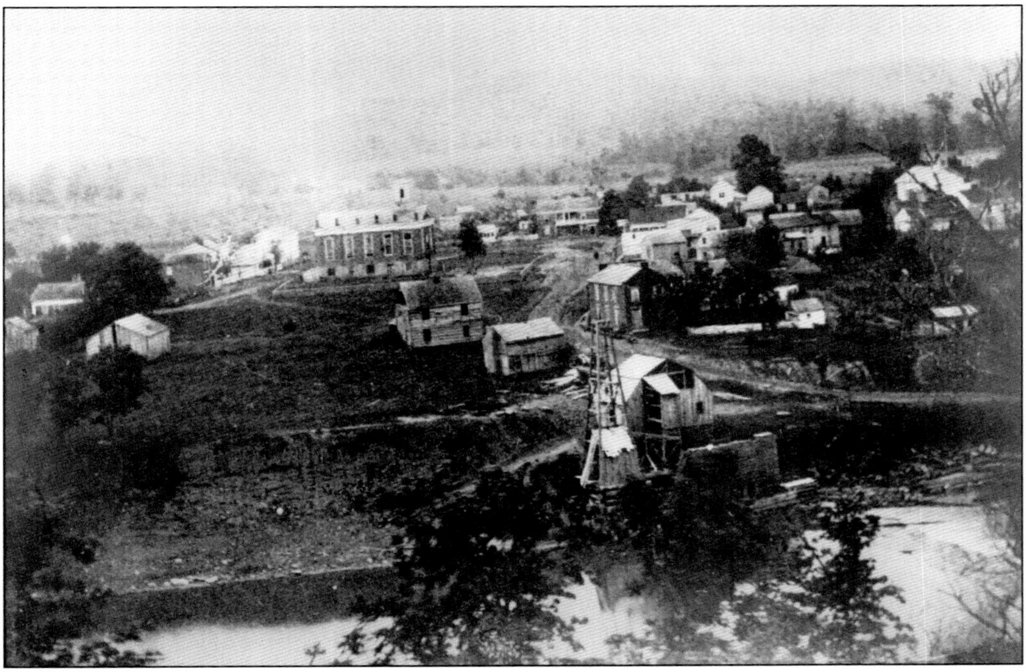

This early photograph of Elizabeth was taken around the Civil War. The town was named in honor of Elizabeth Woodyard Beauchamp in 1822. Prior to its incorporation, the village was known as Beauchamp's Mill. The Beauchamp family operated a water-powered gristmill along the banks of the Little Kanawha River until the mill burned. Traces of the mill can be seen in the lower portion of this photograph. The upper log structure was built about 1800 by Manlove Beauchamp, and the original Wirt County Courthouse can be seen in the distance. (Courtesy of Marjorie F. Mayes.)

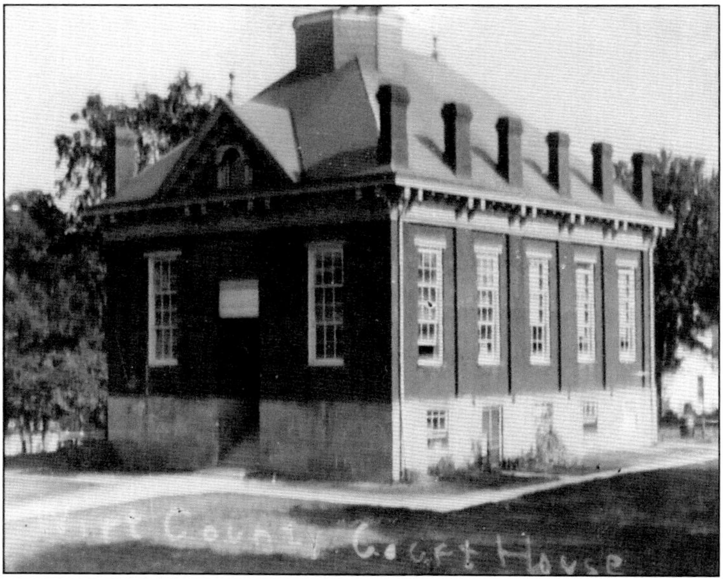

Construction of Wirt County's first courthouse started in 1848, shortly after Thomas Tavenner conveyed 1 acre of land to Justices Henry Steed, William Sheppard, Thomas Boggs, and Charles Rector for a building site for the courthouse. This structure is where fortune seekers turned oil industry moguls recorded some of the world's first oil leases. The courthouse was destroyed by fire in the spring of 1909. (Courtesy of the DAP.)

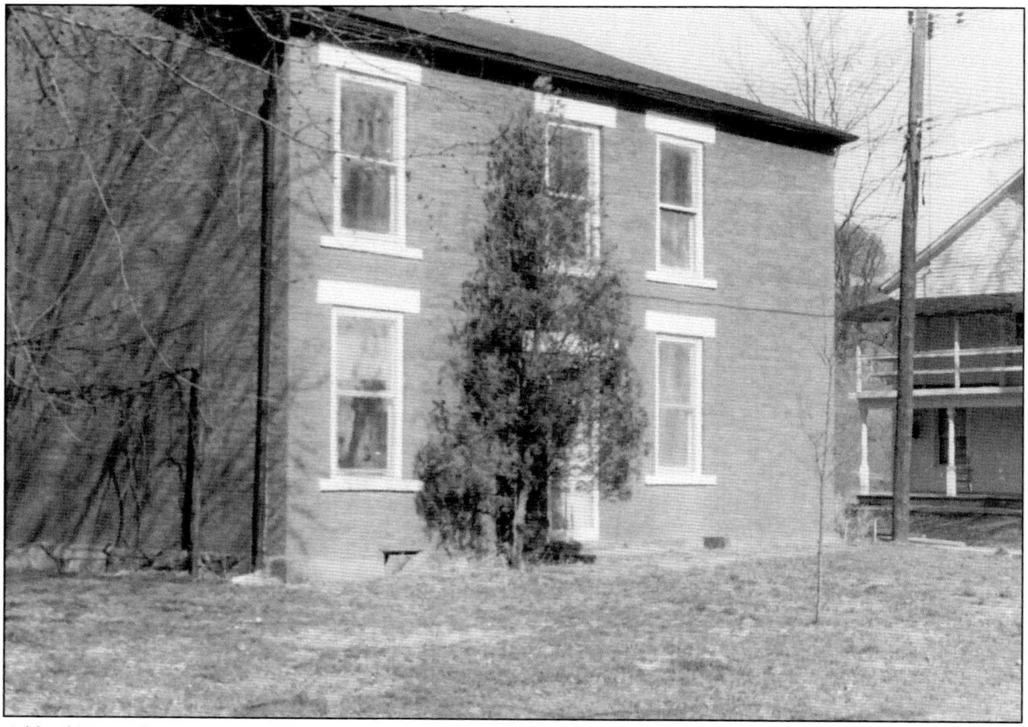

Alfred Beauchamp moved from the area with his father and mother—David and Elizabeth—when he was just 17. Following the death of his father, Alfred returned to his hometown around 1835 and built a grand redbrick home. The Beauchamp home was later selected by the Virginia General Assembly as the meeting place of the first county court of the newly formed Wirt County. It is now the Beauchamp-Newman Museum, which houses many heirlooms from the county's early days. (Courtesy of the DAP.)

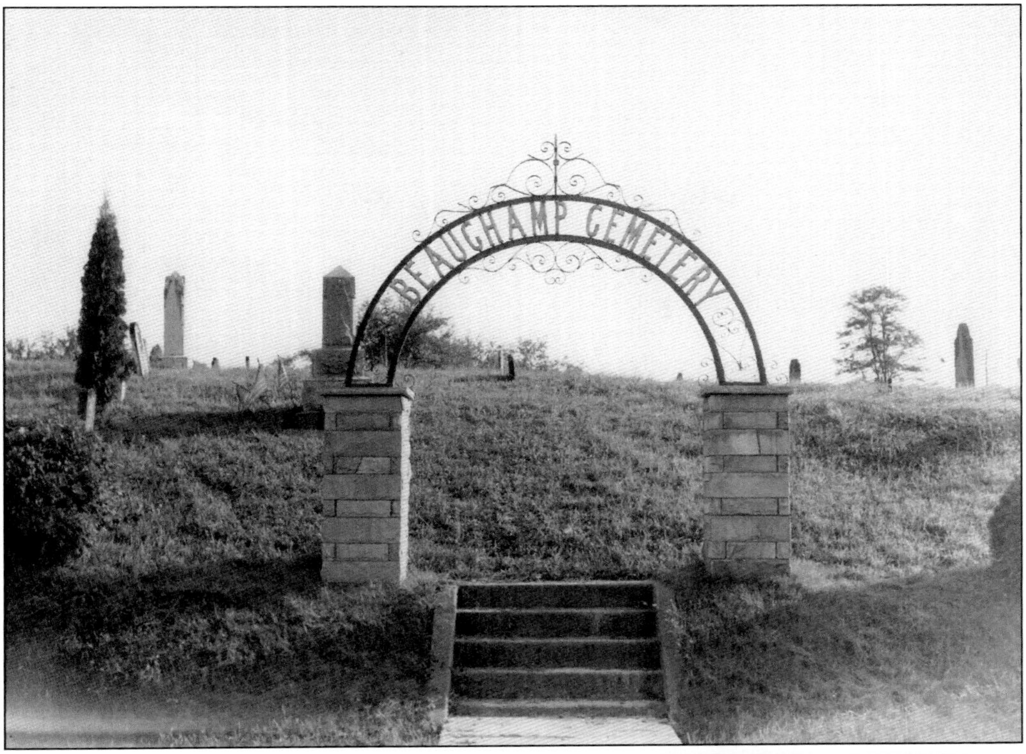

Hailed as a landmark, the Beauchamp-Newman Cemetery inters members of the Beauchamp family along with a number of the county's early settlers. Wirt County's first settler—William Beauchamp—died on October 11, 1808. The cemetery also includes the graves of William's son and daughter-in-law, David Beauchamp and Elizabeth Woodyard Beauchamp. (Courtesy of the DAP.)

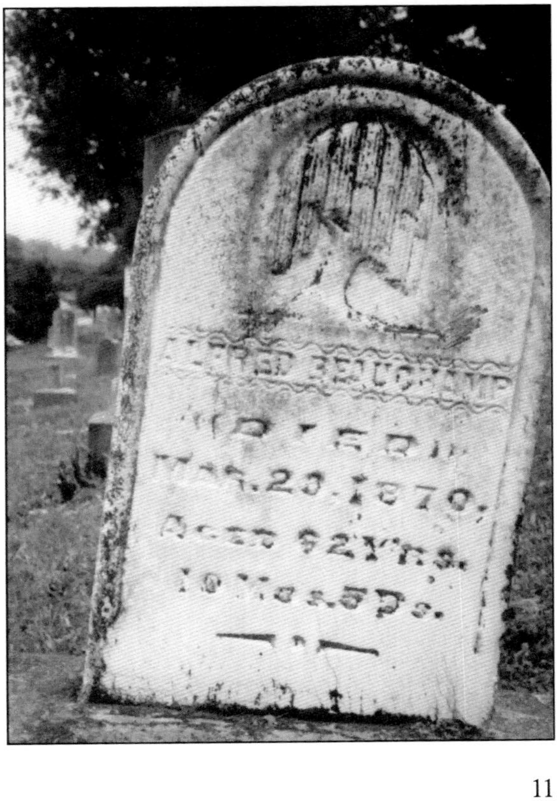

Alfred Beauchamp, grandson of Wirt County's first settler, William Beauchamp, died on March 29, 1870, at the age of 62 years, 10 months, and 5 days. Alfred was a noted community leader whose service was recognized by the Virginia General Assembly in the bill that created Wirt County from parts of Wood and Jackson Counties. The bill called for the justices of the peace to hold court at his grand redbrick home in Elizabeth, which now serves as the Beauchamp-Newman Museum. (Courtesy of the DAP.)

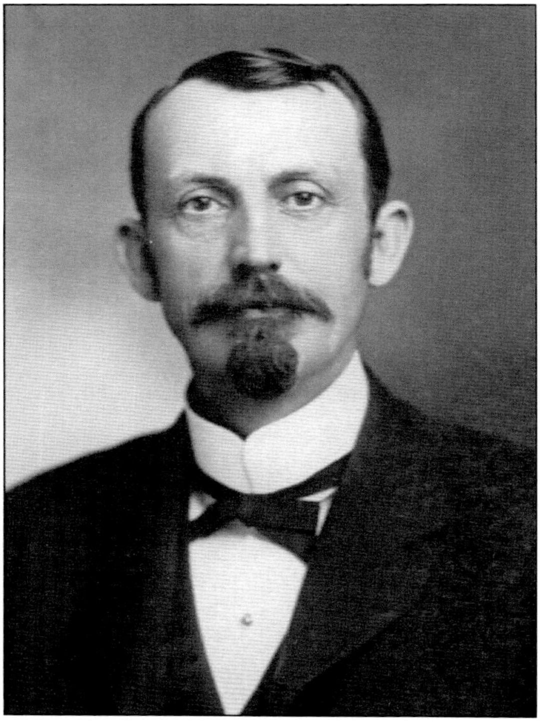

Photographs such as this one of Lewis N. Tavenner were taken during a time when images were transferred onto glass. Lewis was a descendant of Alfred Beauchamp. (Courtesy of the DAP.)

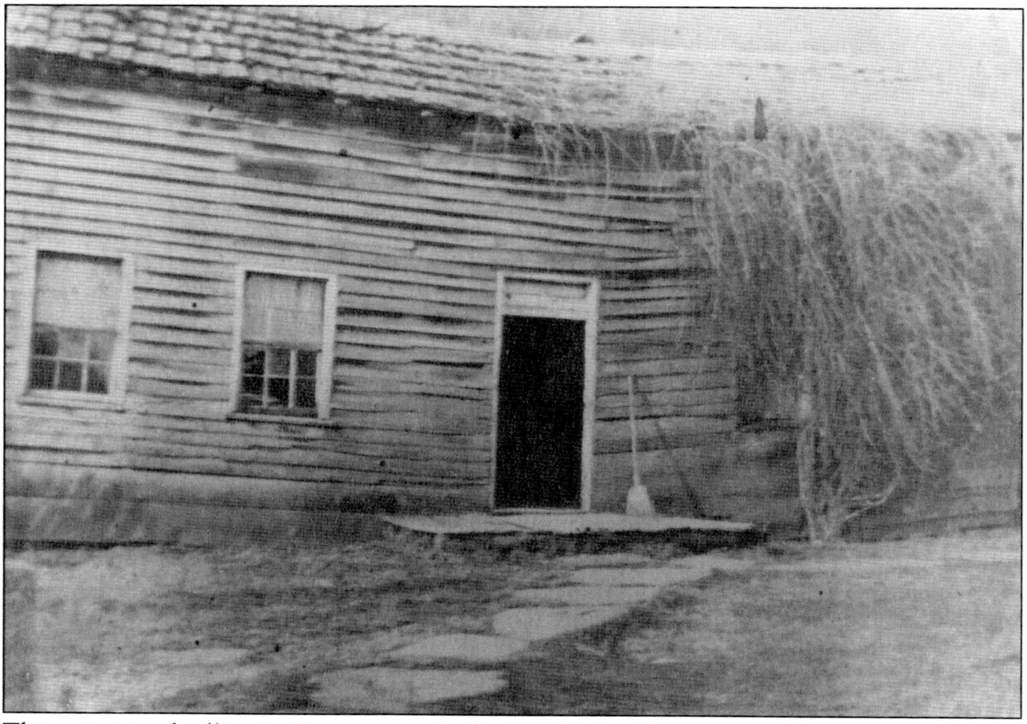

This primitive dwelling in Creston was the home of Robert B. Newman. The house dates back to the late 1800s. (Courtesy of the DAP.)

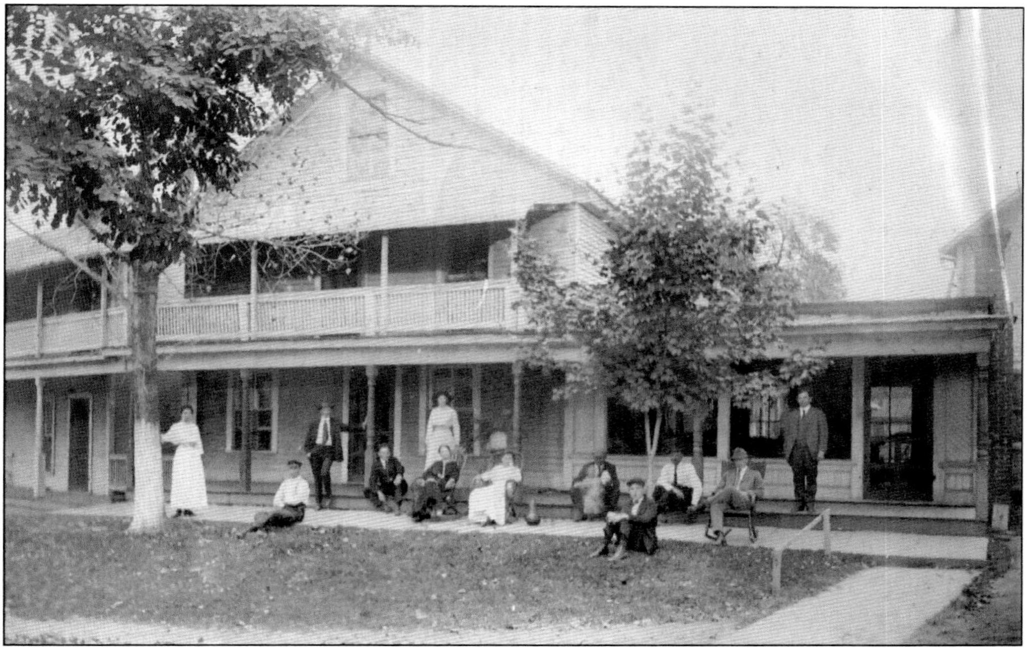

Manlove Beauchamp built this hand-hewn log house around 1800. The house is situated on the east side of Court Street in Elizabeth, on the banks of the Little Kanawha River. It was later converted into the Little Kanawha Hotel and provided a safe haven to travelers visiting the area. The hotel was purchased by Bob and Winnie Murray in the mid-1980s and is still open for tours on special occasions.

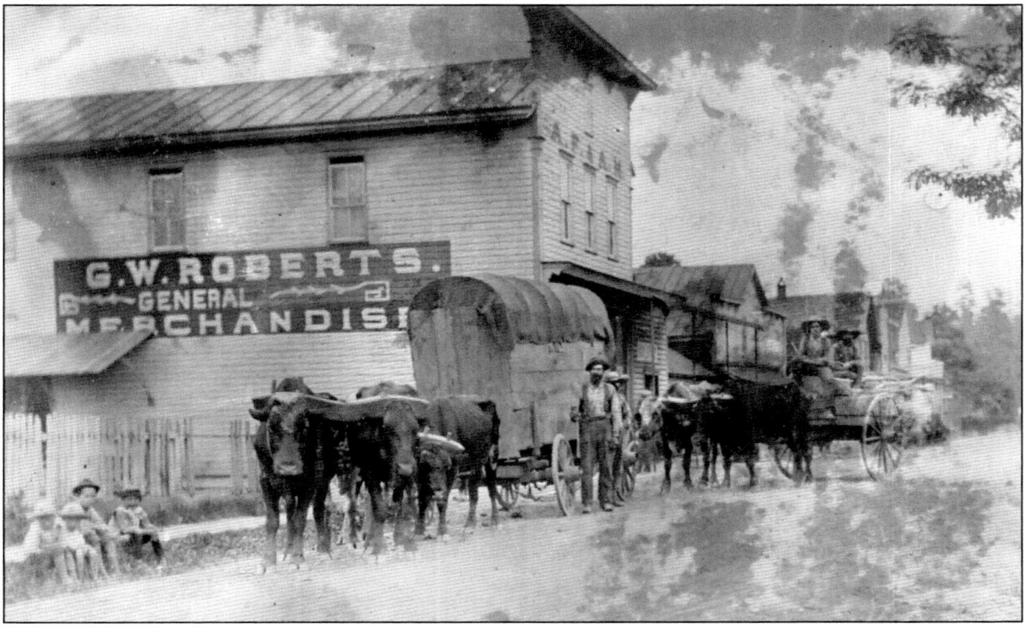

This *c.* 1887 Elizabeth street scene shows a team of oxen in front of Roberts Store. George W. Roberts established the general store on the corner of Court and Juliana Streets in 1886. (Courtesy of Susan Kirby.)

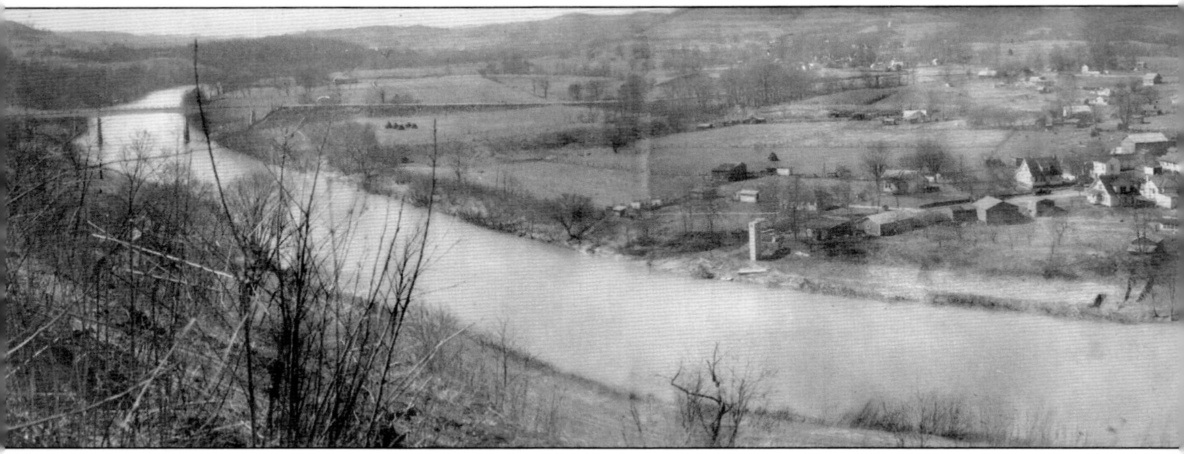

This panoramic view of Elizabeth was taken from atop the hill on State Route 53 in the 1950s. It shows the waters of the Little Kanawha River meandering around the perimeter of the town. The bridge across the Little Kanawha River on State Route 5 was opened on December 1, 1949.

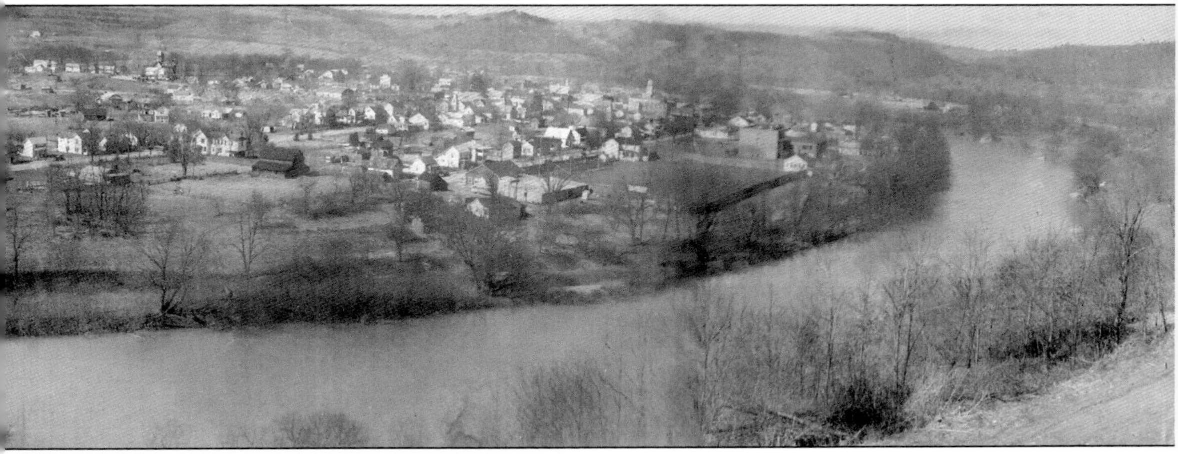

Elizabeth supported several stores, a funeral home, schools, churches, and a post office. (Courtesy of the DAP.)

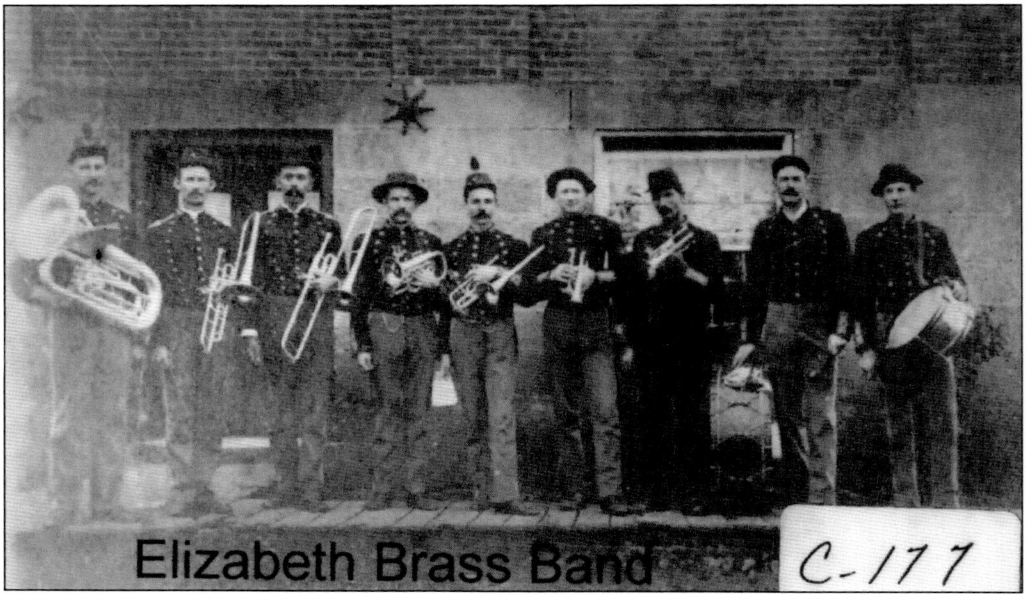

Attorney V. B. Archer purchased a drum from New York that was used by the Elizabeth Brass Band. In 1954, W. O. Davis donated the drum to the newly established Beauchamp-Newman Museum. (Courtesy of the DAP.)

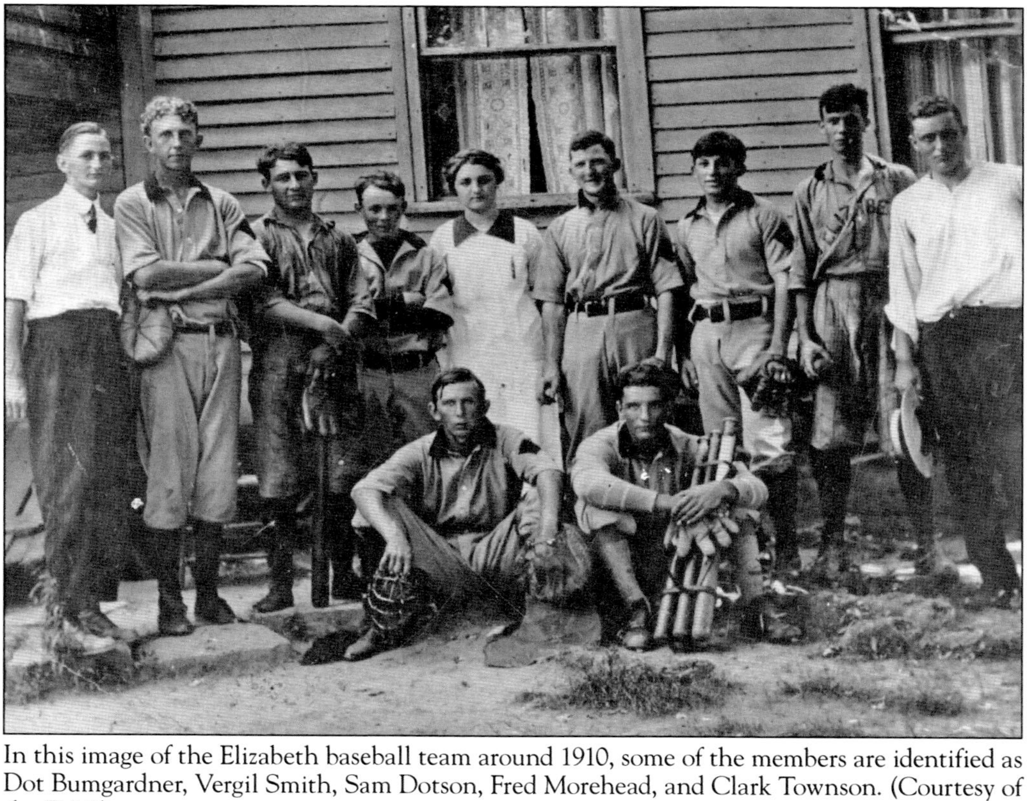

In this image of the Elizabeth baseball team around 1910, some of the members are identified as Dot Bumgardner, Vergil Smith, Sam Dotson, Fred Morehead, and Clark Townson. (Courtesy of the DAP.)

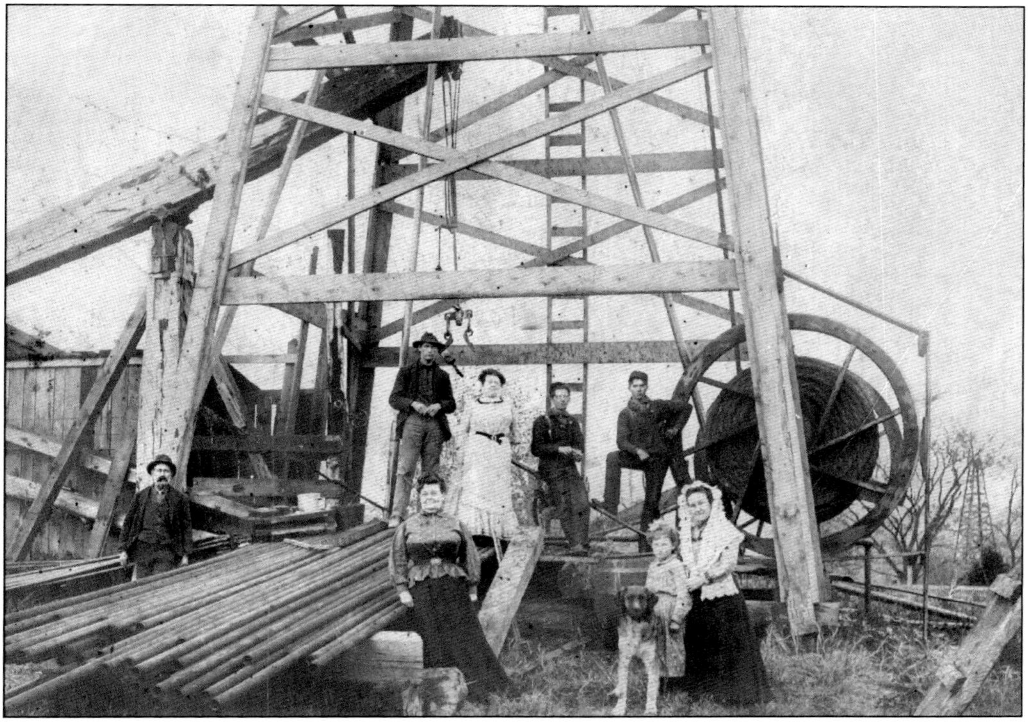

One of the lesser-known oil wells in the Rathbone inventory was the Rathbone Oil Well located at Right Reedy Road just outside of Palestine. Only a few longtime residents of the Palestine area can recall the old oil derrick. (Courtesy of Lori Lee Siers.)

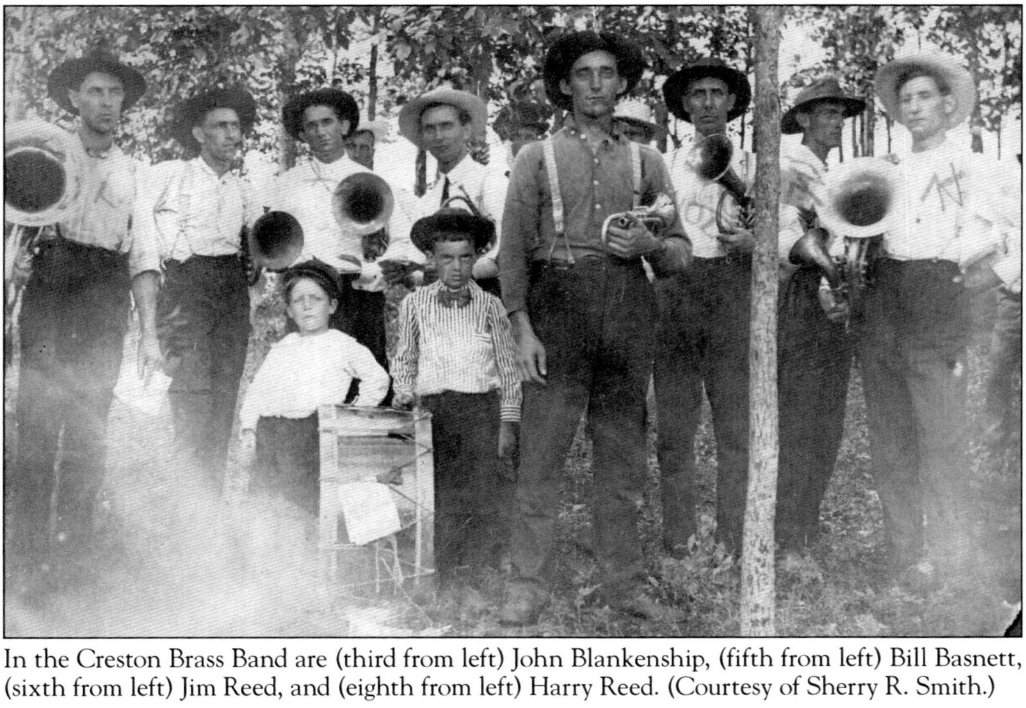

In the Creston Brass Band are (third from left) John Blankenship, (fifth from left) Bill Basnett, (sixth from left) Jim Reed, and (eighth from left) Harry Reed. (Courtesy of Sherry R. Smith.)

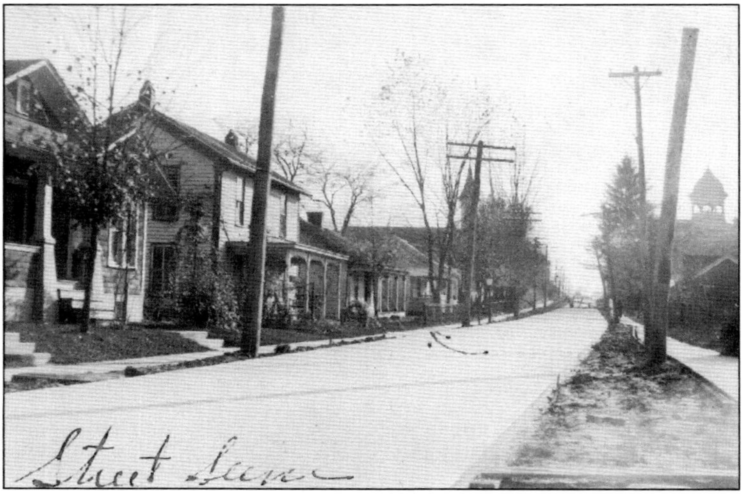

This scene was taken on Court Street in Elizabeth during the 1920s. Pictured from left to right are the family homes of Coplin, Deweese, Vandall, Owens, Tucker, and Reed. The steeple of the South Methodist Church can be seen in the distance. Across the street on the right is the Elizabeth Grade School. (Courtesy of Carole Menefee.)

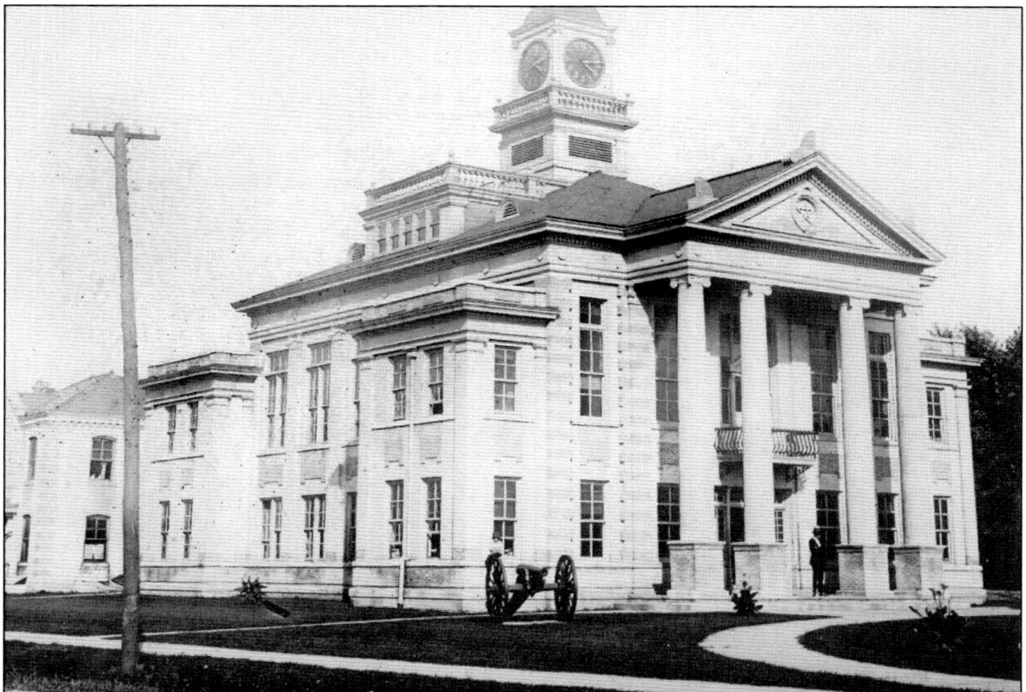

This early photograph of the Wirt County Courthouse shows one of two cannons that have proudly been on display since 1915. Following the Civil War, the Department of the Army loaned the cannons to the people of Wirt County. The Grand Army of the Republic (Union) coordinated the placement of the cannons on the front lawn. The 12-pound bronze Napoleon muzzle-loading cannon was the most popular smoothbore cannon used during the Civil War. It was manufactured by the Revere Copper Company in Boston, Massachusetts, and named after Napoleon III. (Courtesy of Carole Menefee.).

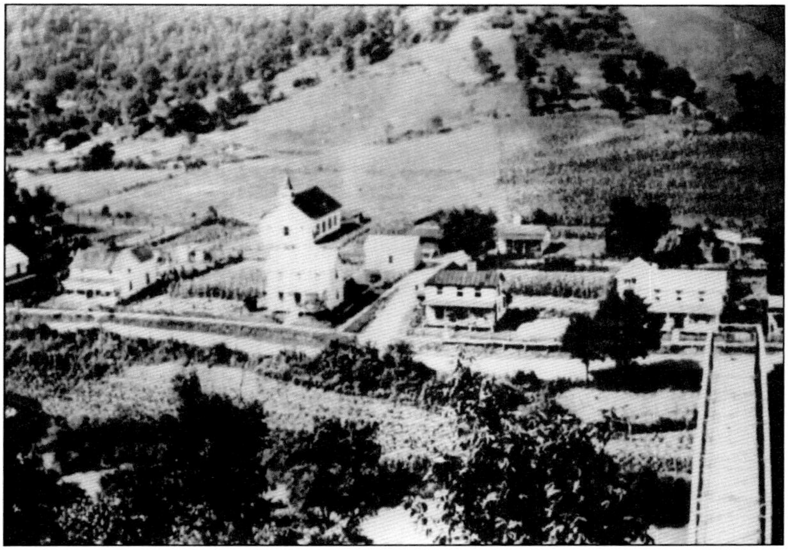

This aerial view of Creston was taken long after the heyday of the 1860s oil boom had faded. The Creston toll bridge can be seen in the lower right-hand corner of the photograph. The Creston United Methodist Church is in the background. (Courtesy of Russ Snyder.)

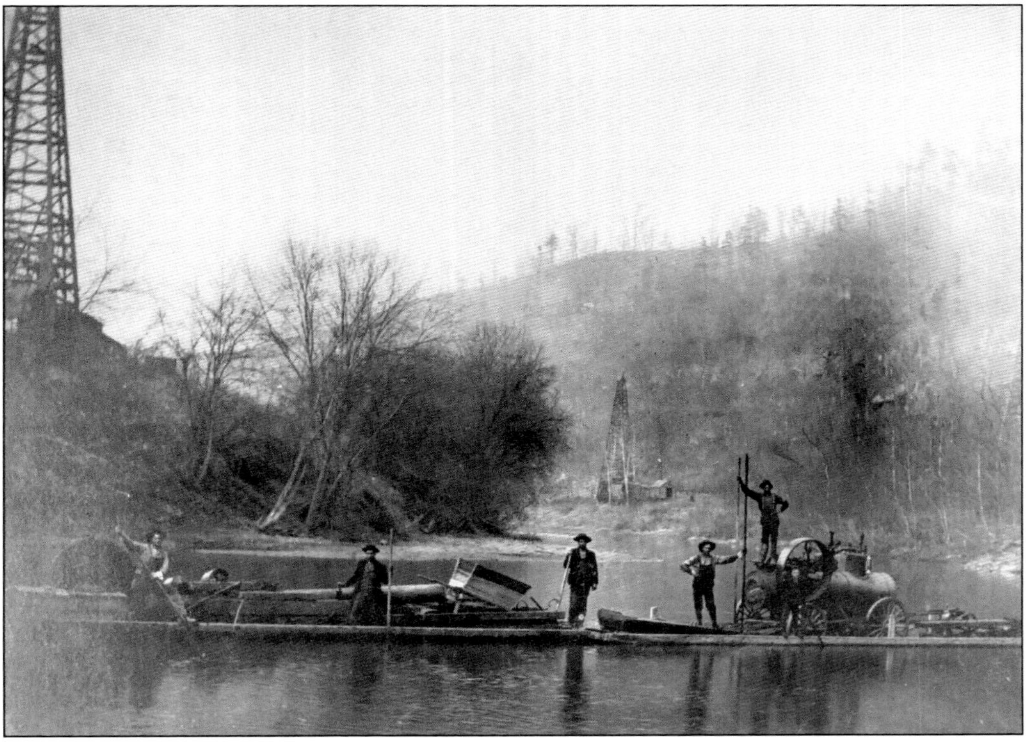

Riverboats were a popular mode of transportation at the time this photograph was taken. The crew of this flatboat is shown navigating across the river at Burning Springs to deliver a steam engine for an oil well. (Courtesy of Susan Kirby.)

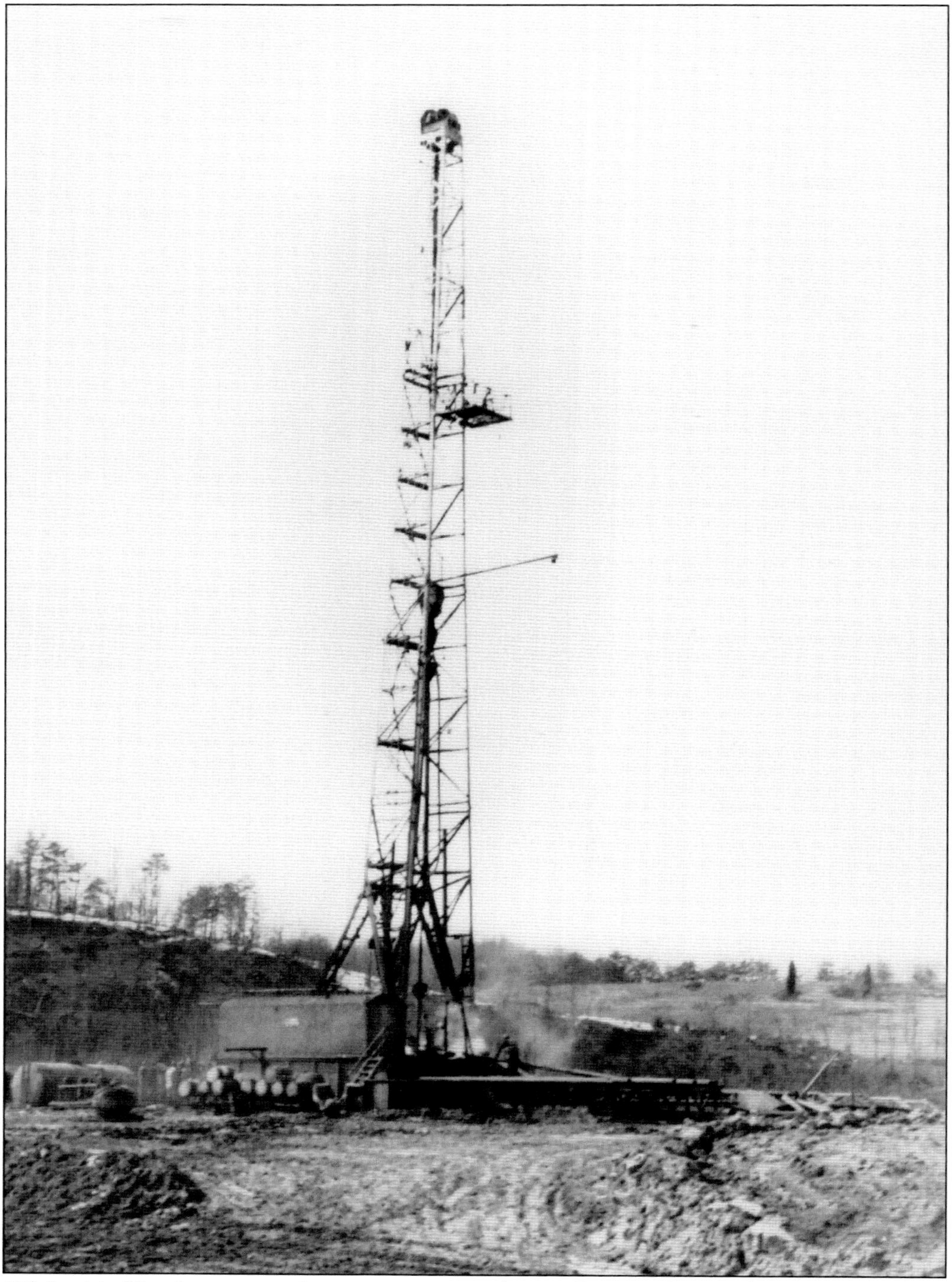

Oil derricks like the one seen here were commonplace in Burning Springs during the oil boom. The steel derrick stood 130 feet tall and featured a double pulley system. The water barrels at the base of the derrick were used to keep the ground saturated while drilling for oil. (Courtesy of the DAP.)

Two

Religion and Churches

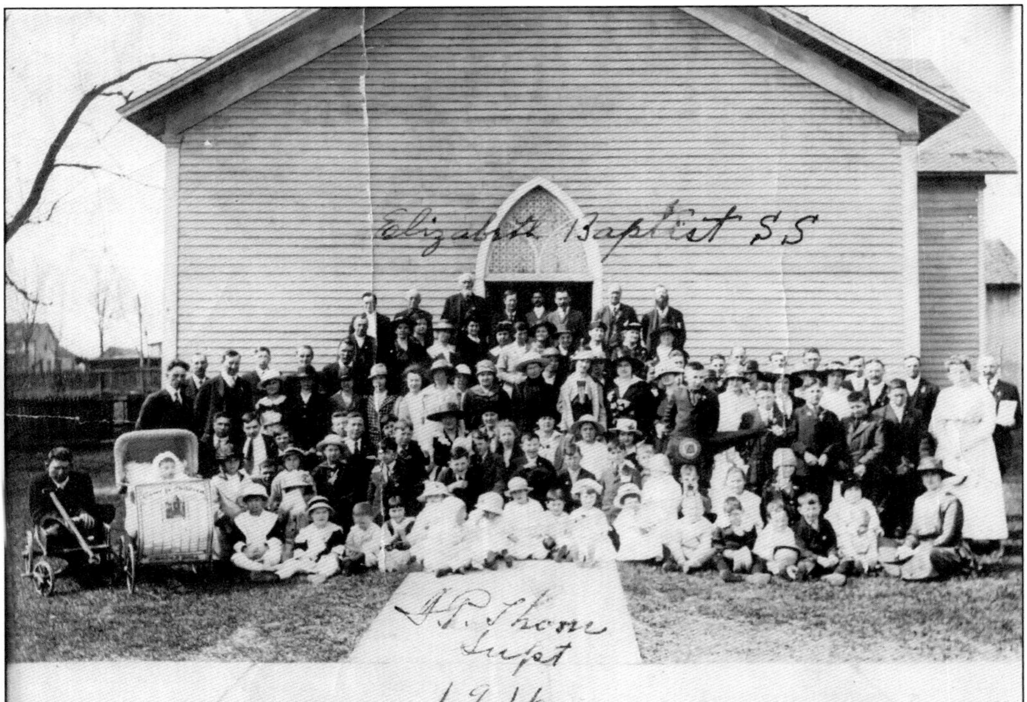

The Elizabeth Baptist Church, located on Mulberry Street in Elizabeth, was built in 1867. This photograph from 1916 shows the congregation during a period of time when I. P. Thorn served as superintendent of the church. Some folks may still remember Buddy Wilson (the boy on the left in the cart) as a noted character in the community who was unable to walk and used a cart to get around Elizabeth. (Courtesy of Betty Thorn.)

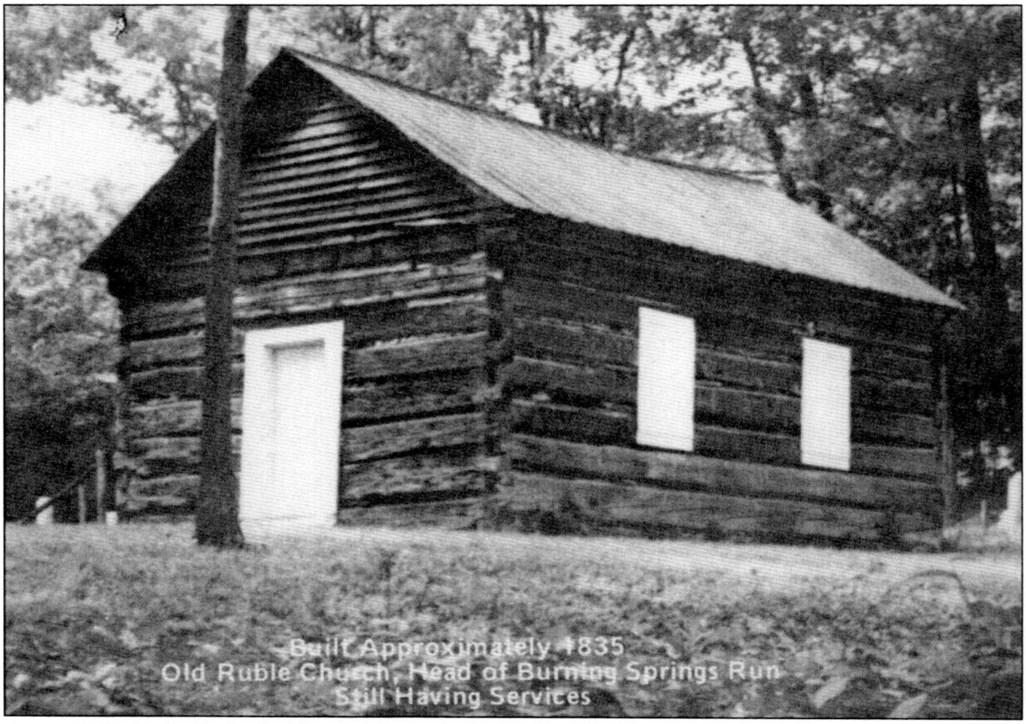

Aaron S. Ruble built the Ruble Church at the head of Burning Springs Run in 1835. The hand-hewn log structure measures 18 by 24 feet and was heated by a potbellied stove and lighted by kerosene lamps. The deed book states that all denominations, except those of "Northern Principles," were welcome. (Courtesy of Sue Douglas.)

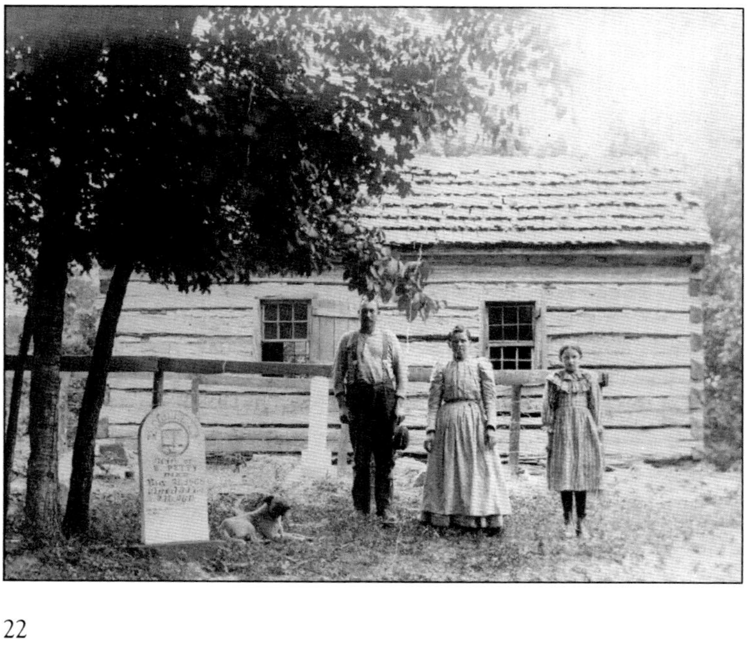

This photograph of the cemetery at the Ruble Church was taken in 1900. Pictured from left to right are Jasper Whitecotton, Rose Conley Whitecotton, and Elle Whitecotton. The church was built on land belonging to William and Richard Doane Petty. Many of the graves in the church cemetery are members of the Petty family and predate the Civil War. (Courtesy of Susan Kirby.)

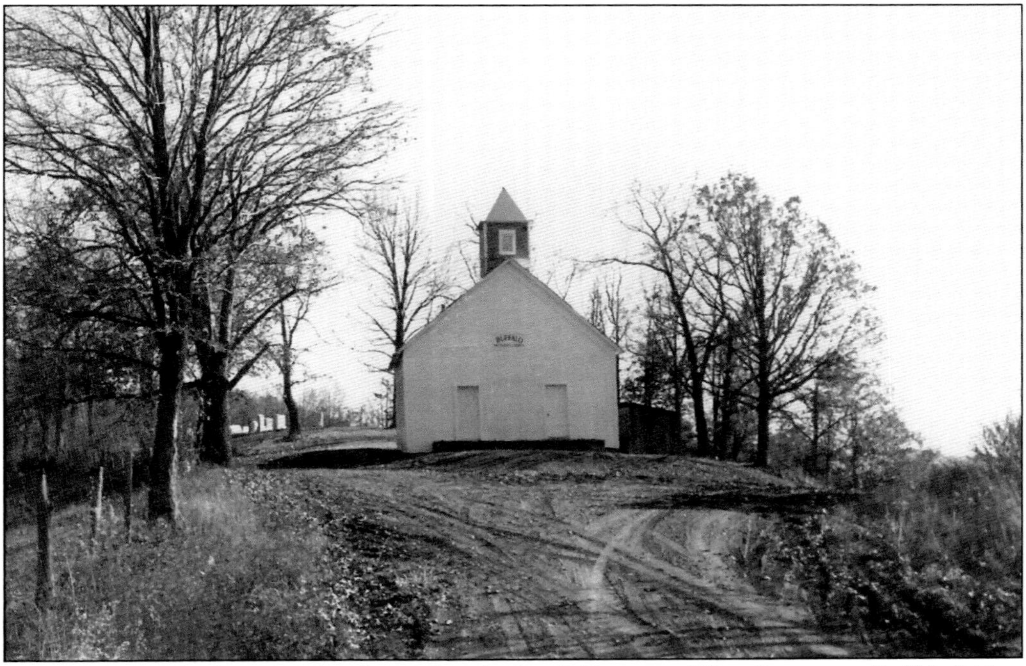

The Buffalo Methodist Church is located in the Reedy District of Wirt County on Buffalo Ridge. The one-story log structure was originally built between 1884 and 1886 and has two entrance doors—one for women and one for men. The church looks much like it did in 1909 after beech wood weatherboarding was added to the exterior. The interior features the original brackets and hooks to support oil lanterns. (Courtesy of Linda Sams.)

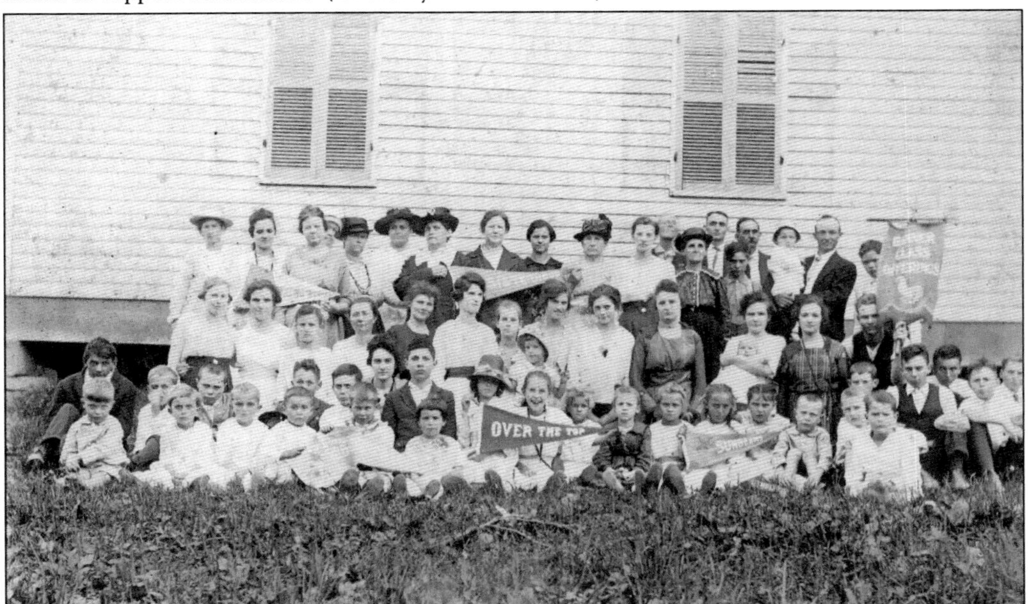

Members of the Thorn, Somerville, Young, and Sheppard families can be seen here posing for a group photograph in front of the Mount Pisgah United Methodist Church around 1916. (Courtesy of the DAP.)

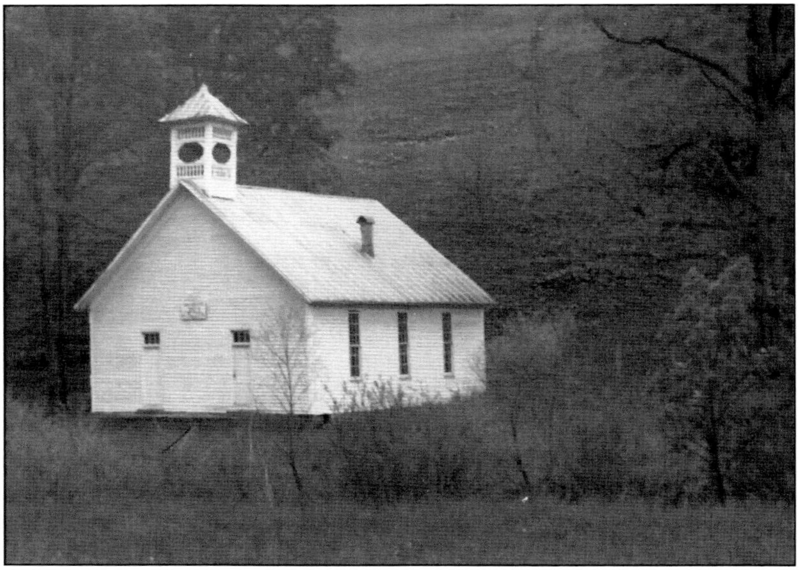

The Standing Stone Baptist Church is situated in the Burning Springs District of Wirt County. The church was built on property deeded to the trustees by J. W. and Teresa Veon in 1893. (Courtesy of Linda Sams.)

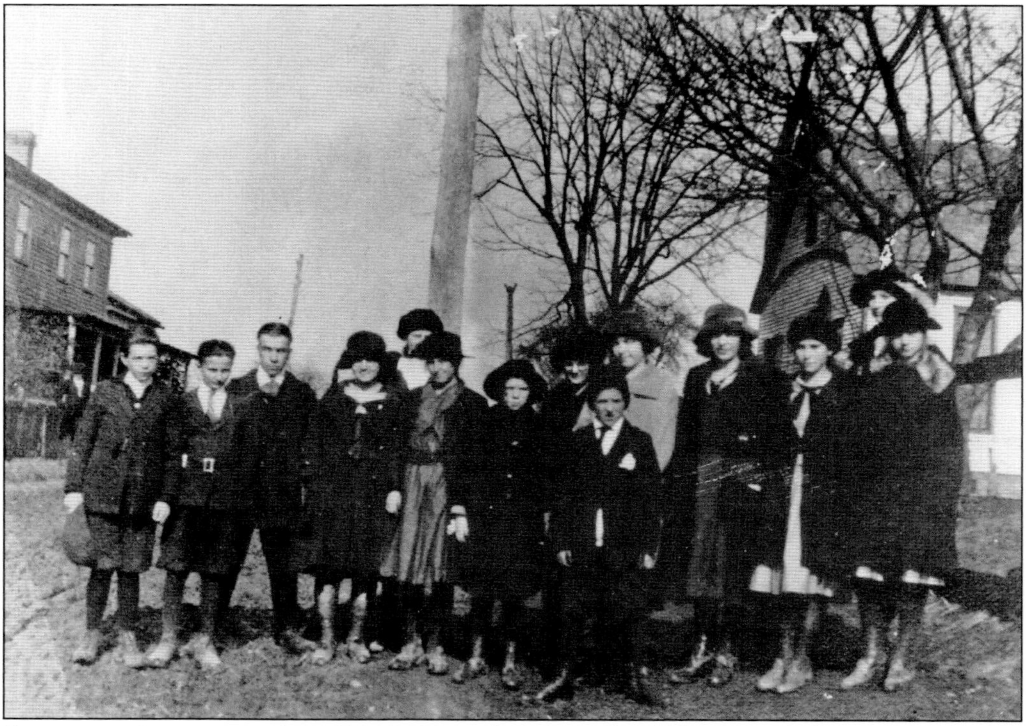

Since it was first organized in 1879, the Newark Baptist Church has provided its members with a place to worship. This photograph, taken in the 1920s, shows, from left to right, (first row) Ray Hannaman, Okey Fought, Palomaneda Clayton, Winnie Morgan, ? Hannaman, George Morgan, Claudie Buck, Gracie Morgan, and Icy Buck; (second row) Vinia Morgan, ? Hannaman, Maggie Fought, Carrie Fought, and Ernest Hall. The Bailey Hotel, operated by Etsie Hannaman Bailey, can be seen on the left-hand side of the photograph. (Courtesy of Marjorie F. Mayes.)

Three

Living and Learning

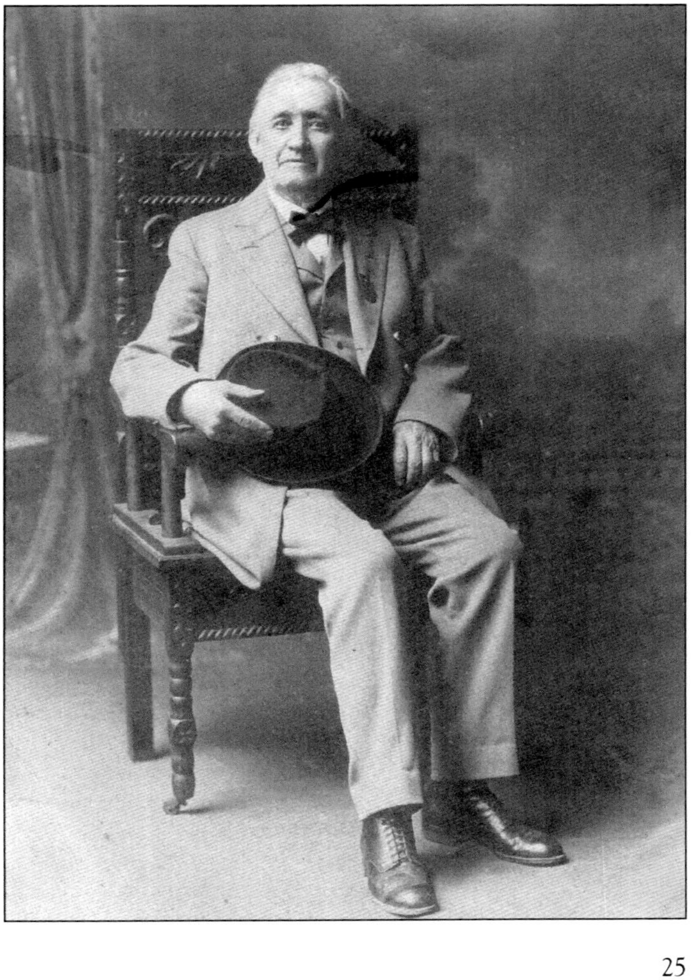

Edgar Heermans, an early educator in the county, was thought to be one of the best teachers ever to teach in Wirt County. Heermans was in the school system from 1844 until his retirement in 1900. During that time, he was principal of the schools of Elizabeth and Burning Springs. He also founded the Seminary and Business School in Elizabeth. (Courtesy of the DAP.)

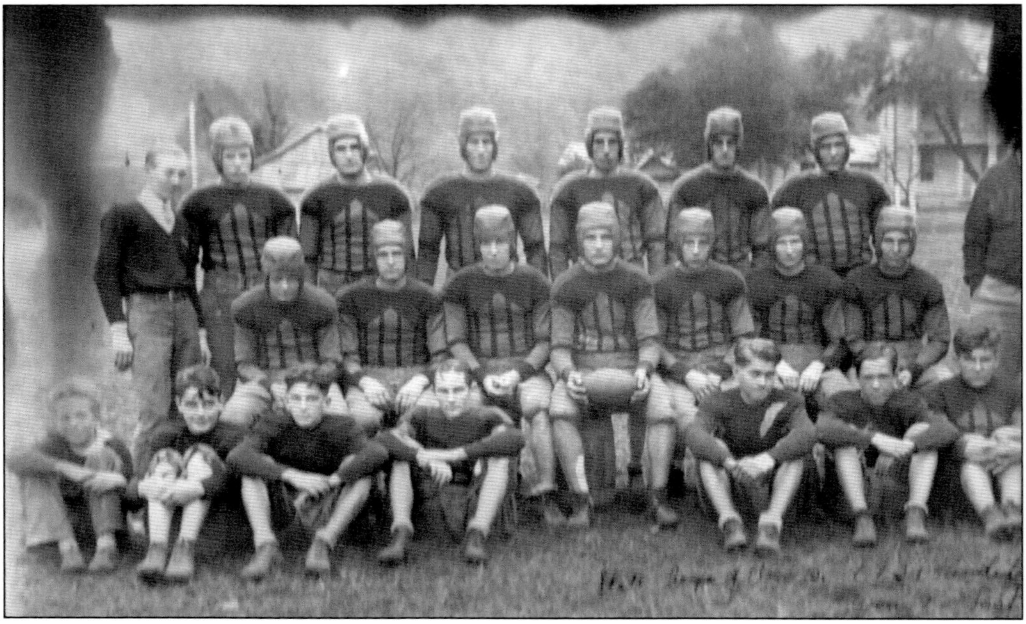

Members of the 1931 Wirt County High School football team are pictured here. The starting lineup included left end Joe Mace; left tackle Speedy Vaught; center Woody Burton; right guard Ken Morgan; right tackle George Morgan; right end Edward McClung; and backs Gilbert Lockhart, Charles King, Chuck Cheuvront, and Charles Bumgarner. (Courtesy of the DAP.)

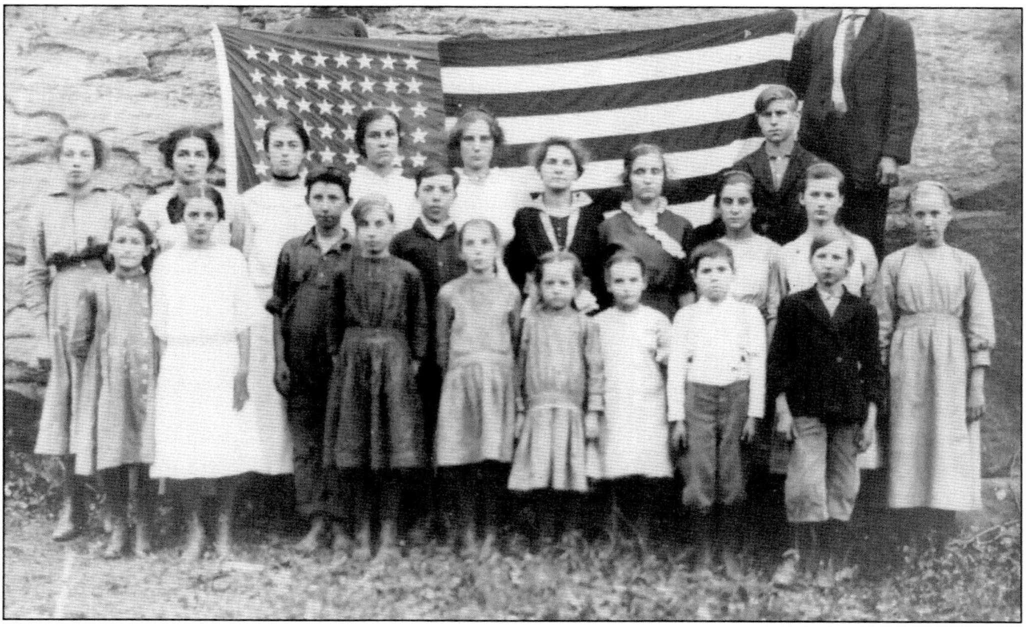

The Cool Springs School was located at the fork of Otter Run and Standing Stone Road. In 1933, it was one of a handful of country schoolhouses that was allowed to remain open. Most schools of its kind were closed in the 1950s, when students were transported to larger, more modern facilities in Elizabeth. The identity of the gentlemen holding the flag may never be known, as the photographer inadvertently cut them off when taking this photograph. (Courtesy of Susan Kirby.)

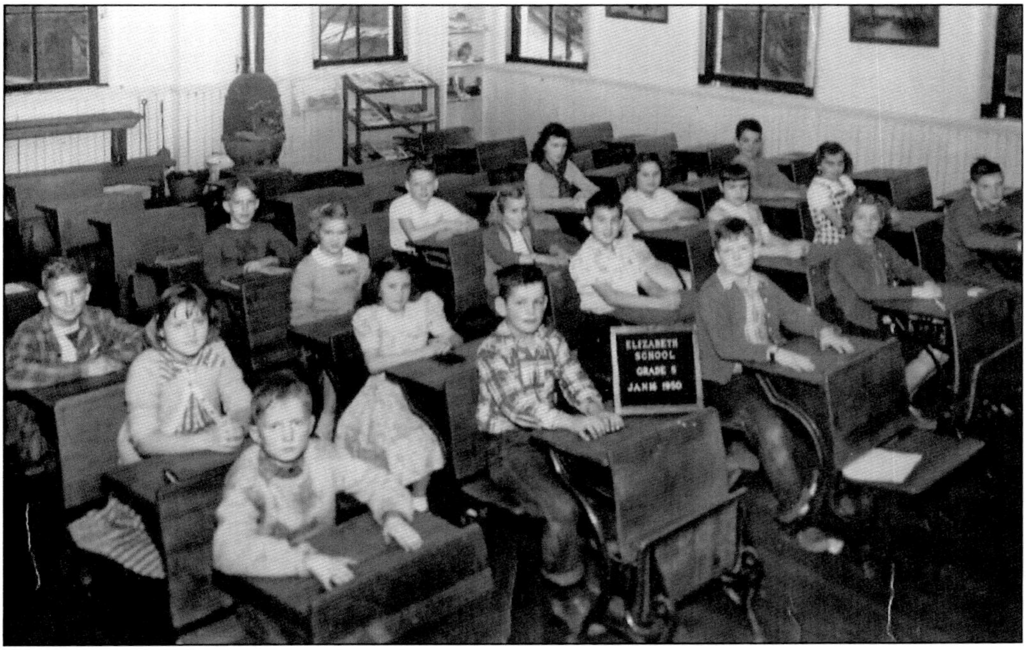

Carolyn Smith and the rest of her fifth-grade class posed for this school picture at the Elizabeth Grade School in January 1950. Carolyn is seated at the second desk from left in the second row. (Courtesy of Debbie Hennen.)

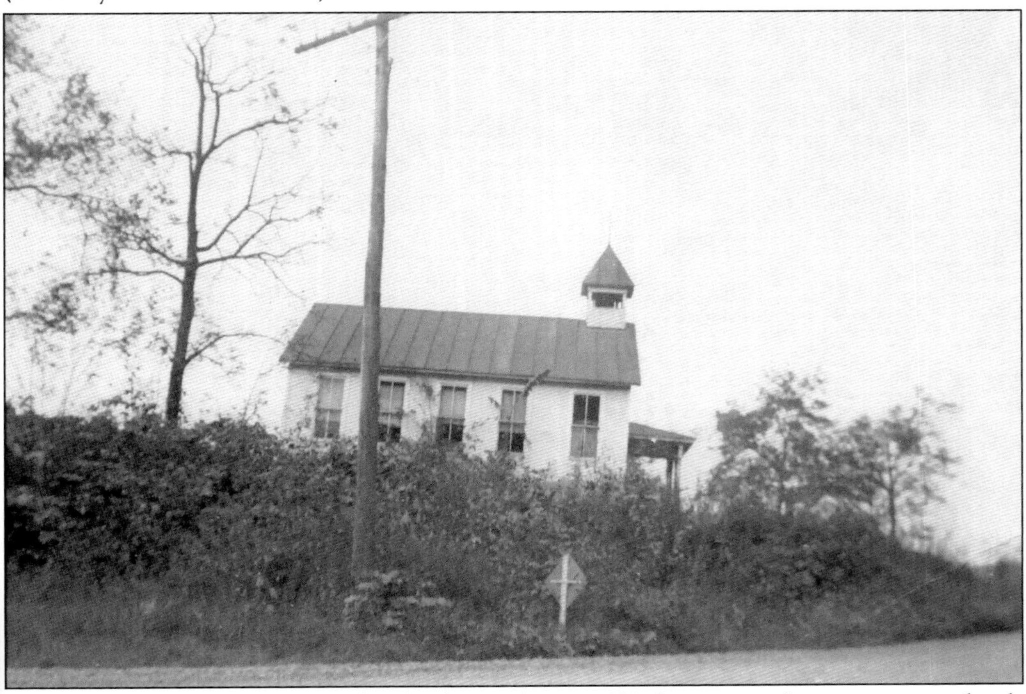

This photograph of the Cedar Hill School was taken in 1950. It was one of many country schools throughout Wirt County that provided children the opportunity to obtain an education. (Courtesy of Carole Menefee.)

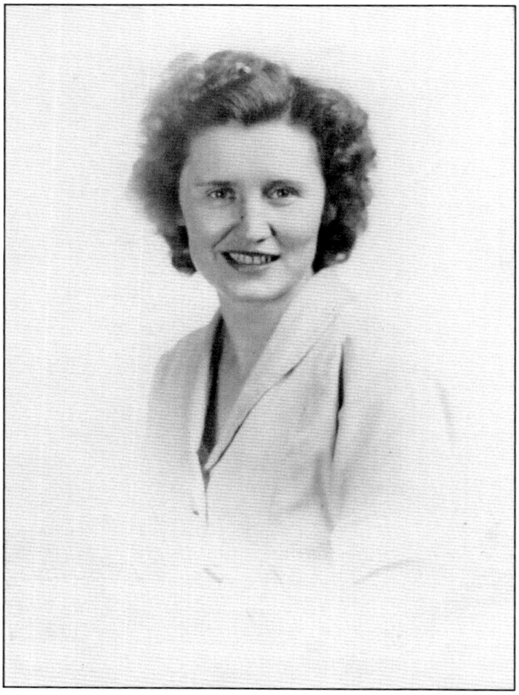

During her tenure, Lois Mace was one of the most revered teachers at the Wirt County High School. This is evident in the senior class dedication of the 1965 *Elizabethan*. It reads as follows: "Because she has become a part of Wirt County High School through her years of service to the student body, annual staff, and senior class, and because she possesses the qualities of an ideal teacher, we the seniors, take pleasure in dedicating this 1965 annual to Mrs. Lois Mace." (Courtesy of Gayle Lowe.)

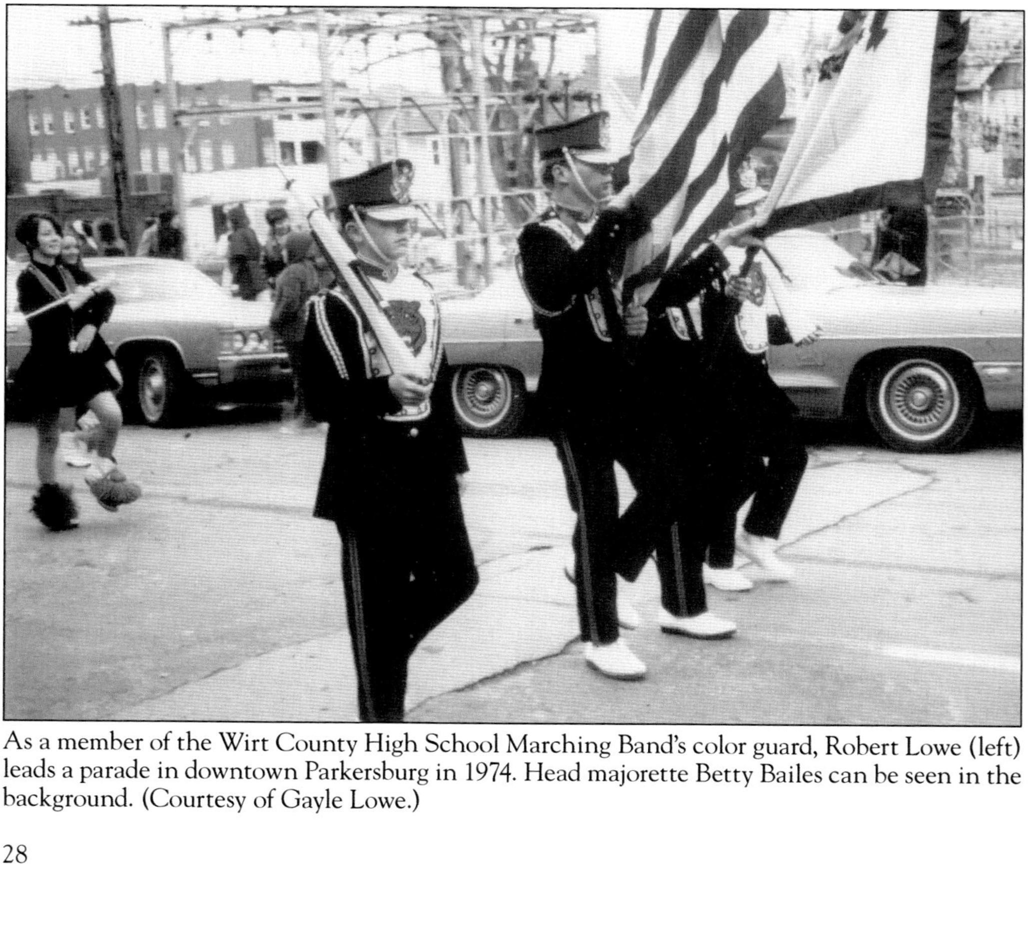

As a member of the Wirt County High School Marching Band's color guard, Robert Lowe (left) leads a parade in downtown Parkersburg in 1974. Head majorette Betty Bailes can be seen in the background. (Courtesy of Gayle Lowe.)

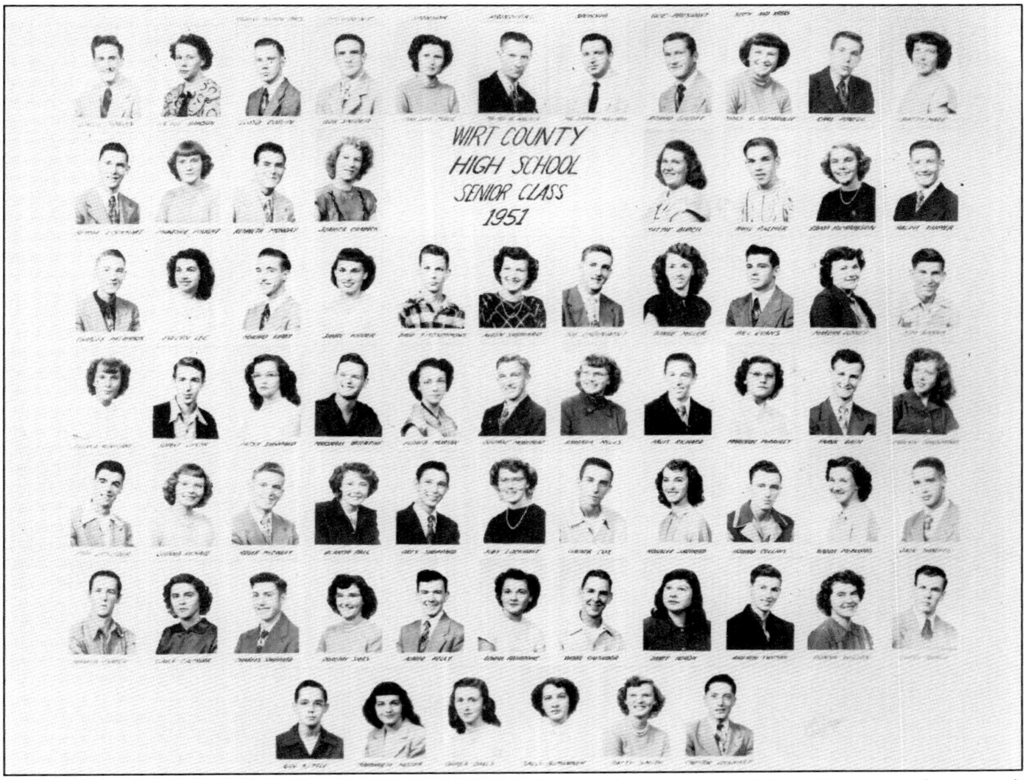

The Wirt County High School class of 1951 included, from left to right, (first row from top) Lowell Morgan, Luciele Dawson, Lloyd Coplin, Bob Snider, Lois Mace, Ray W. Walter, Sammy Williams, Richard Elliott, Mary H. Somerville, Carl Powell, and Patty Mace; (second row) Remma Lockhart, Marjorie Fought, Kenneth Munday, Juanita Chadock, Mattie Burch, Paul Palmer, Edna Richardson, and Ralph Tanner; (third row) Charles Patterson, Evelyn Lee, Howard Kirby, Janice Kidder, David Fitzsimmons, Aleen Sheppard, Joe Cheuvront, Bonnie Miller, Bill Evans, Martha Duskey, and Jim Hanna; (fourth row) Glenna Windland, Robert Lynch, Patsy Sheppard, Marshall Valentine, Eldred Morgan, George Morehead, Barbara Mills, Arlis Richard, Marilynn McCauley, Frank Bain, and Evelyn Townsend; (fifth row) Park Licklider, Glenna Richard, Roger McCauley, Blanche Hall, Okey Sheppard, Judy Lockhart, Grover Cox, Rosalee Sheppard, Howard Collins, Wanda McClung, and Jack Menefee; (six row) Franklin Frazier, Gayle Caltrider, Charles Sheppard, Dorothy Siers, Alfred Kelly, Donna Rathbone, Wayne Caltrider, Janet Heron, Andrew Twyman, Donna Wilson, and Larry Ruble; (seventh row) Guy Kittle, Margariete Nester, Orpha Davis, Sally Bumgarner, Patty Smith, and Chester Lockhart. (Courtesy of Gayle Lowe.)

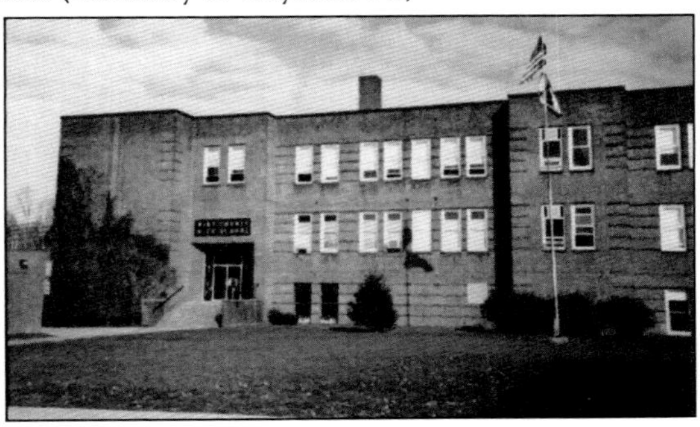

Wirt County High School was built in 1938 with federal and county funds. The new school opened with 13 classrooms—a gymnasium was added in 1948, a vocational building during the 1958–1959 school term, and a new library in 1962. (Courtesy of the Ludwig family.)

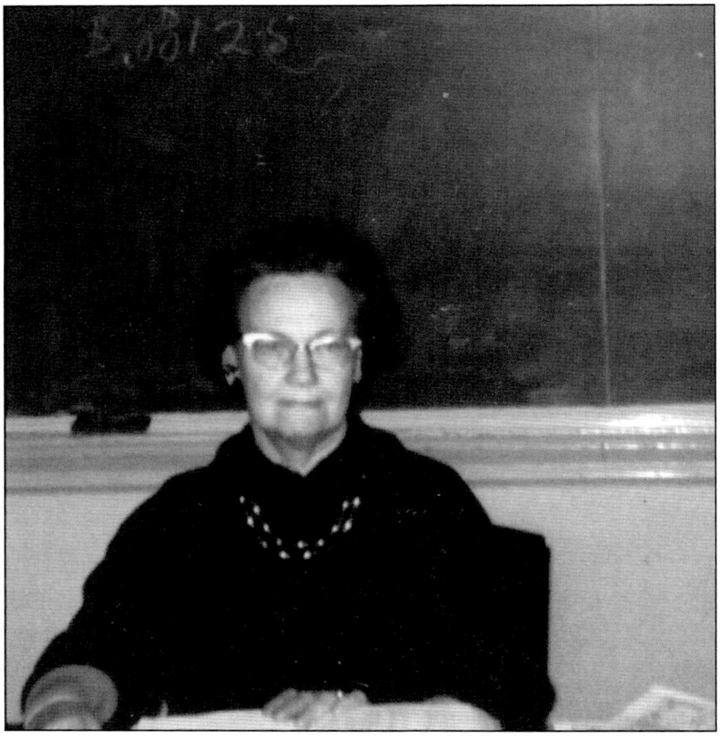

Ethel "Heck" Cheuvront had a passion for teaching West Virginia history. Following her death in 1974, the Ethel Cheuvront Memorial Award was established at Wirt County High School to recognize the highest scoring Golden Horseshoe winner. (Courtesy of the Ludwig family.)

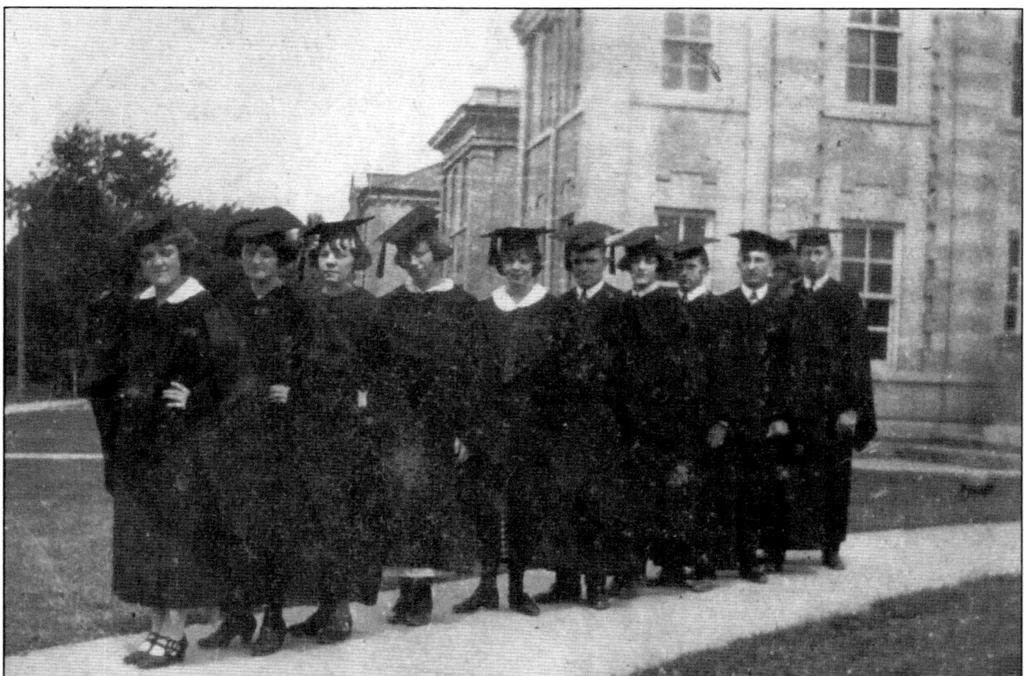

These high school graduates are shown leaving the Wirt County Courthouse auditorium following their commencement exercises in the 1930s. (Courtesy of the DAP.)

William "Bill" Higgins is seen here wearing his football jersey and is ready to proudly represent Wirt County High School during a football game in the early 1950s. (Courtesy of Gayle Lowe.)

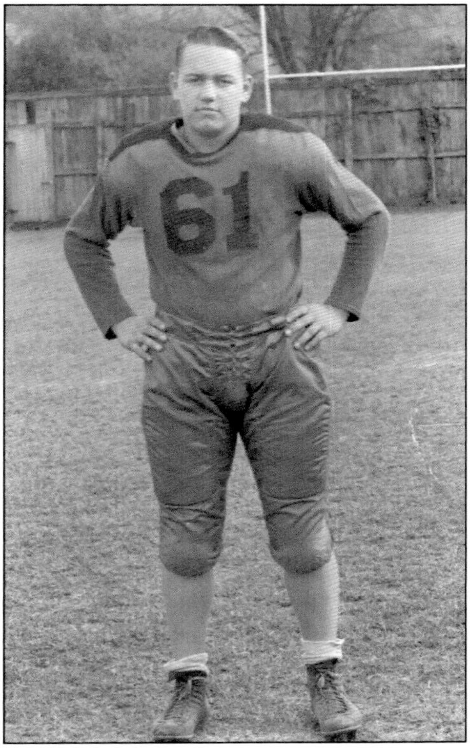

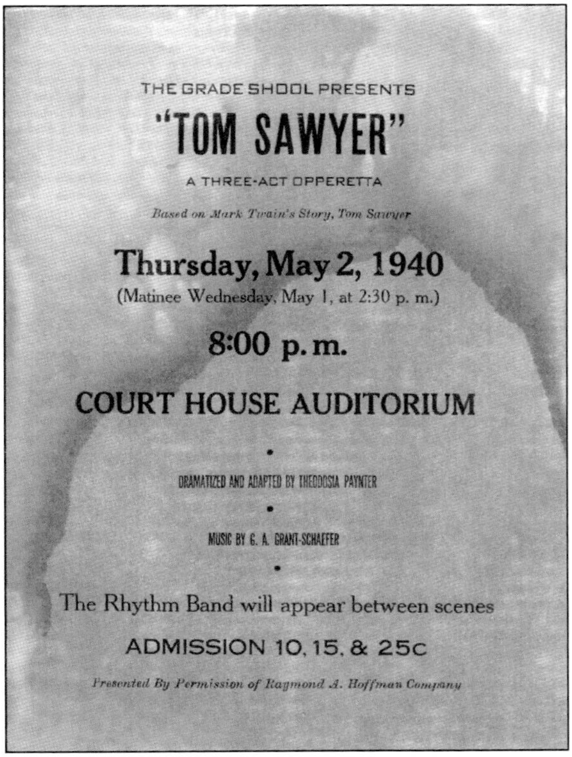
THE GRADE SHOOL PRESENTS
"TOM SAWYER"
A THREE-ACT OPPERETTA
Based on Mark Twain's Story, Tom Sawyer
Thursday, May 2, 1940
(Matinee Wednesday, May 1, at 2:30 p. m.)
8:00 p.m.
COURT HOUSE AUDITORIUM
DRAMATIZED AND ADAPTED BY THEODOSIA PAYNTER
MUSIC BY G. A. GRANT-SCHAEFER
The Rhythm Band will appear between scenes
ADMISSION 10, 15, & 25c
Presented By Permission of Raymond A. Hoffman Company

This playbill from 1940 advertised a three-act operetta entitled *Tom Sawyer* that was presented by the Elizabeth Grade School children at the county courthouse auditorium. The courthouse was regularly used for school plays until the gymnasium was built at the Wirt County High School in 1948.

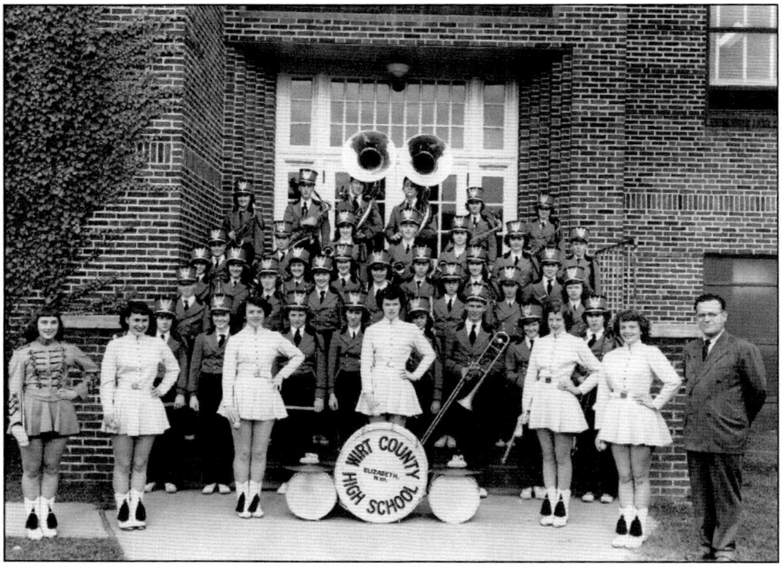

The majorettes from the 1950–1951 school term are pictured here with the Wirt County High School Marching Band. From left to right are Lucille Cooper, Janice Kidder, Hester Blair, Pauline Radabaugh, Lorraine Murray, and Geraldine Hickman. The band was under the direction of Joseph Henry. (Courtesy of Betty Thorn.)

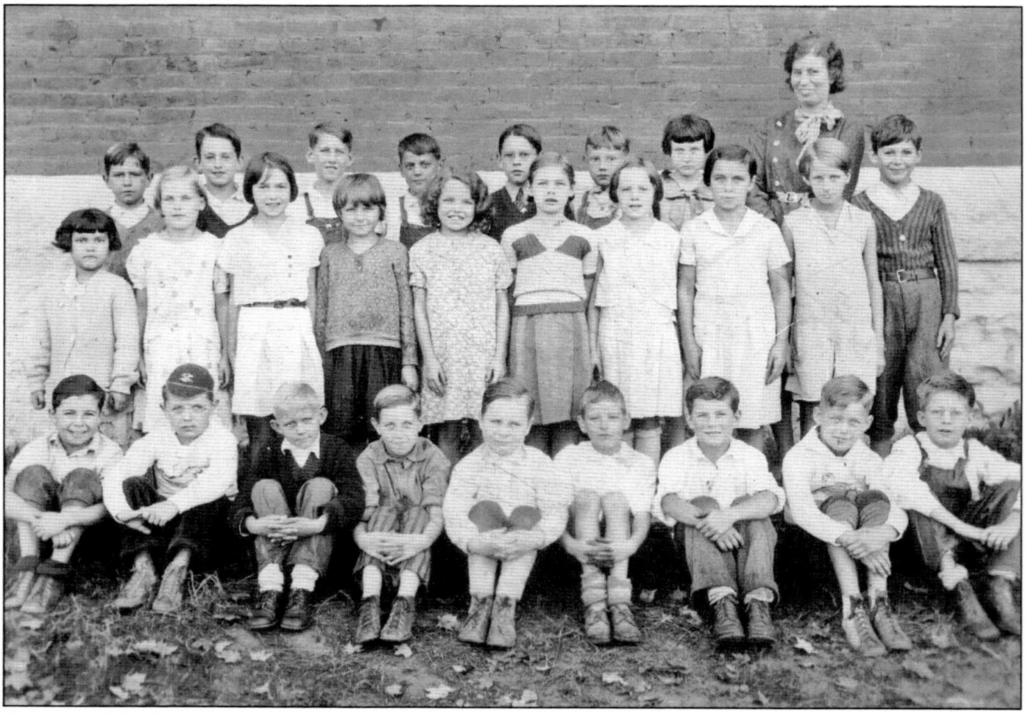

"Miss Mildred" Cline's third-grade class, pictured here from left to right, includes (first row) Marshal Boggs, Jimmie Muncie, Walter Dailey, June Lemon, Eugene Sims, Reynolds Brooks, Billy Townsend, John Roberts, and Donald Coe; (second row) Geraldine Petty, Mary Elenor Castle, Gwendolyn Roberts, Lucy Woodring, Doris Goodwin, Virginia Thorn, Delores Williams, Susie Wagner, Elsie Copen, and Everett Cooper; (third row) June Gainer, June Roberts, Raymond Reed, Seymour Kirchener, Richard Thorn, Benjamin Hale, Orma Morgan, and Mildred Cline, the teacher. (Courtesy of Betty Thorn.)

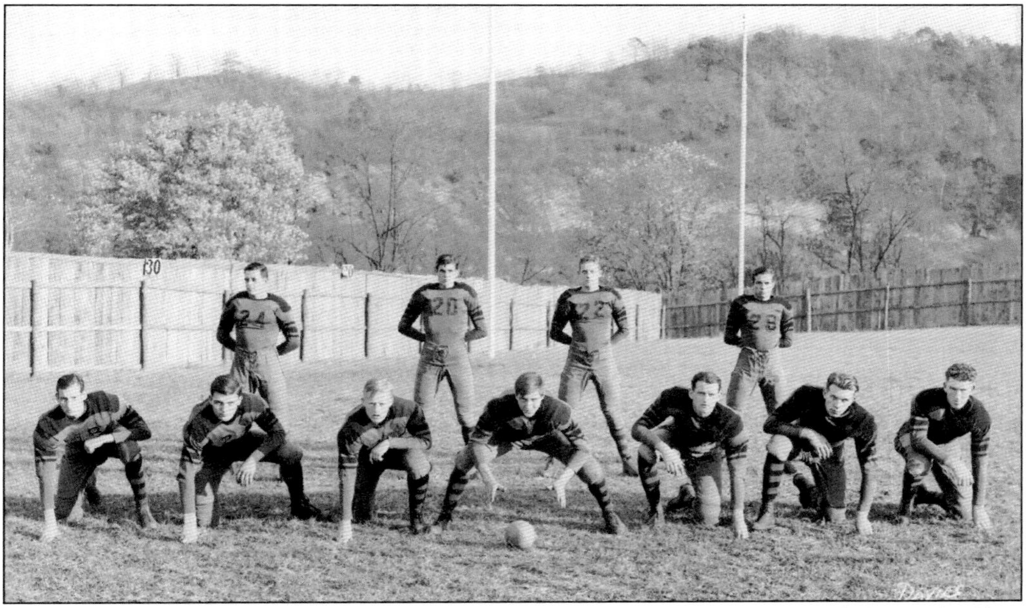

The Wirt County High School football team of 1941–1942 is pictured here from left to right: (first row) Kenneth Fitzwater, Henry Green, Bob Kinney, Curt Mace, Richard Thorn, Oscar Hickman, and Ralph Lockhart; (second row) Wally Rathbone, Bob Wix, John Roberts, and June Gainer. (Courtesy of Betty Thorn.)

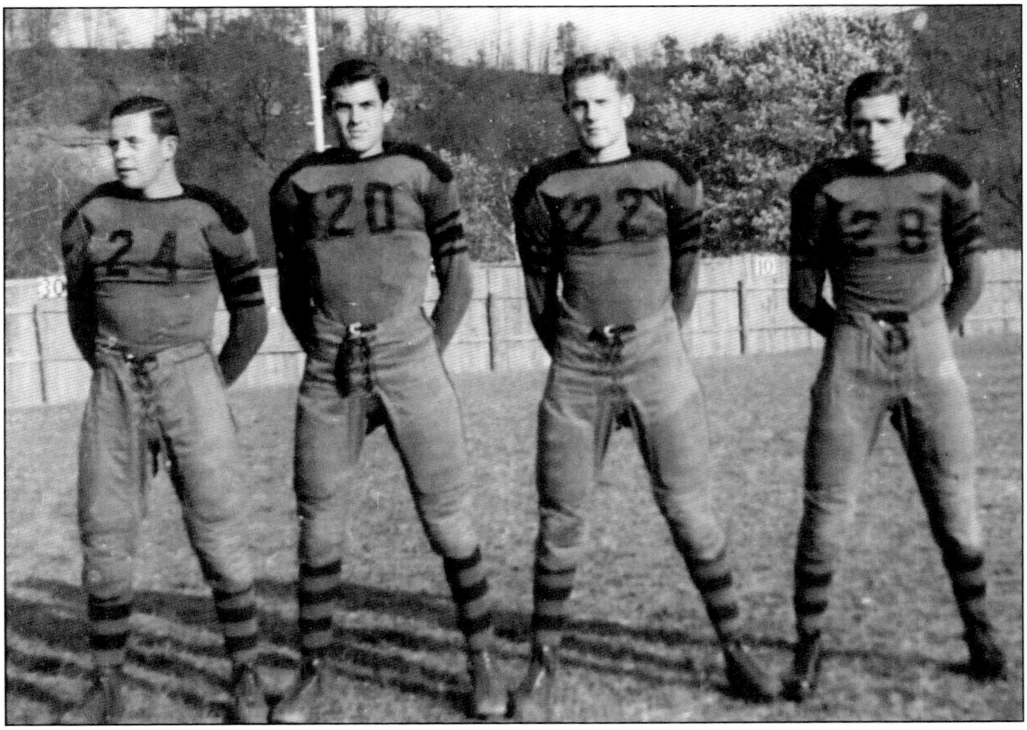

Shown here is the 1941–1942 Wirt County High School football team's backfield. From left to right are Wally Rathbone, Bob Wix, John Roberts, and June Gainer. (Courtesy of Betty Thorn.)

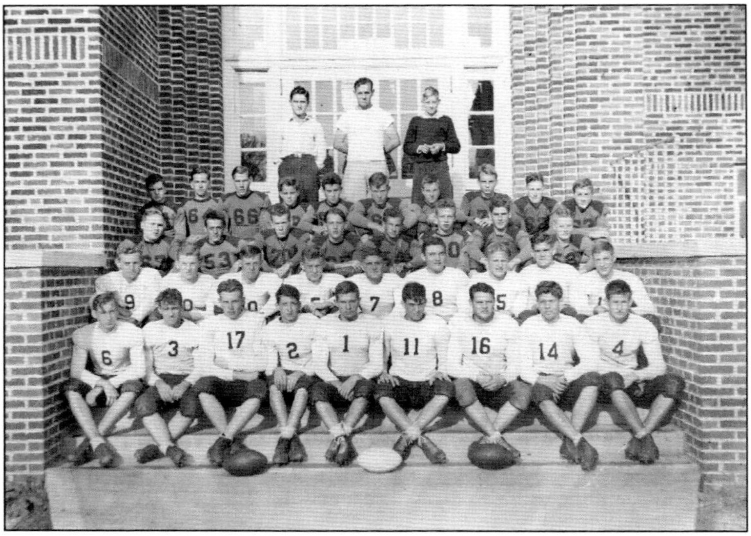

The Wirt County High School football team during the 1939–1940 season was led by coach Gordon Eismon (top row center) and manager Walter Dailey (right of Eismon). (Courtesy of Betty Thorn.)

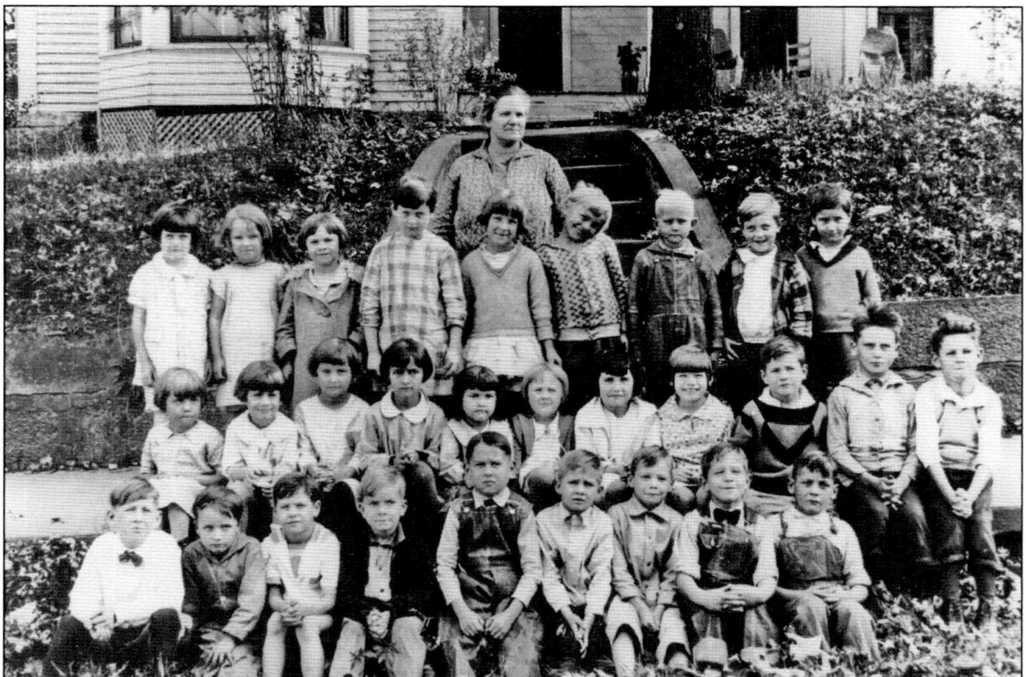

This group photograph of an Elizabeth Grade School class was taken on Court Street across from the schoolhouse. Pictured from left to right are (first row) Raymond Reed, Harold Coplin, June Dotson, Adrain Thorn, Richard Thorn, Donald Coe, Jack Williams, June Gainer, and Theodore Kirchner; (second row) Jean Gainer, Wilma Prather, Opal Wright, Francis Petty, Geraldine Petty, Kathleen Corbett, Betty Gunoe, Virginia Thorn, Bill Townsend, Jesse Cooper, and Everett Cooper; (third row) Betty Roberts, Orva Givens, Dorcas Cooper, Orma Morgan, ? Chenoweth, Joan Kirchner, Walter Dailey, June Lemon, Edgar Boston, and Val Sayre Hammond, teacher. (Courtesy of Sherry R. Smith.)

Denzil Sims can be seen here driving the 1965 cheerleaders in the Wirt County High School homecoming parade. Pictured from left to right are Sherry Reed, Lynda Villers, Delores Owen, and Loretta Hunt. The building in the background housed Lowe's Shoe Repair and Sales, owned and operated by Bernard Lowe. (Courtesy of Sherry R. Smith.)

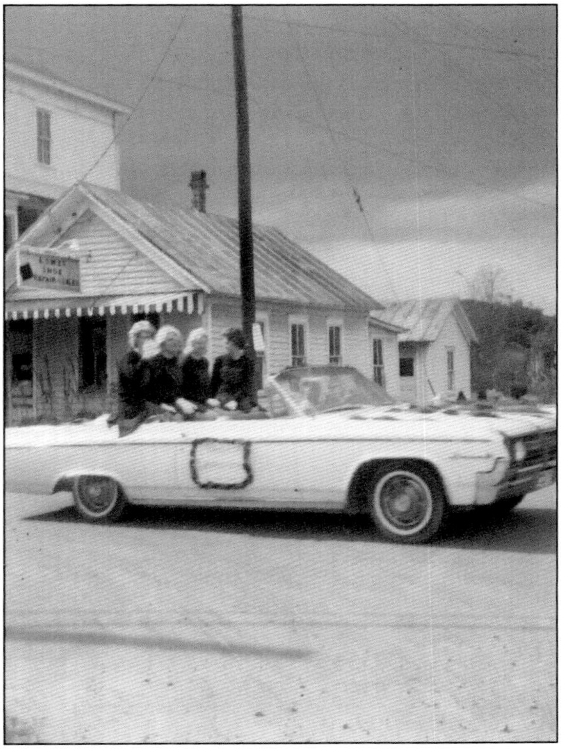

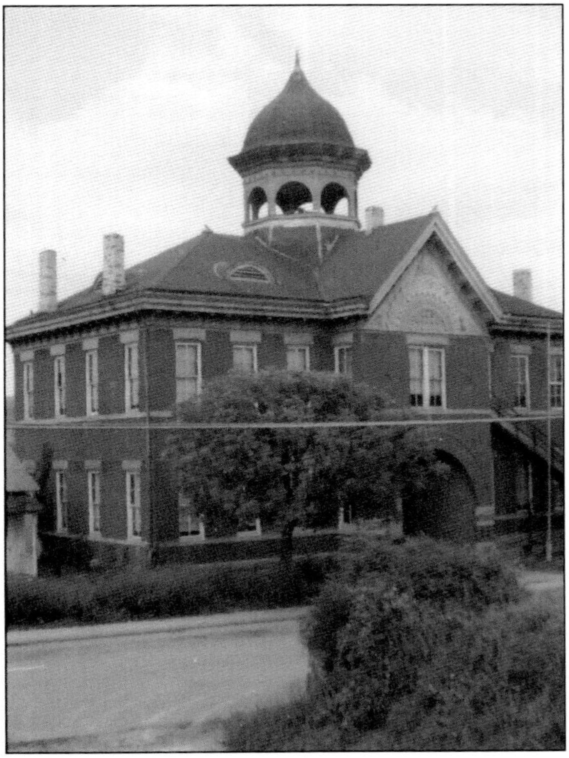

This brick schoolhouse was originally built in 1896 and consisted of five classrooms. Many students will remember sliding down the fire escape during fire drills. The last school term held in this facility was 1962. Elizabeth Elementary School moved to its current location on Schoolview Street in 1963. (Courtesy of Sherry R. Smith.)

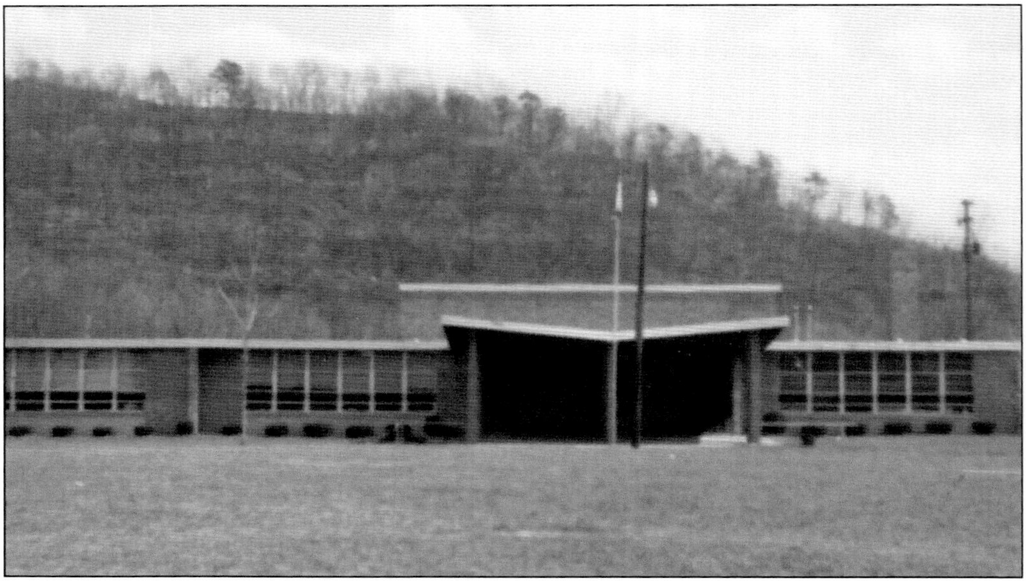

The Elizabeth Elementary School was built in 1963 on a 13-acre tract of land. This photograph shows the single-story structure before an expansion project in 1977. At that time, additional classrooms, a resource center, and a cafeteria were added. Louis Rollins was the principal from the time the school was constructed until his retirement in 1985. (Courtesy of Linda Sams.)

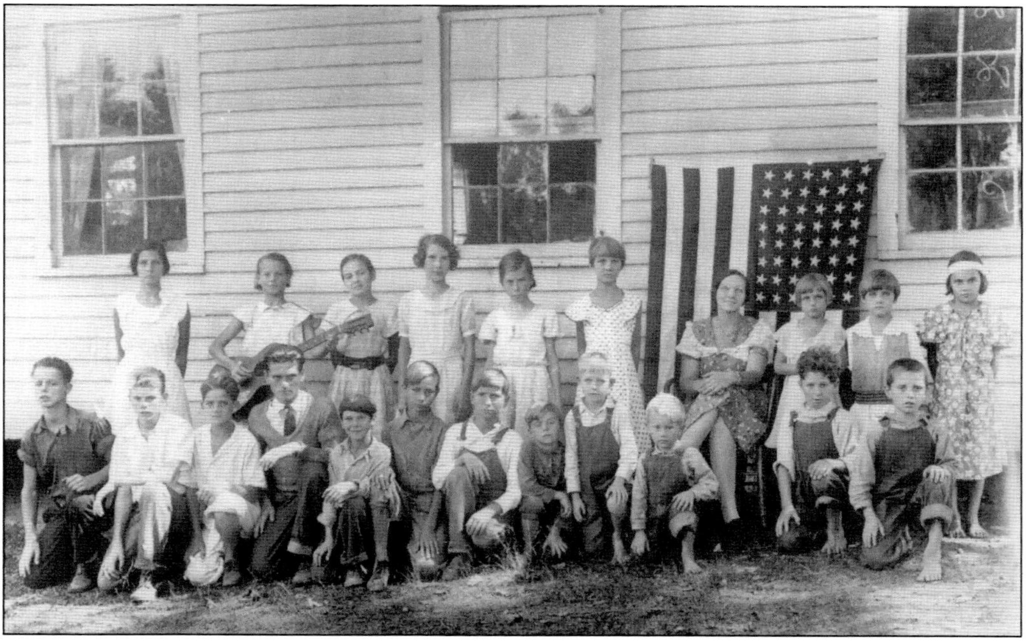

Pictured here in the fall of 1933 is Ruth Dennis's class at the Flatwoods School in Walker. From left to right are (first row) Junior Trippett, Johnnie Jones, Dorr Fultz, Raymond Jones, Denny Johnson, Carl Mitchell, Russell Fought, Thomas Cain, Heyman Jeffries, Eddy Jones, William Lemley, and Bernard Jones; (second row) Beulah Fultz, Garnet Trippett, Sylvia Eneix, Muriel Fought, Helen Cain, Nina Fultz, teacher Ruth Dennis, Louise Jeffries, Norma Fultz, and Sylvia Lemley. (Courtesy of Marjorie F. Mayes.)

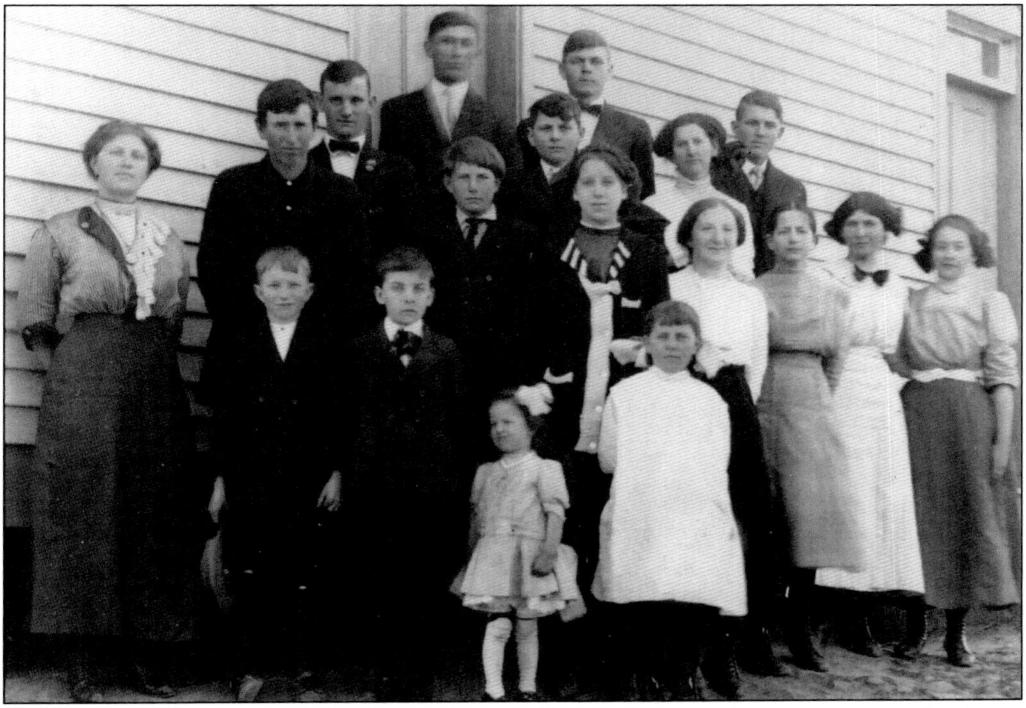

Attendees of the Two Runs School appear here in 1916. Included in the picture are teacher Mary Trickett, Blondie Edwards, Ernest Hall, Hattie Edwards, Garnett Trickett, Gretta Boso, Anna Springston, Mattie McCoy, Bessie Hall, Bertie Edwards, Everett Cox, Walter Trickett, Tennie Selby, Frank Trickett, Thurman Haney, Estella Springston, and Carl Trickett. (Courtesy of Marjorie F. Mayes.)

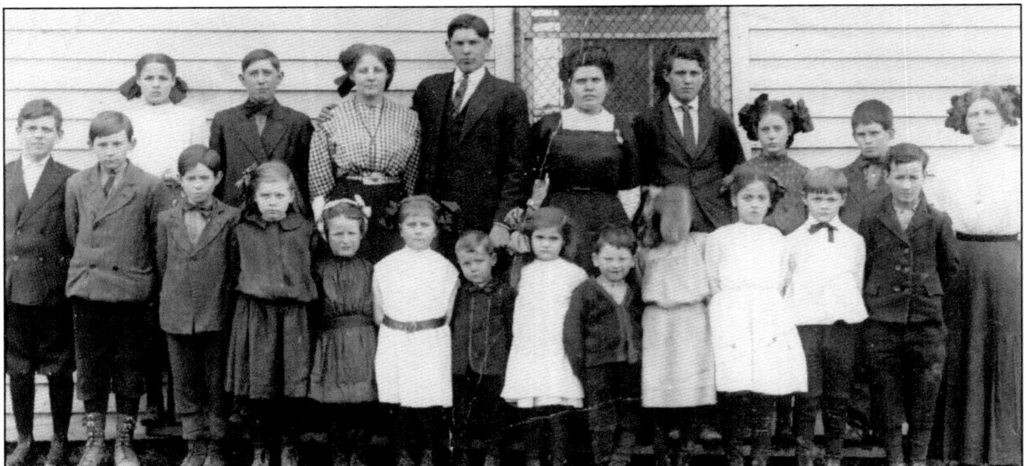

Sycamore (also known as Fought) School, pictured here around 1912, was located about 2 miles north of Two Runs Church on State Route 14. Pictured from left to right are (first row) Henry Sheppard, Gay Morehead, Richard Hall, Ruth Sheppard, Alma Hall, Garnett Trickett, Ernest Board, Carrie Sims, James Sheppard, Ruby Board, Erma Sims, Omer Sims, and Kelsie Board; (second row) Estella Sims, Herbert Sheppard, Pearl Sims, Talmadge Sheppard, Estella Sheppard, Carl Trickett, Laveda Hall, Bud Hall, and teacher Mary Trickett. (Courtesy of Marjorie F. Mayes.)

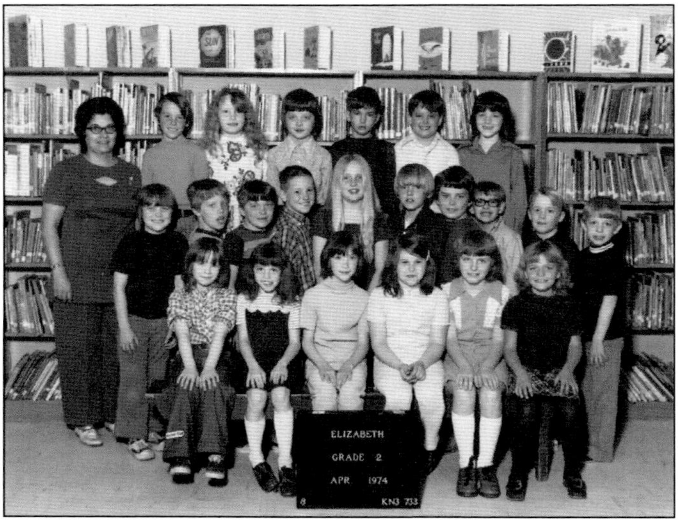

Pearllena Hickman's second-grade class is shown here in April 1974. Pictured from left to right are (first row) Teressa Kelley, Teresa Doty, Teresa Marks, Shelly Kuphner, Janet Conner, and Darlene Miller; (second row) Steve Shears, Donald Hopkins, Randy Villers, David Fought, Brenda Spencer, Richard Ice, Richard Coplin, Danny Bock, Darin Shaw, and Jeff Tanner; (third row) Pearllena Hickman, Kevin Seirs, Brenda Ross, Gary Watkins, Mike Hall, Richard Lowe, and Kelly Sims.

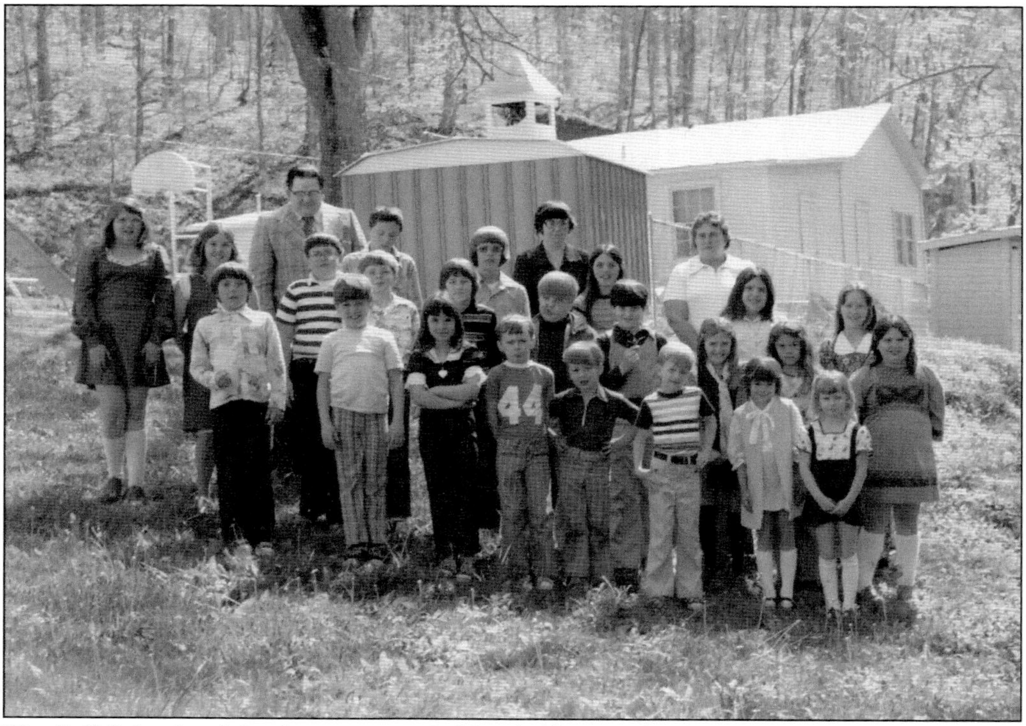

The Bell School in Munday was attended by children in the first through sixth grades. This photograph pictures students and staff from the 1976–1977 term. From left to right are (first row) Delbert Bunner Jr., Brenda Rose, Herbie Toney, Paul Bunner, Randy Lockhart, Sissy Ash, and Tracy Toney; (second row) Eddie Mathess, Tim Bunner, Brian Bunner, Scott Maze, Chris Bunner, Mike Munday, Kelly Toney, Charlene Enoch, and Kim Bunner; (third row) Angie Bunner, Debbie Bunner, Leo Mason, Jay Metz, Gregg Busch, Loretta Boggs, Missy Munday, Mable Bunner (cook), Glenna Rose, and Brenda Toney. (Courtesy of Debbie Hartshorn.)

Four

Business and Industry

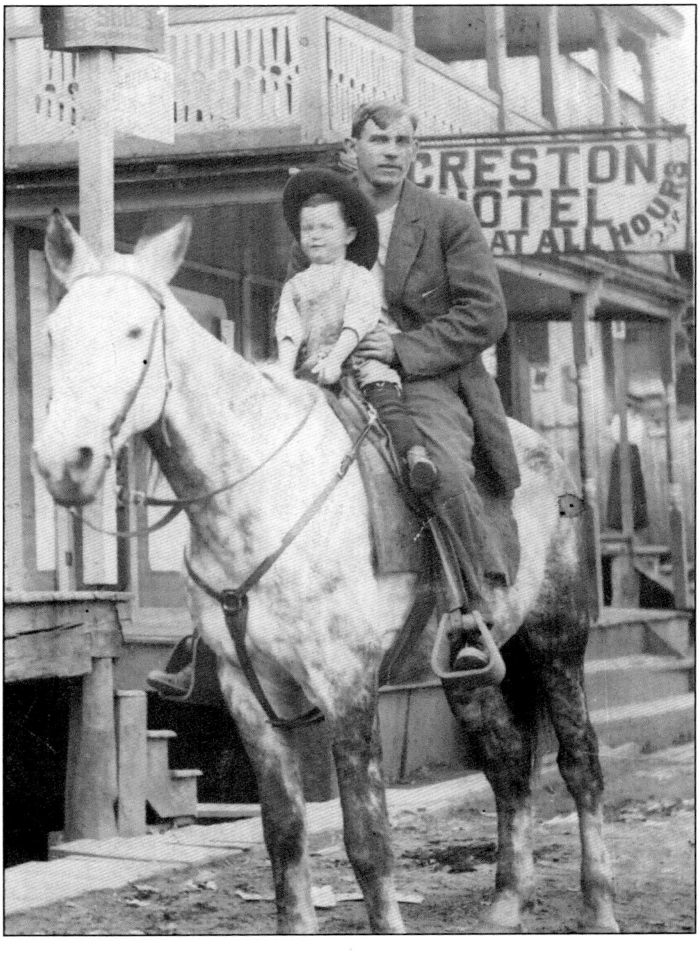

Lloyd Gibson (the child) is photographed on a horse in front of the Stevens Hotel prior to the 1917 fire that destroyed nearly the entire village of Creston. The Stevens Hotel, operated by Capt. and Mrs. Henry Stevens, burned to the ground when a gas jet ignited a fire in an upstairs bedroom. The following businesses were also destroyed in the fire: J. P. Campbell Store, Guy Rader's Hardware and Funeral Parlor, Armstrong Hotel, Eustace Gibson's store and post office, and the Rader Hotel. (Courtesy of Sherry R. Smith.)

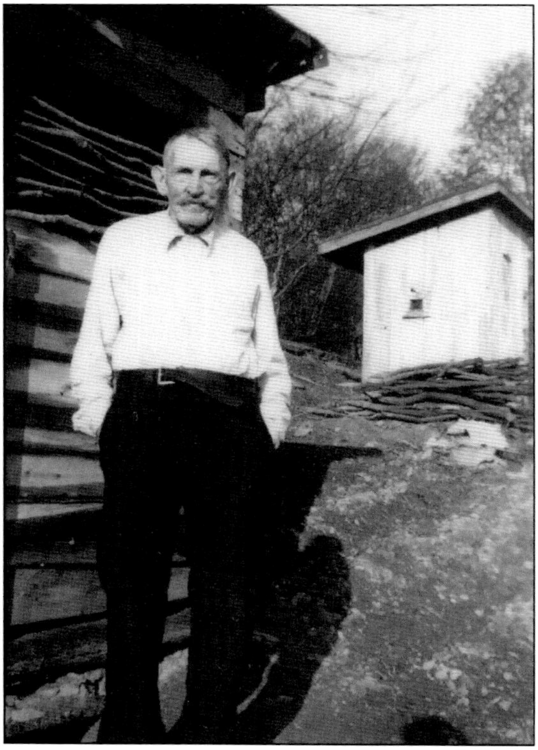

Charles Clarence Menefee owned and operated the C. C. Menefee Store in Burning Springs in the early 1900s. (Courtesy of Carole Menefee.)

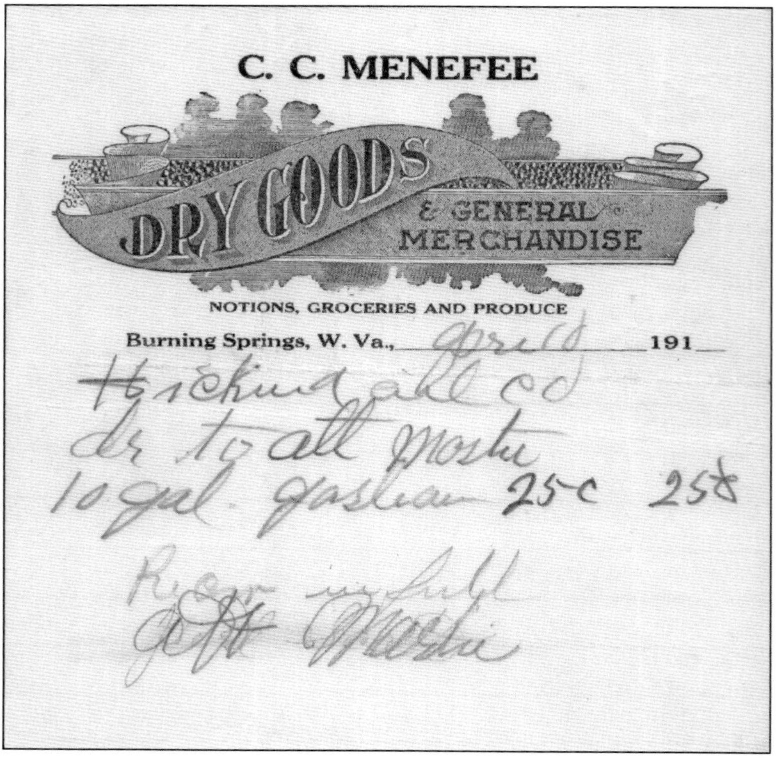

This c. 1910 store receipt from the C. C. Menefee Dry Goods and General Merchandise in Burning Springs shows the price for a gallon of gasoline at 25¢. (Courtesy of Carole Menefee.)

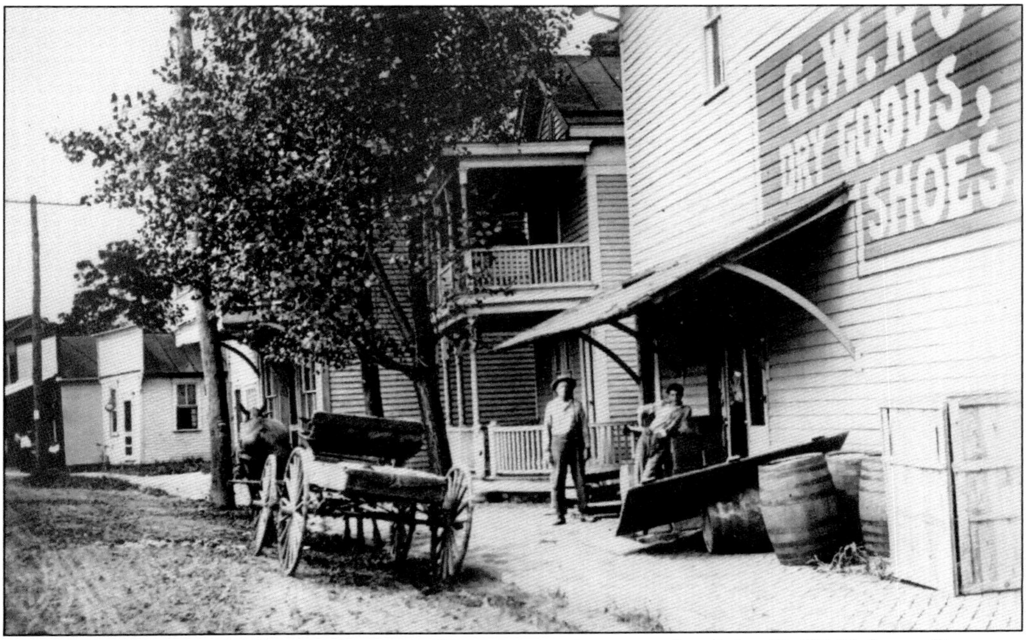

This early photograph shows a horse and wagon waiting outside of the G. W. Roberts Store on Juliana Street in Elizabeth. (Courtesy of Susan Kirby.)

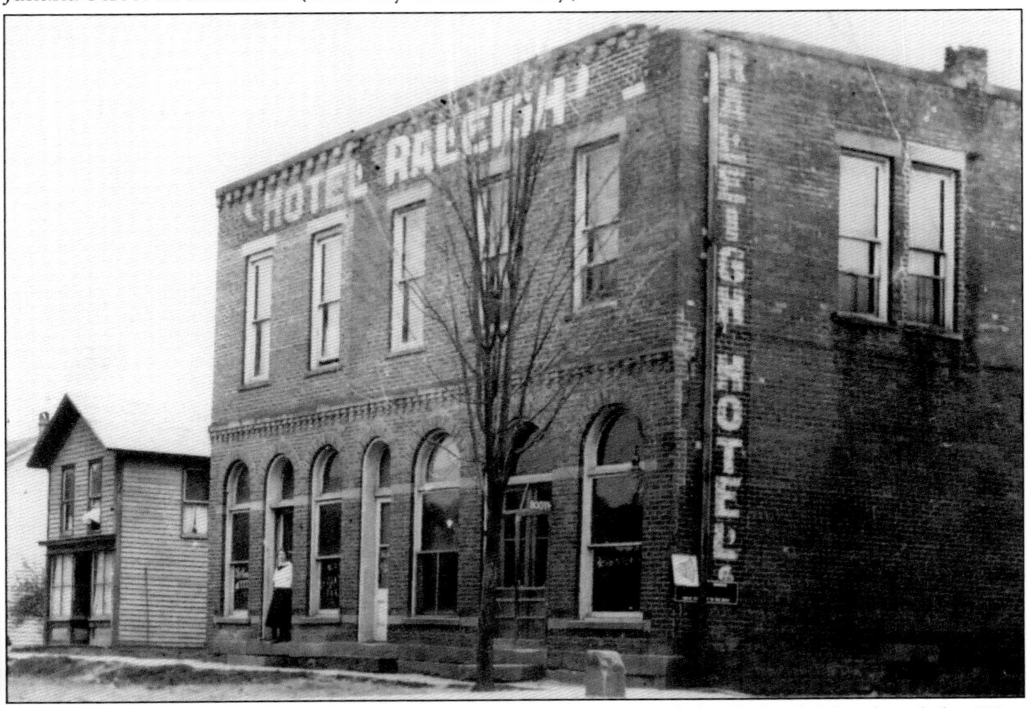

Originally built by W. H. Vernon in 1869, this structure housed the Raleigh Hotel and the Wirt County Bank. In recent years, it housed the Matheny-Pomroy Funeral Home, *Wirt County Journal*, and the Elizabeth Hope Shop. Due to its age and poor condition, the structure was torn down in 2006. (Courtesy of the DAP.)

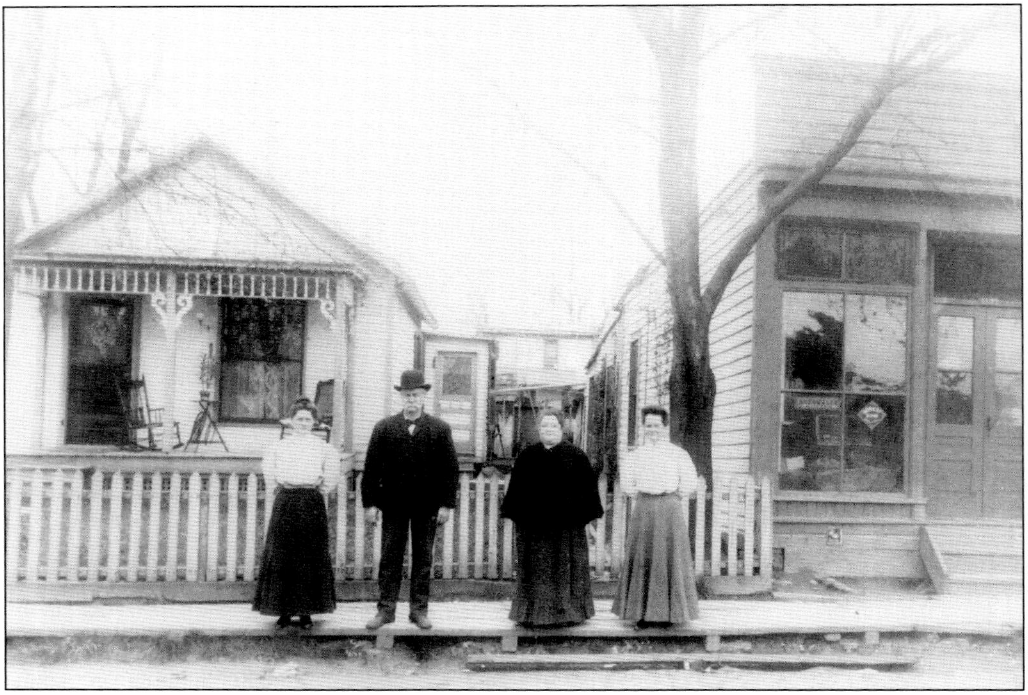

This early photograph of Fought's Store at Burning Springs pictures owner Willie Fought and his wife, Mamie, with daughters Elsie (left) and Emily Keys Fought (right). (Courtesy of Susan Kirby.)

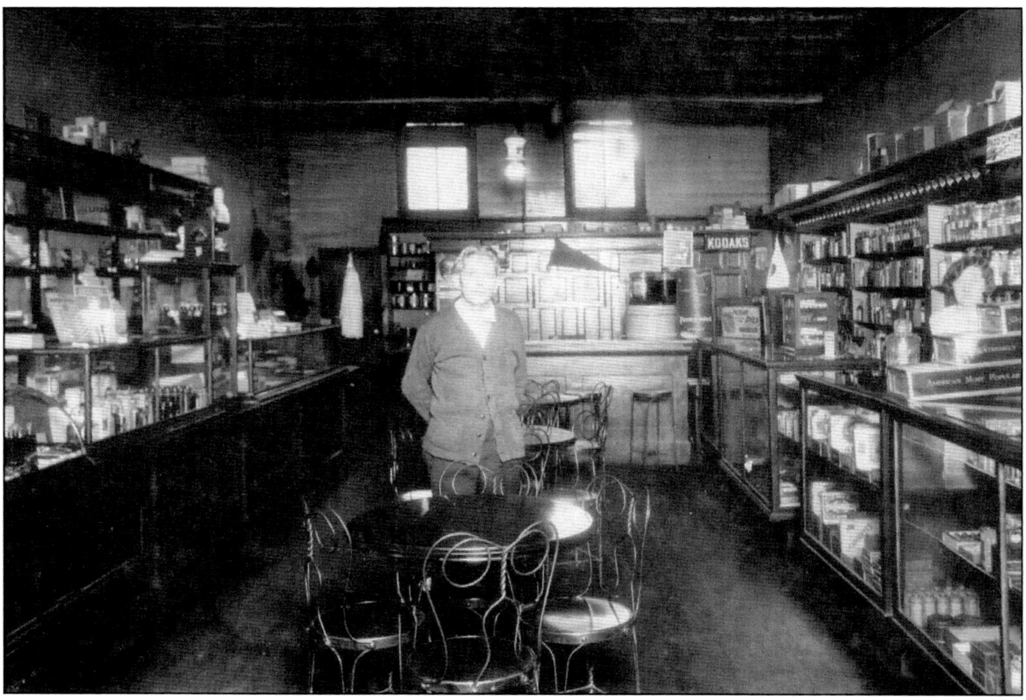

This interior view of the Elizabeth Drug Store shows druggist John Eastman in 1918. (Courtesy of the DAP.)

William Marian Pomroy established the Pomroy Funeral Home in 1907. Following his death, his son, Donald Roscoe Pomroy, took over management until his death in 1969. Ruby Pomroy, Donald's wife, operated the funeral home until it was sold in 1979. This photograph of the funeral home was taken in 1976. (Courtesy of Waneta Thorn Lawrence.)

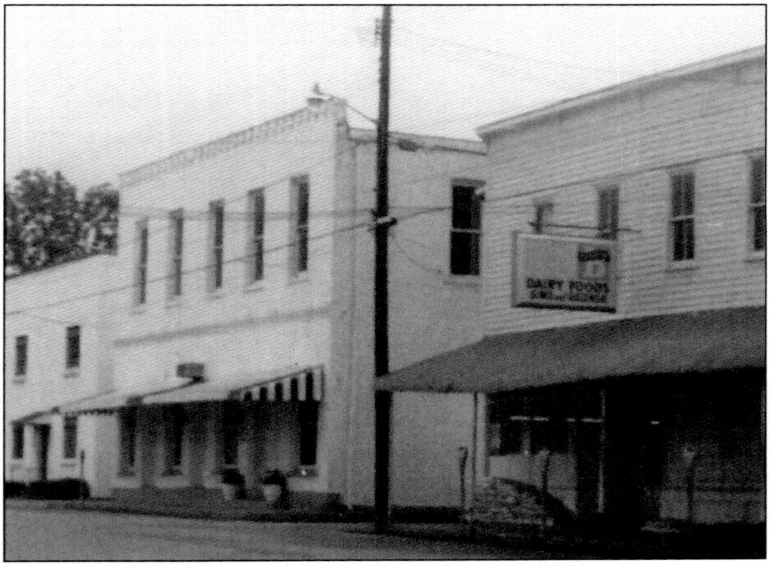

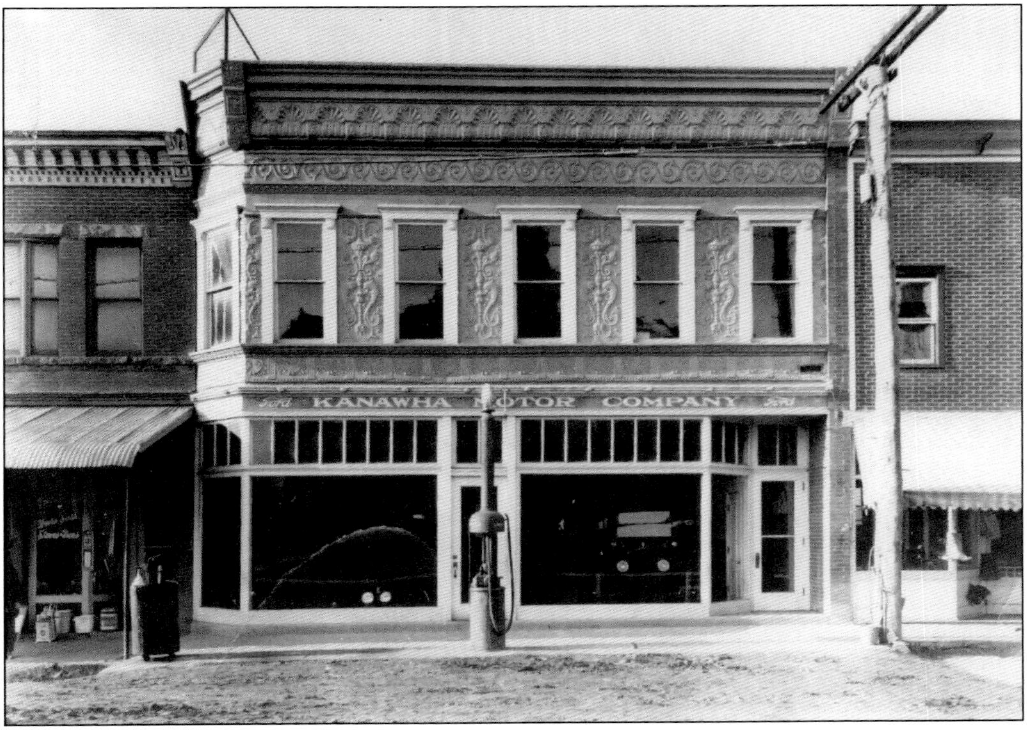

The Kanawha Motor Company was a successful automobile dealership in Elizabeth. It was owned and operated by Howard Mills and offered Lincoln, Ford, and Fordson cars, trucks, and tractors. The dealership also sold gasoline. The hand-operated gasoline pump in the center of this photograph allowed customers to pump their gasoline into a glass cylinder. The gasoline was then gravity-fed into the tank of the automobile. (Courtesy of the DAP.)

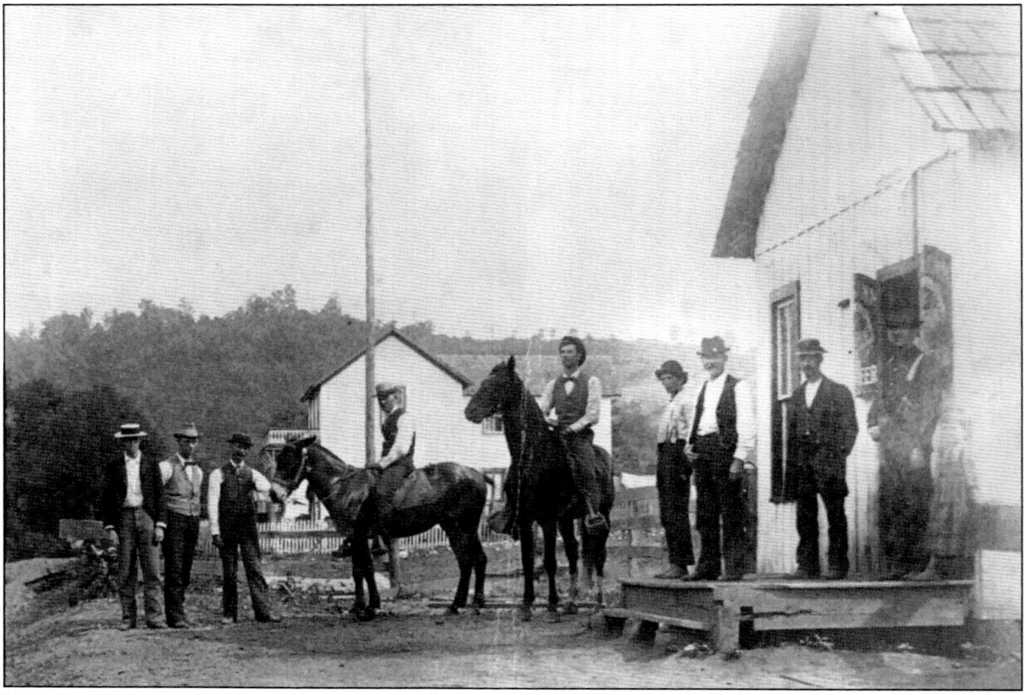

New businesses, like the saloon pictured here, sprang up in Creston during the 1860s oil boom. Creston also had several hotels, dance halls, and brothels. (Courtesy of the DAP.)

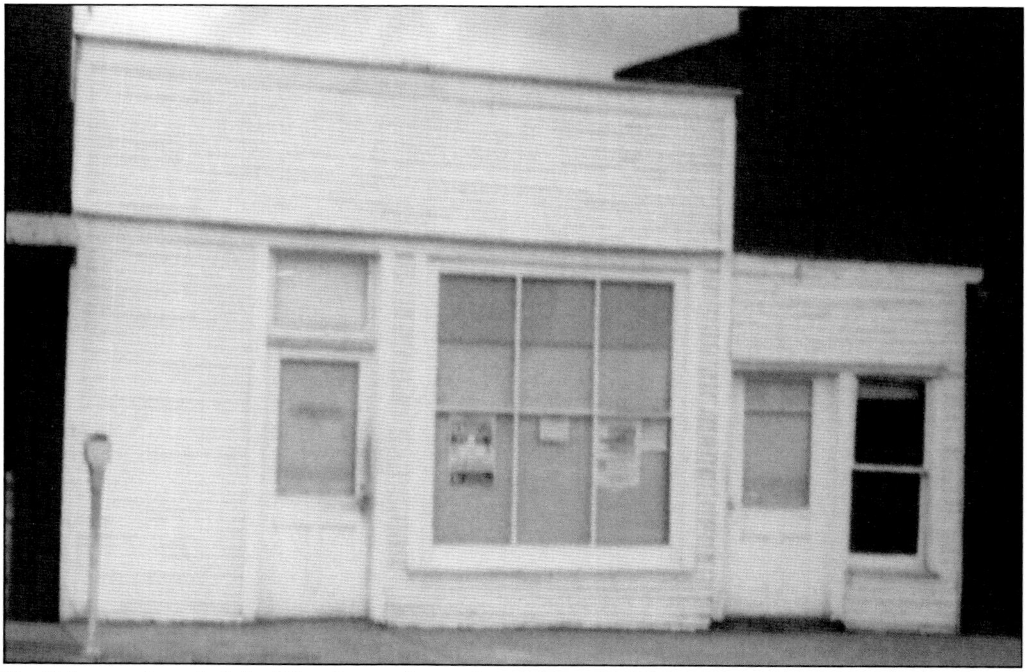

Fred Haverty founded the *Wirt County Journal* in 1908 and sold the newspaper in 1917. Ross Wilson and C. H. Snodgrass published the *Journal* until 1946, when Wilson retired. The 1916 price per copy was 1¢, and a yearly subscription in 1966 was $2.50. (Courtesy of Waneta Thorn Lawrence.)

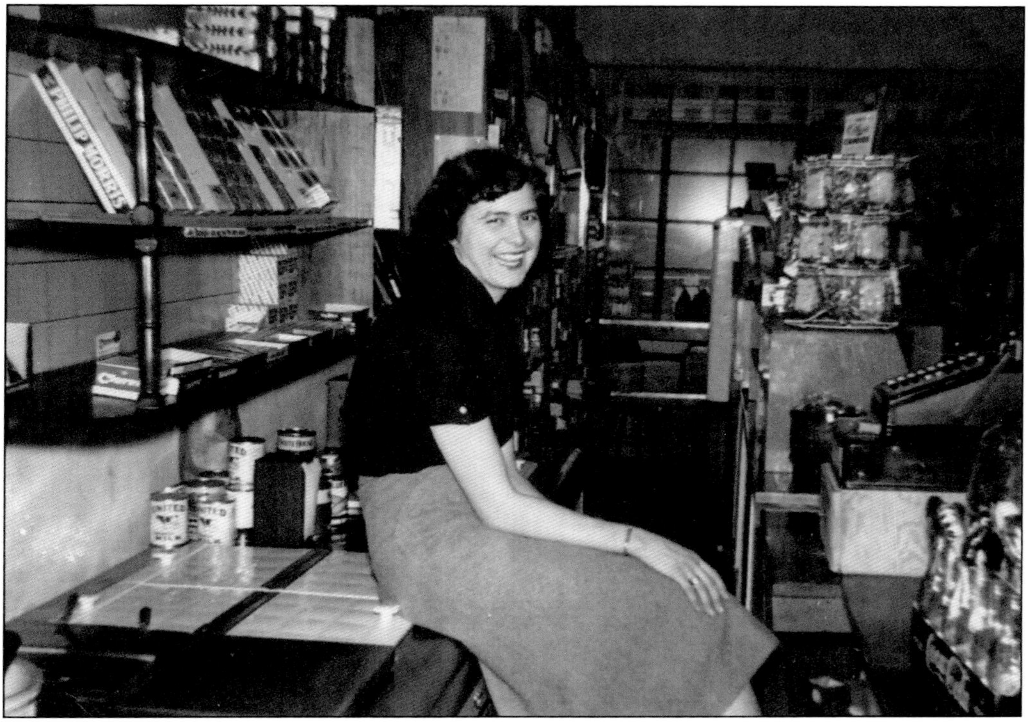

The Theater Restaurant was owned and operated by Robert "Bob" Lowe and his wife, Gayle (above), in the early 1950s. The restaurant was usually busy after football games and when the movies let out. The menu included 15¢ hamburgers, 25¢ milkshakes, 5¢ double-scoop ice cream cones, and 5¢ cups of coffee with free refills. The restaurant closed in 1958, when Bob accepted employment with DuPont in Washington, West Virginia. (Courtesy of Gayle Lowe.)

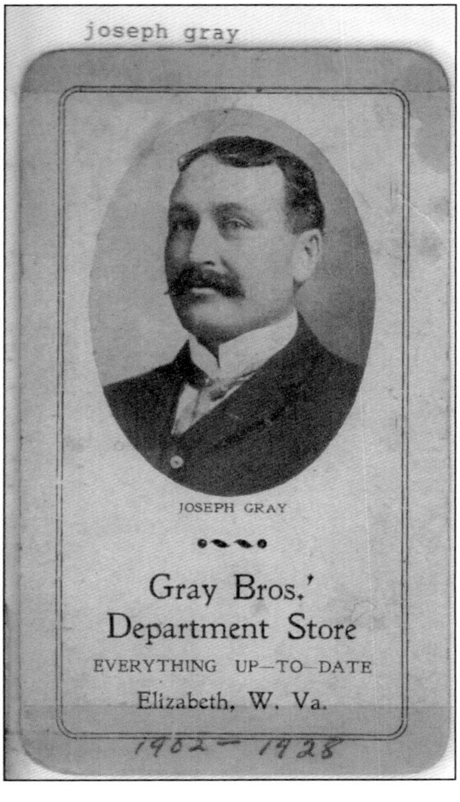

Joseph Gray was the owner of the Gray Brothers Department Store in Elizabeth from 1902 to 1928. The retail store prided itself on offering up-to-date merchandise such as clothing, millinery, and ladies' wraps. (Courtesy of the DAP.)

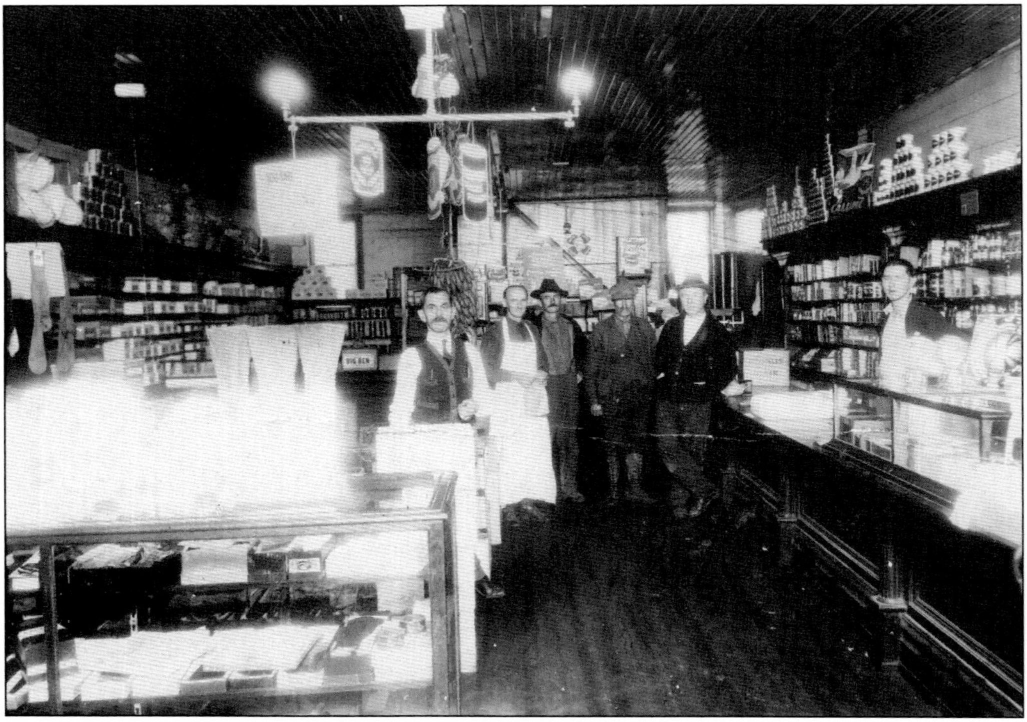

I. P. Thorn and his son, Van W. Thorn, operated the I. P. Thorn Store beside the Kanawha Motor Company in Elizabeth. I. P. continued in the grocery business until his death in 1937. (Courtesy of Betty Thorn.)

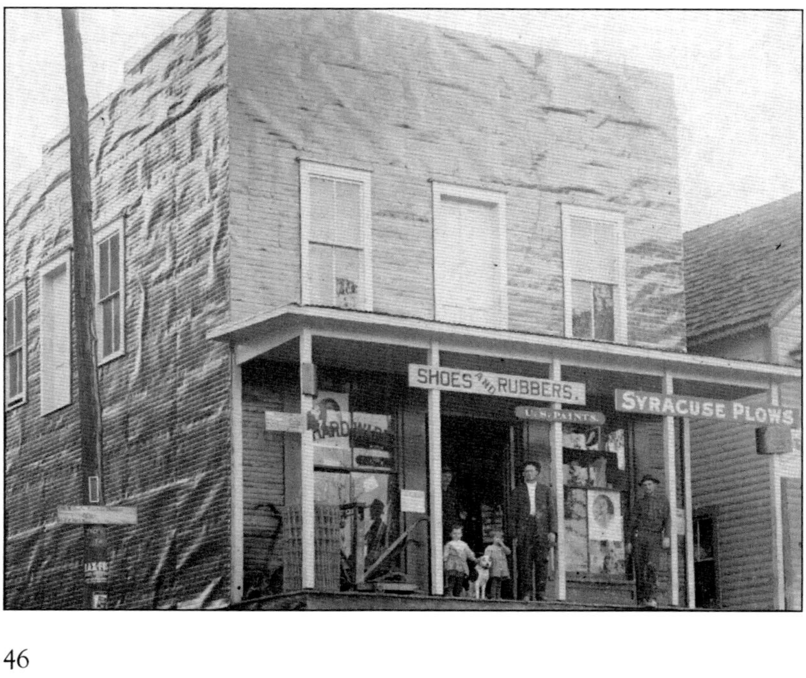

This 1913 photograph of the Creston Store shows Jim Blankenship standing at the entrance of the store with two small children. The little boy on the left with the dog is Lloyd Gibson. The back portion of the store served as living quarters for Jim and Viola Reed. (Courtesy of Sherry R. Smith.)

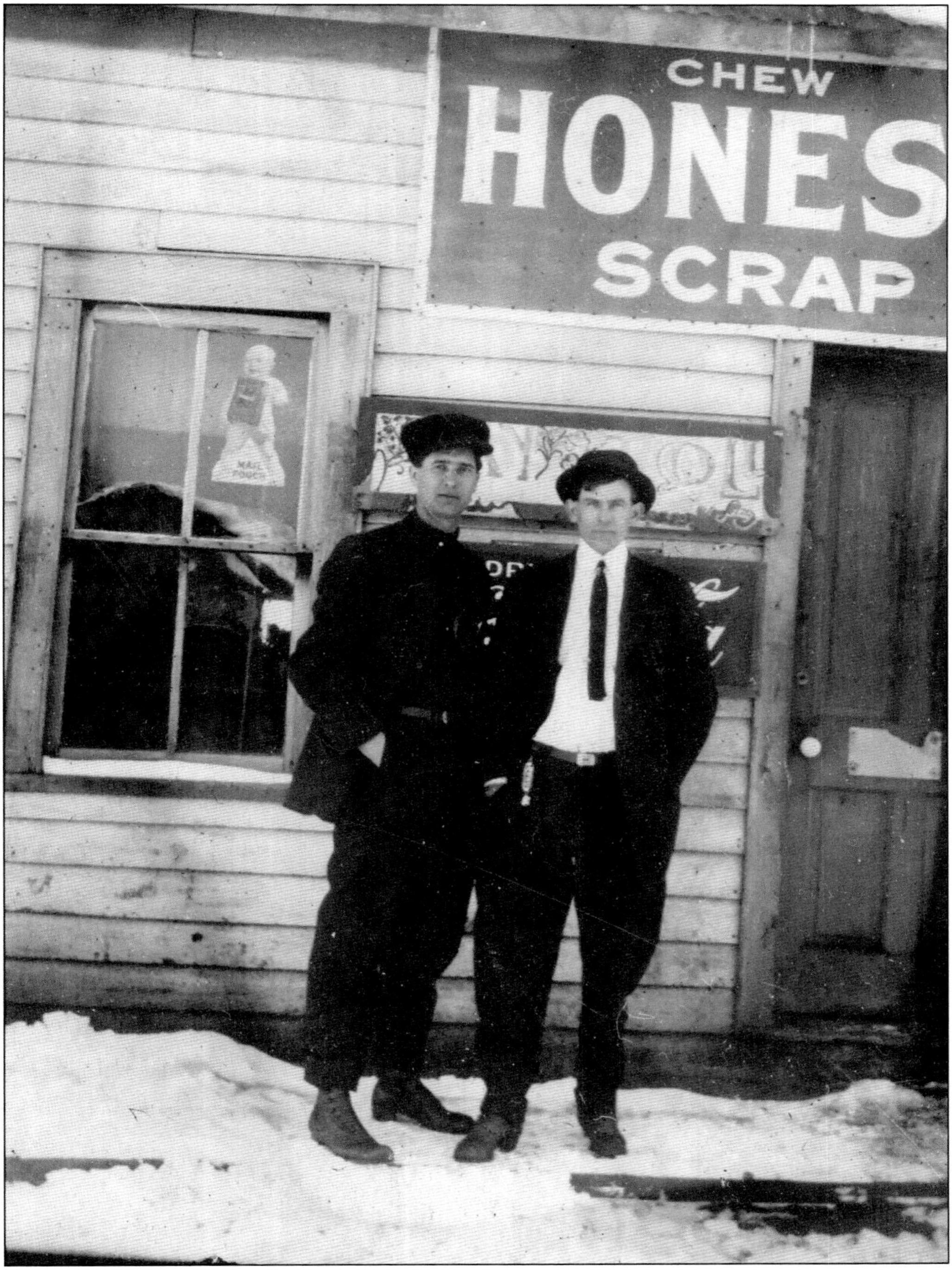

Locals Harry Reed (left) and Al Criss stand in front of the old general store at Creston during the winter. The store advertisement featured Hones Scrap—a popular brand of chewing tobacco. Scrap, or loose-leaf chewing tobacco, was originally the excess of plug tobacco that was sweetened with a molasses-based syrup for flavor. (Courtesy of Sherry R. Smith.)

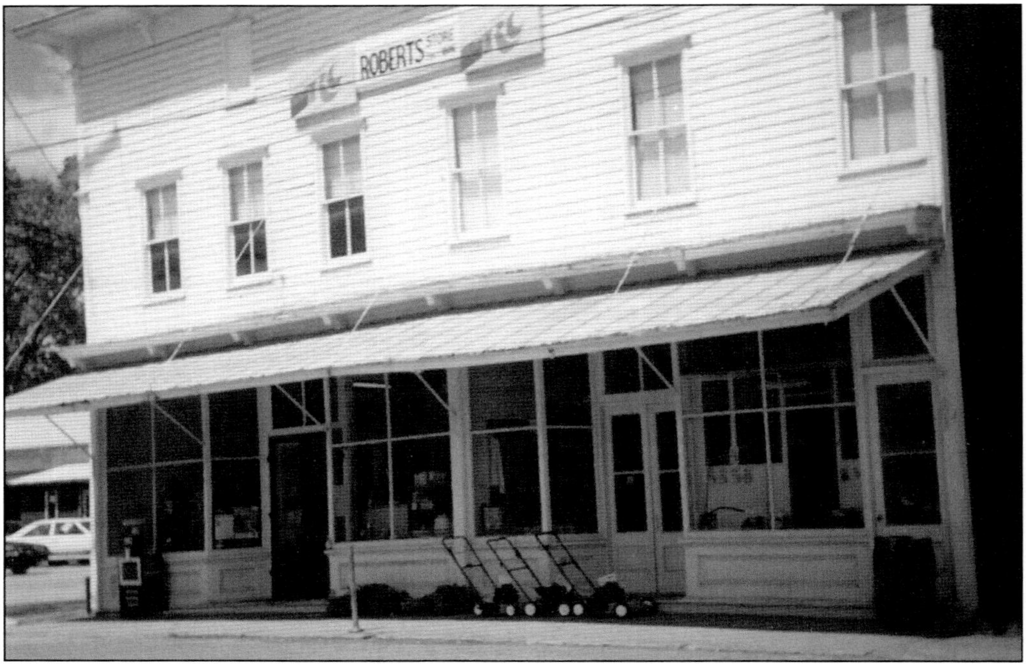

Whether one was looking for chicken feed, fencing, sewing notions, or garden supplies, Roberts Store could always be depended upon for just about anything one might need. Although the store was destroyed in an early-morning fire on June 14, 2006, its staff and their service to the community for over 120 years will long be remembered. (Courtesy of Sherry R. Smith.)

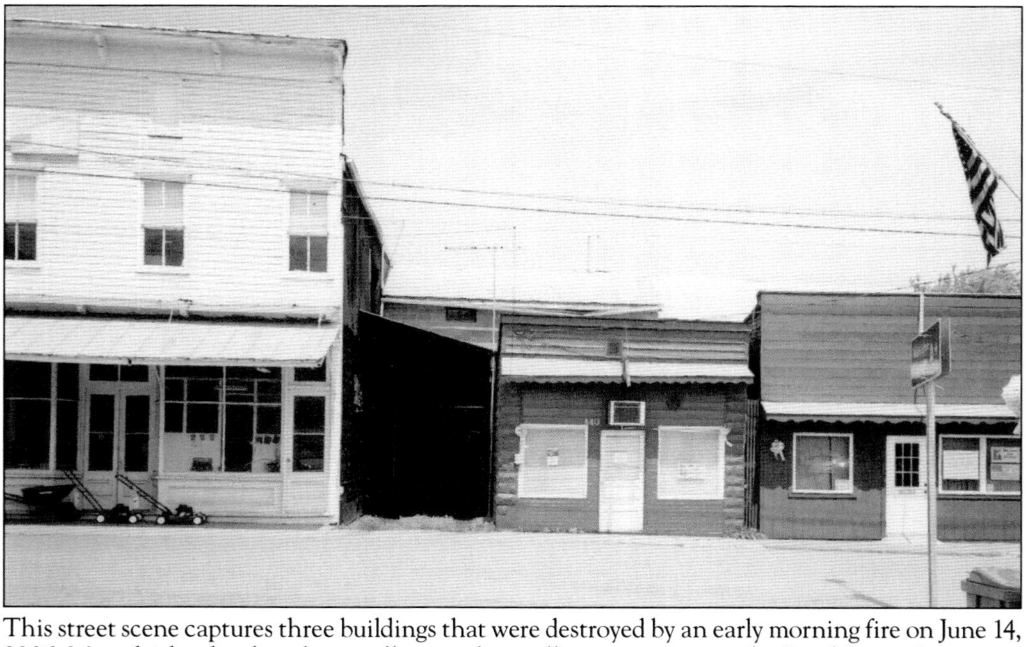

This street scene captures three buildings that were destroyed by an early morning fire on June 14, 2006. Many high school students will remember walking uptown past the Reed Sturm Insurance office and the Satin Swirl Beauty Salon to get a Grape Nehi soda from Roberts Store. (Courtesy of Sherry R. Smith.)

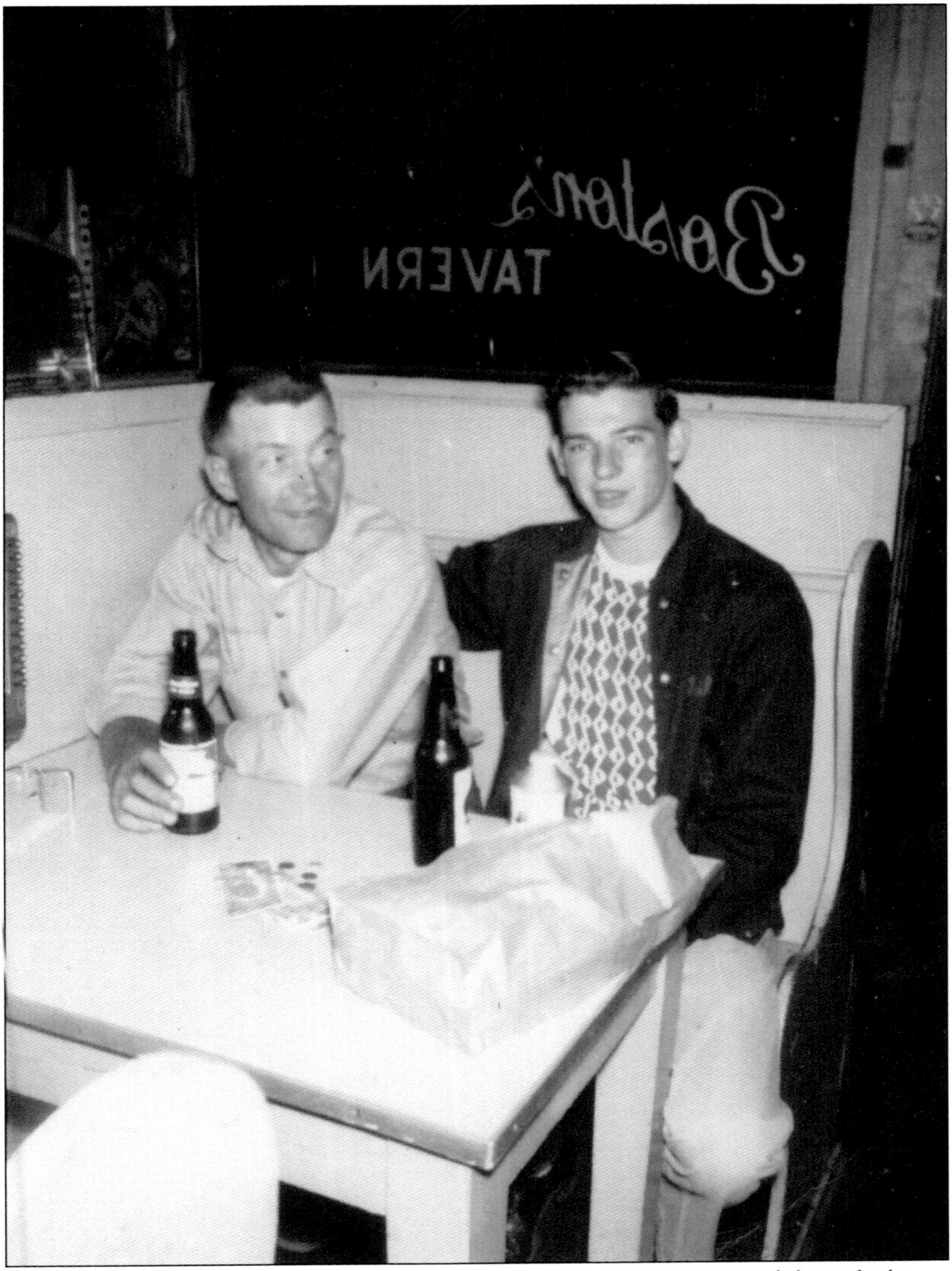

In the 1950s, patrons frequented Boston's Tavern to enjoy a cold beverage and shoot the breeze with owners Ethel and Lloyd "Pudd" Boston. (Courtesy of Basil Cline.)

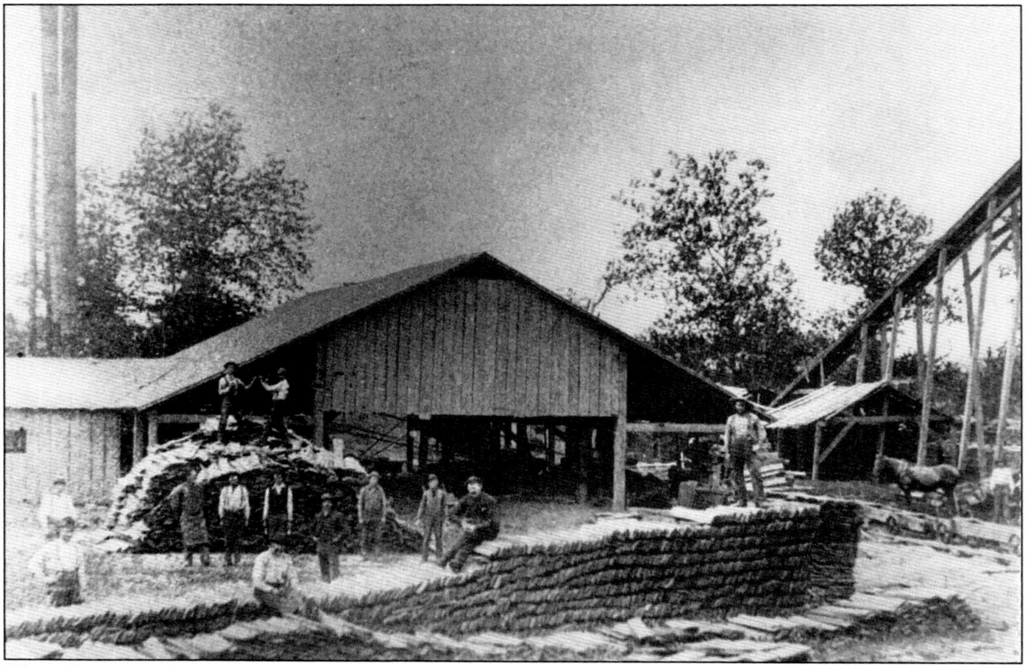

This photograph of the sawmill at Greencastle was taken around 1892. The mill was owned by a Mr. Beckwith. His mill foreman, John Adams, and crew produced barrel staves from timbers that had been cut and floated down the Hughes River to the mill. (Courtesy of Marjorie F. Mayes.)

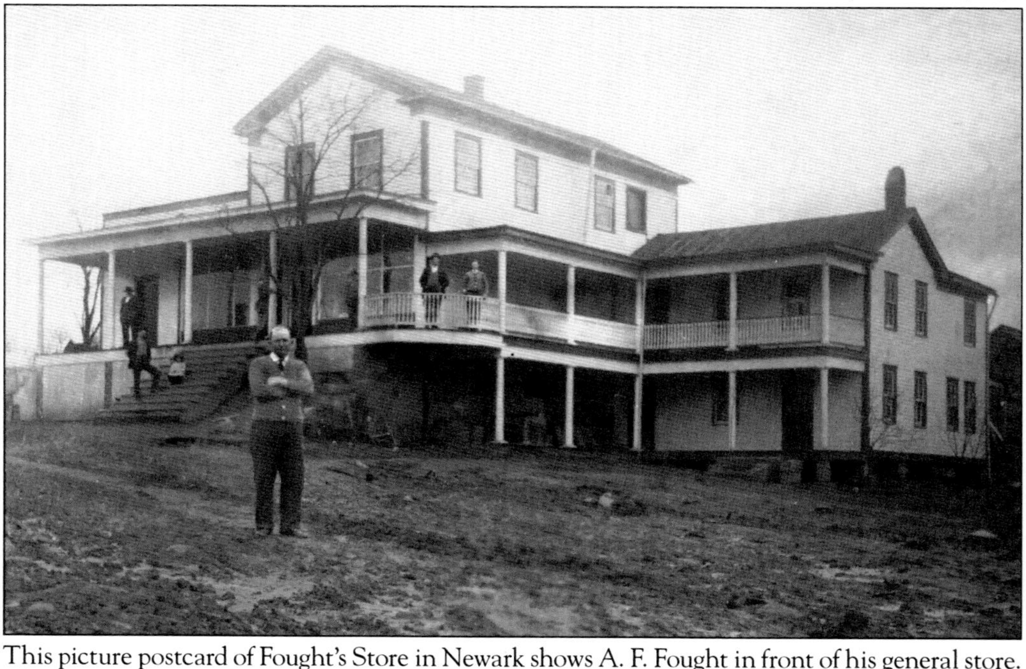

This picture postcard of Fought's Store in Newark shows A. F. Fought in front of his general store. John Keys is pictured on the steps with his daughter Pauline. This postcard, cancelled in 1910, was purchased by Fought's daughter Marjorie Mayes from a gentleman in Maine. (Courtesy of Marjorie F. Mayes.)

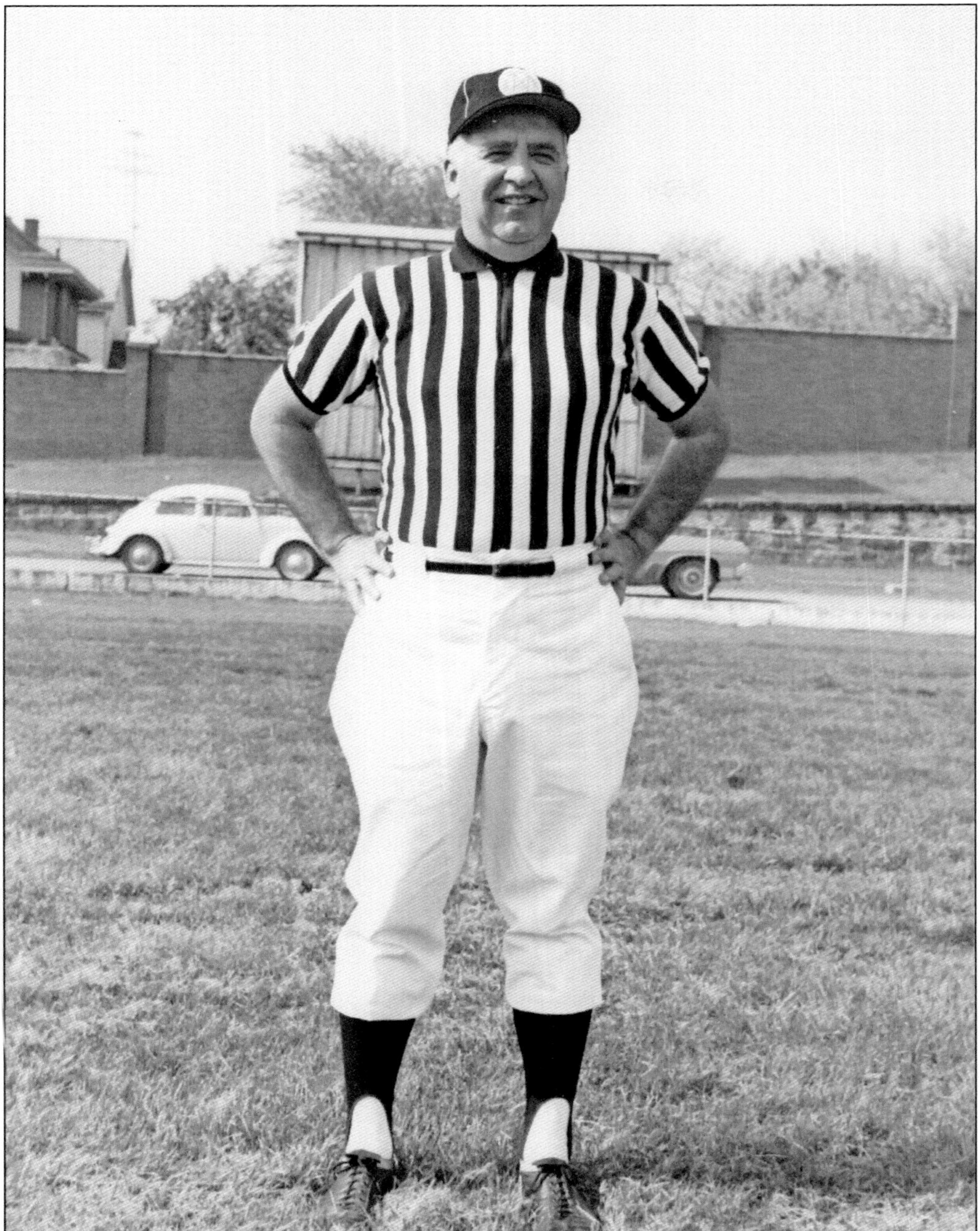

Longtime county resident Sam Williams was a well-known football official. After graduating from Glenville State College in 1946, Sam entered the sports industry as a football coach at Wirt County High School. He went on to obtain a master's degree from West Virginia University and served as the executive secretary of the West Virginia Secondary Schools Activities Commission from 1968 until his retirement in 1985. During the years 1947 to 1975, Sam officiated in high school football games, state championships, the West Virginia Athletic Conference, the Central Ohio League, and the Mid-American Conference.

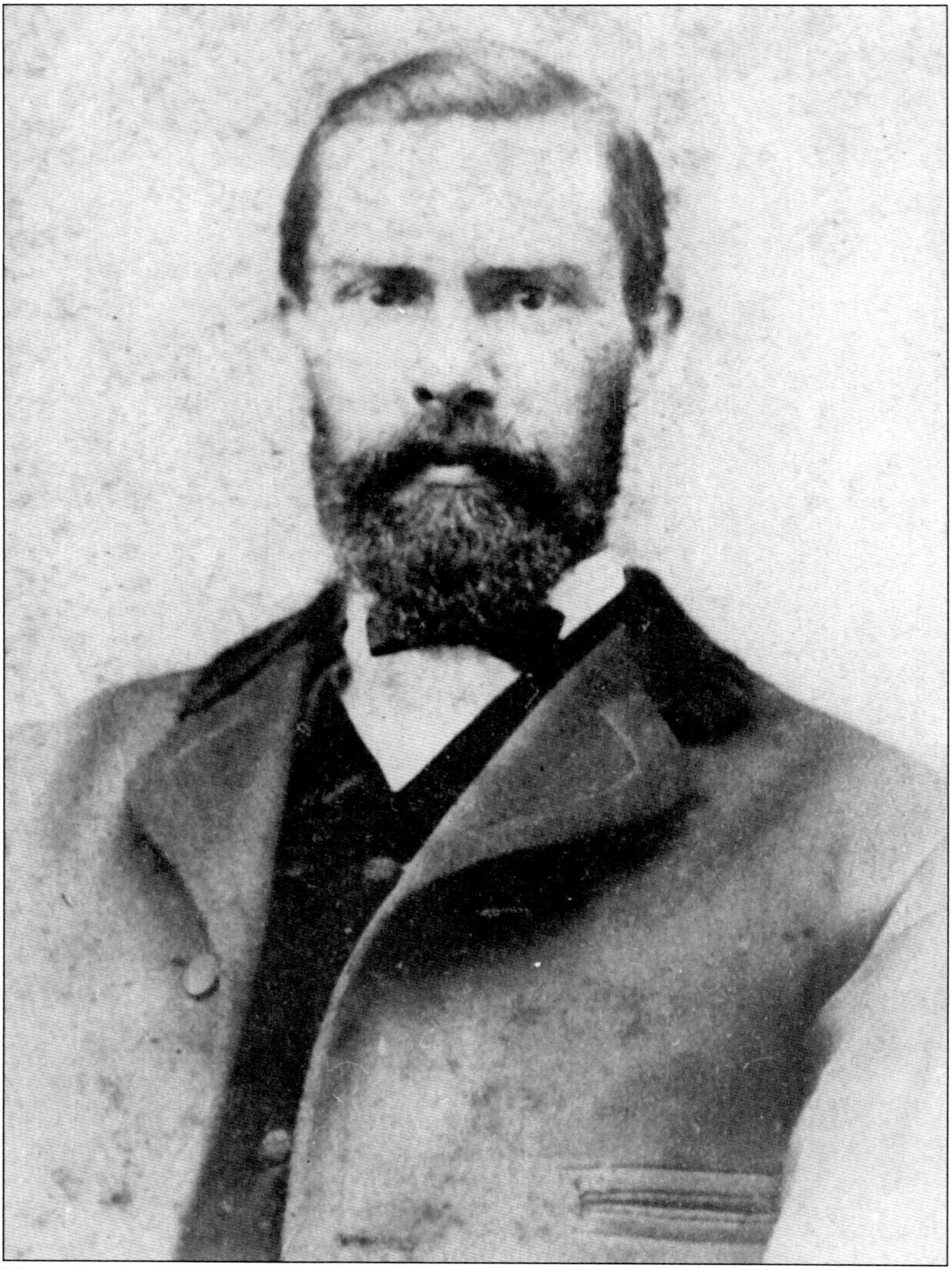

Hiram Butcher Pribble (October 12, 1841–February 11, 1903) was the son of Hiram and Deborah Pribble. He lived in the Greencastle area of Wirt County and was known as "Bee" by most folks. (Courtesy of Marjorie F. Mayes.)

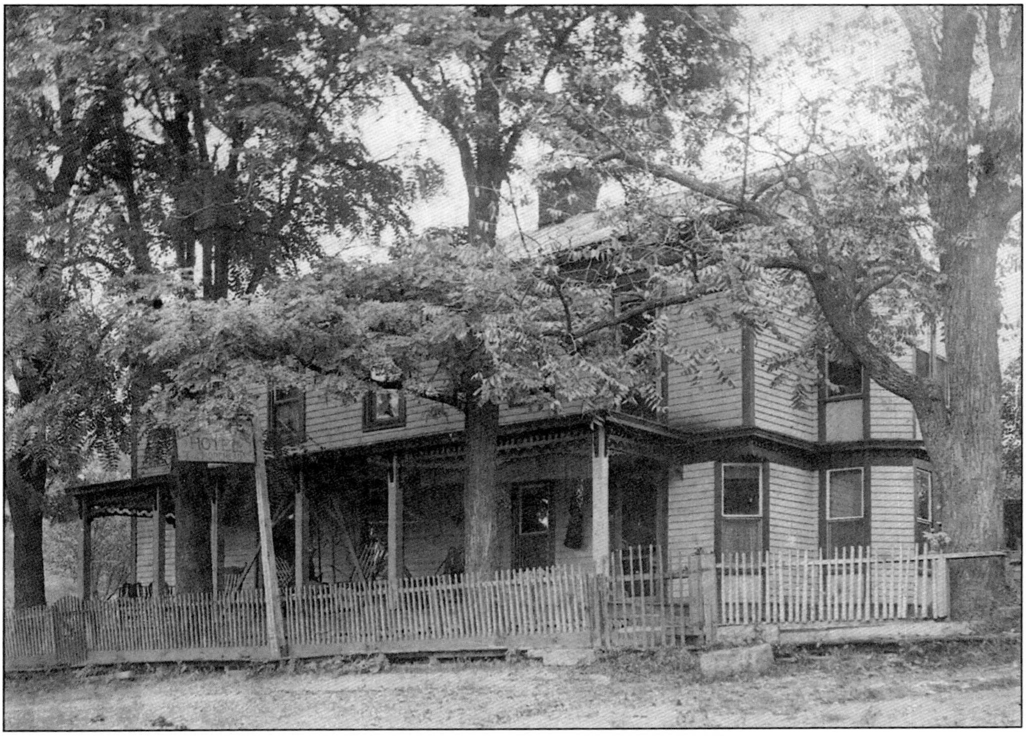

This photograph of the Greencastle Hotel was taken from the ferry road about 1890. Thomas J. Morehead operated the hotel for several years. (Courtesy of Marjorie F. Mayes.)

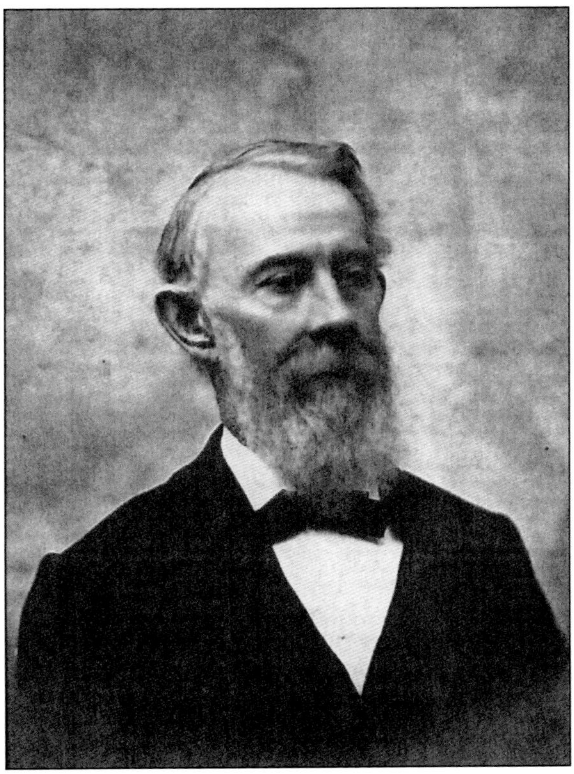

Thomas J. Morehead was born on August 8, 1830. Following his service to his country in the Civil War, he operated the Greencastle Hotel. He died on May 20, 1904, and is buried in the Fought Cemetery. (Courtesy of Marjorie F. Mayes.)

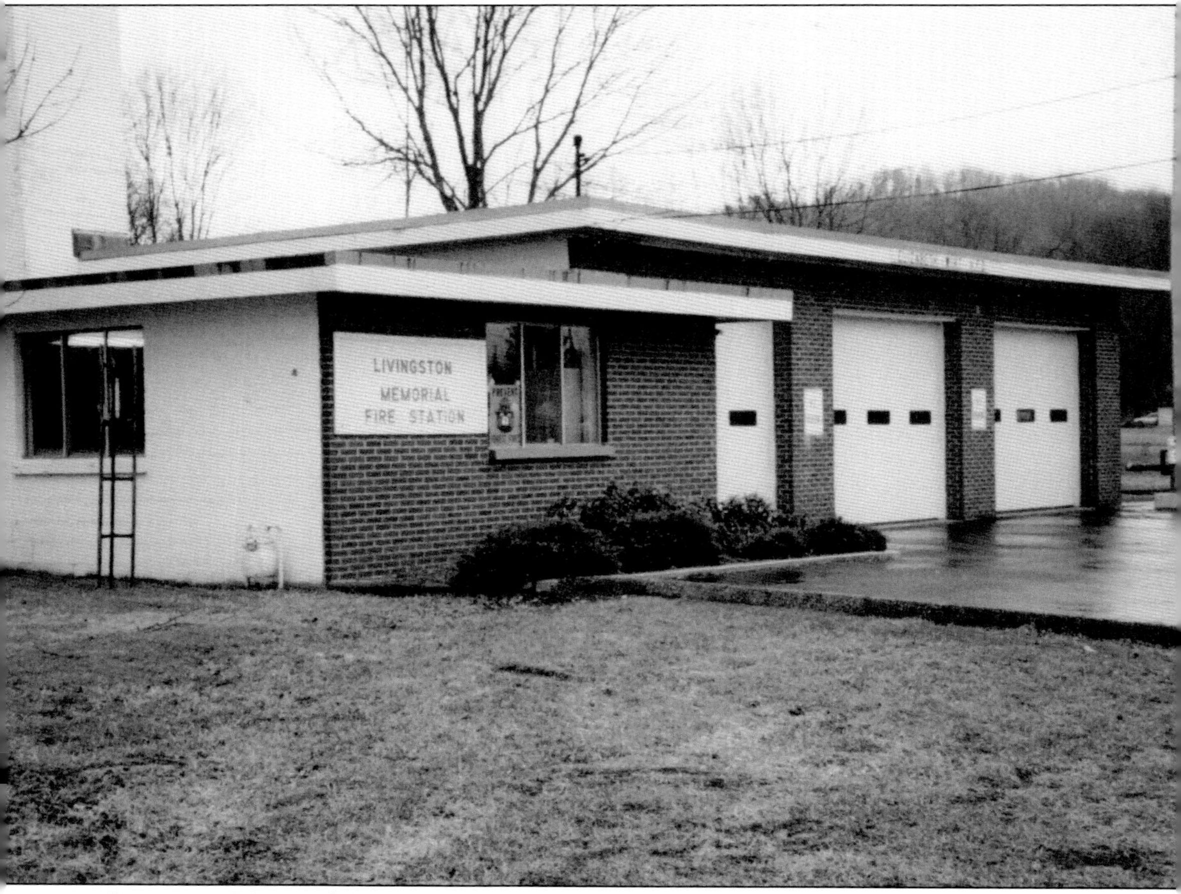

Livingston Memorial Fire Station was named in honor of Minnie Livingston, who donated land for the station in November 1965. The original floor plan measured 34 feet, 4 inches by 62 feet, allowing enough space to house the fire trucks and equipment. The first meeting was held in the new fire station on January 24, 1966. This photograph was taken after remodeling. (Courtesy of the Elizabeth-Wirt VFD.)

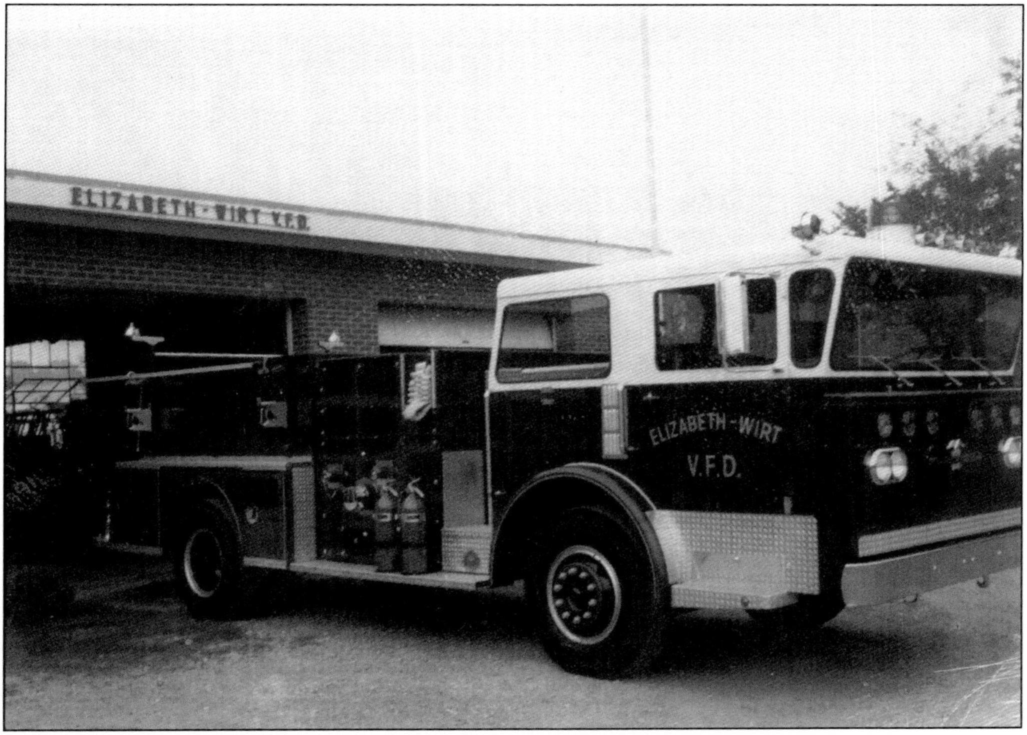

This American LaFrance was added to the fire department's fleet of trucks in June 1977. (Courtesy of the Elizabeth-Wirt VFD.)

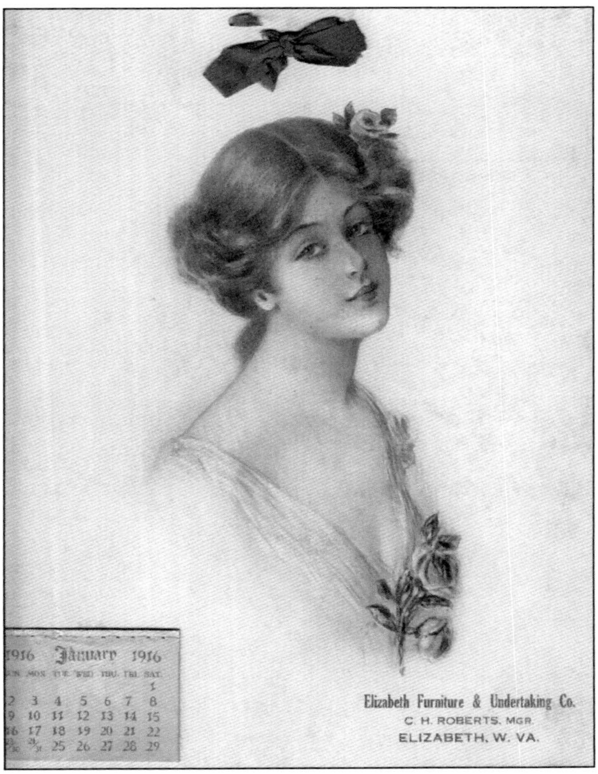

Advertisement calendars such as this one from 1916 were giveaways offered to customers of the Elizabeth Furniture and Undertaking Company in Elizabeth. (Courtesy of the DAP.)

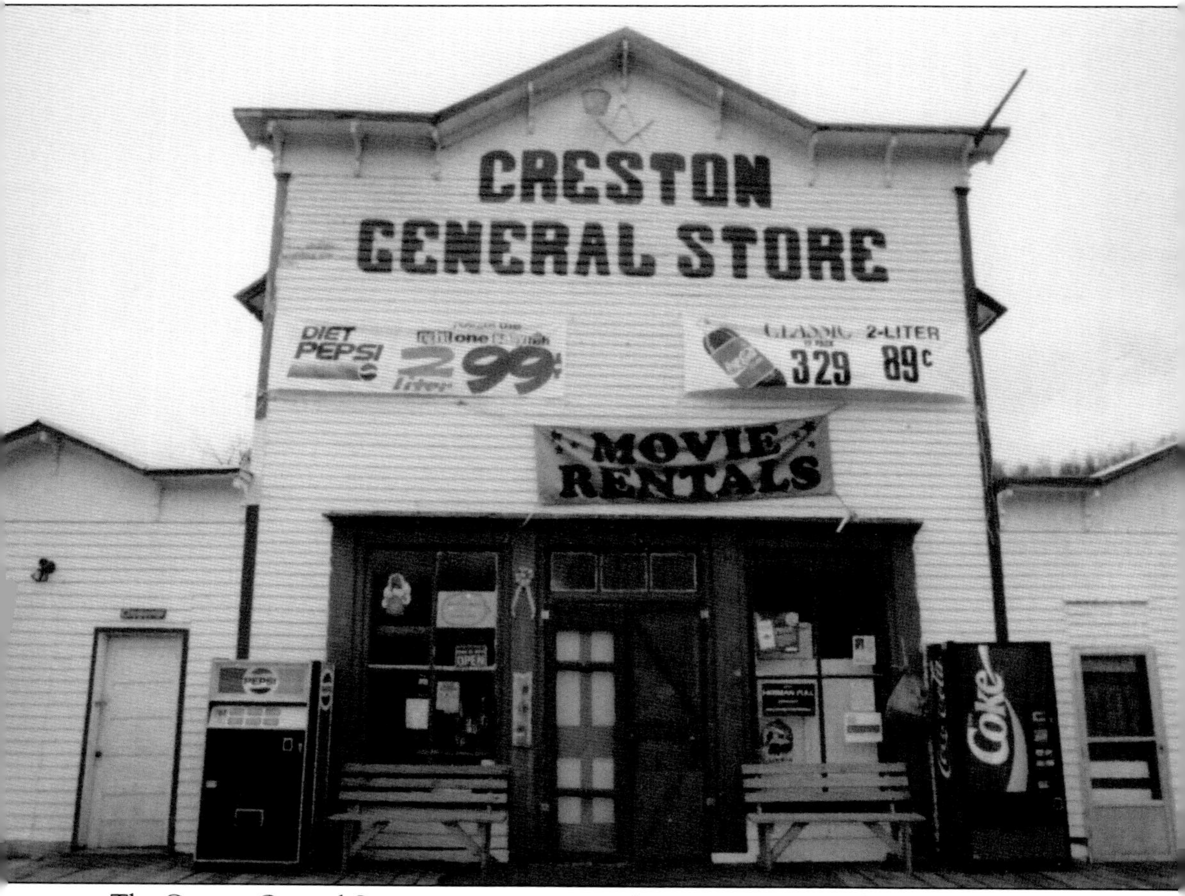

The Creston General Store was a mainstay in the community since being built in the 1880s. Through the years, the store was home to a furniture business, drugstore, undertaking establishment, meeting hall, and post office. At the time of this photograph, Carl and Donna Ferrell operated the store. The store fell to arson in September 2008. (Courtesy of Russ Snyder.)

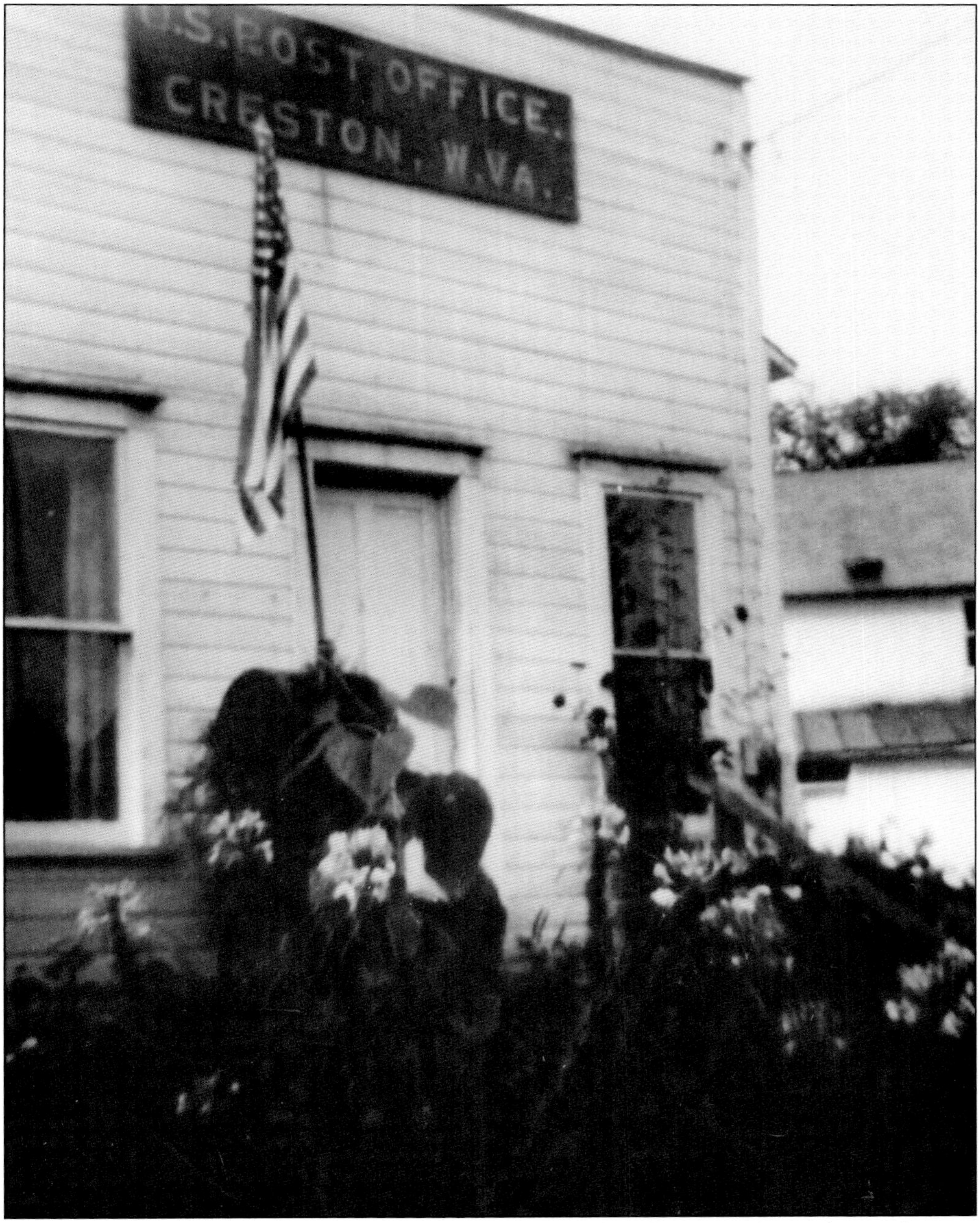

The first post office in Creston was established in 1882. The office was relocated several times. This location was home of the post office in its final days before being ordered closed in the fall of 2007. Many customers fondly remember postmistresses Mary Emma Lynch and Mildred Lynch and rural route carrier Oris Meadows. (Courtesy of Russ Snyder.)

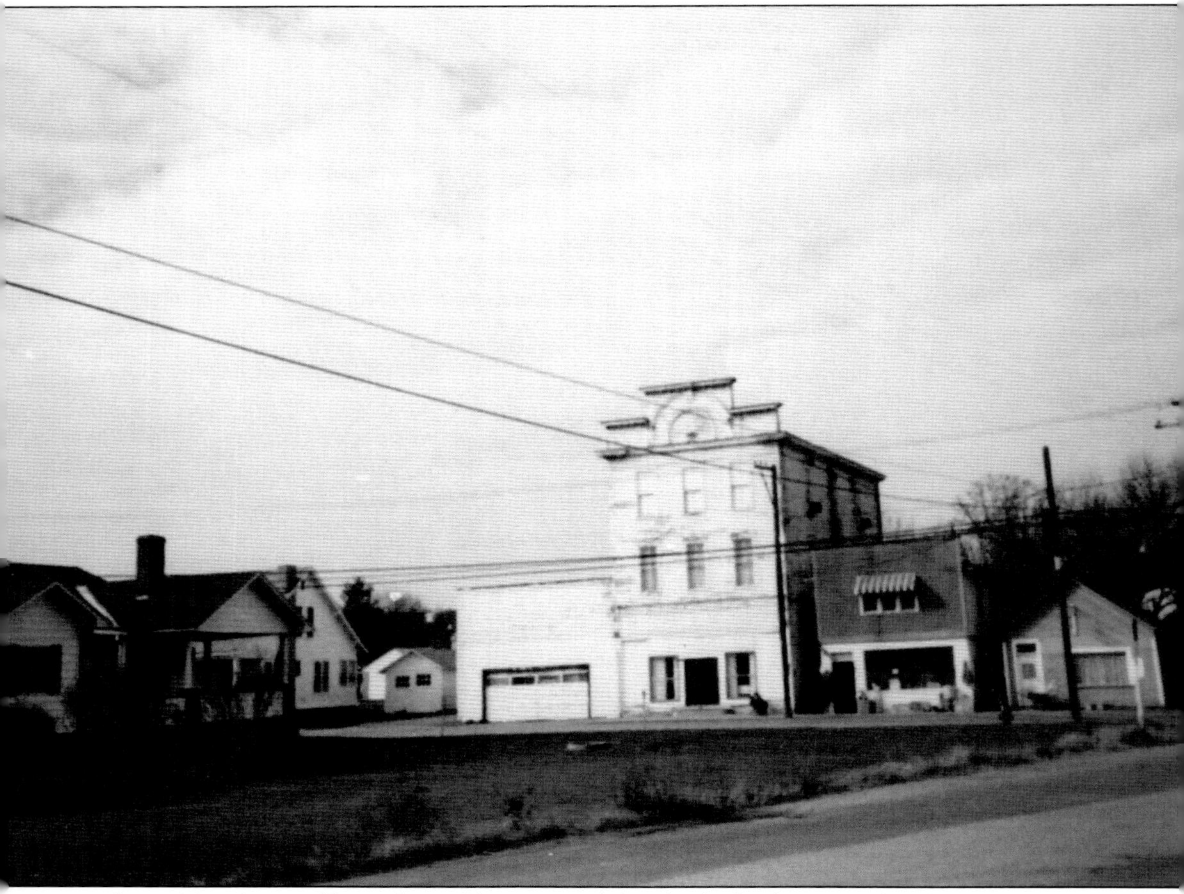

James Vogeding and his wife, Freddie, operated the Elizabeth Theater in this three-story structure from the early 1940s until closing the business in 1961. Admission to the movies was 25¢ for adults and 10¢ for children under 12. Although the building no longer stands, many will remember it as the Elizabeth State Police Detachment. (Courtesy of the Ludwig family.)

Five

People around the County

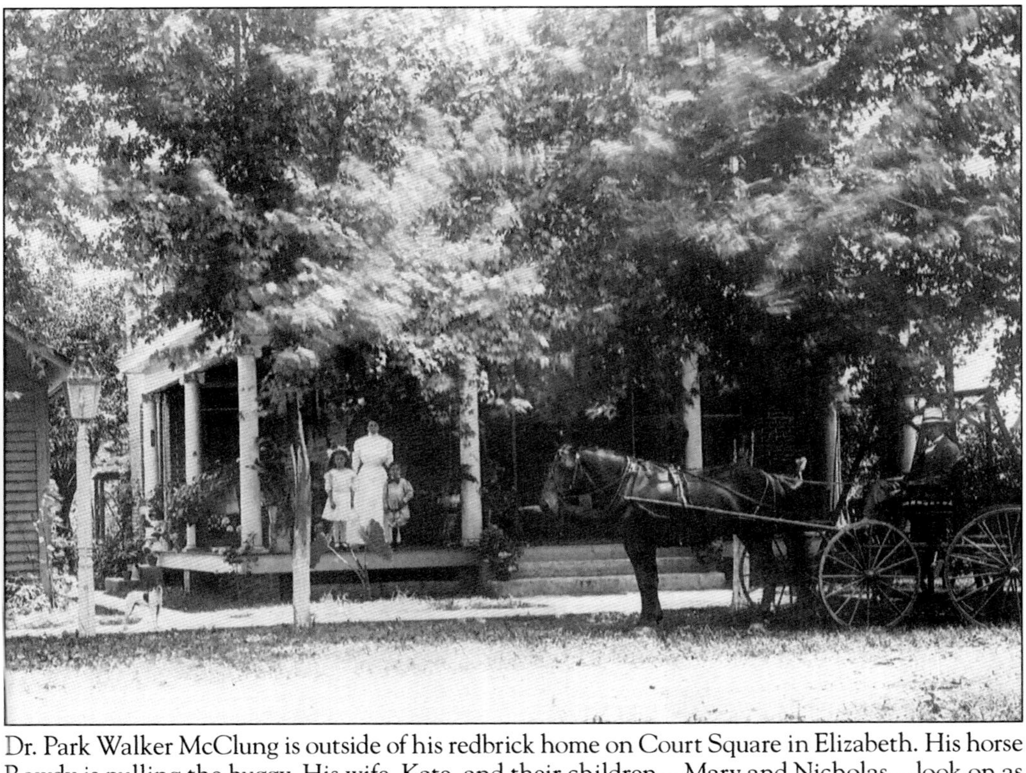

Dr. Park Walker McClung is outside of his redbrick home on Court Square in Elizabeth. His horse Rowdy is pulling the buggy. His wife, Kate, and their children—Mary and Nicholas—look on as he heads off to make house calls to his patients. (Courtesy of Paula Licklider Smith.)

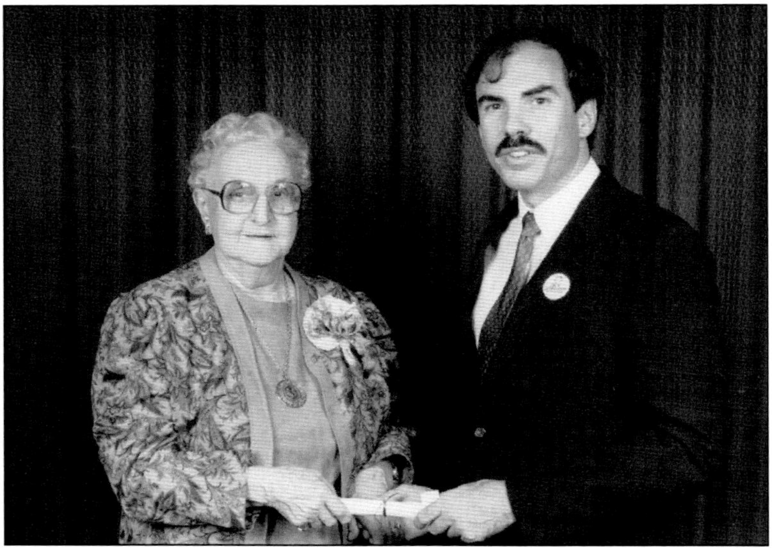

Longtime Wirt County Democrat Florence Cline was named West Virginia's Democrat of the Year in 1987. Congressman Bob Wise was on hand at the Democratic Party's annual Jefferson-Jackson dinner to present Florence with this honor. Arkansas governor Bill Clinton was the guest speaker at the dinner. (Courtesy of Basil Cline.)

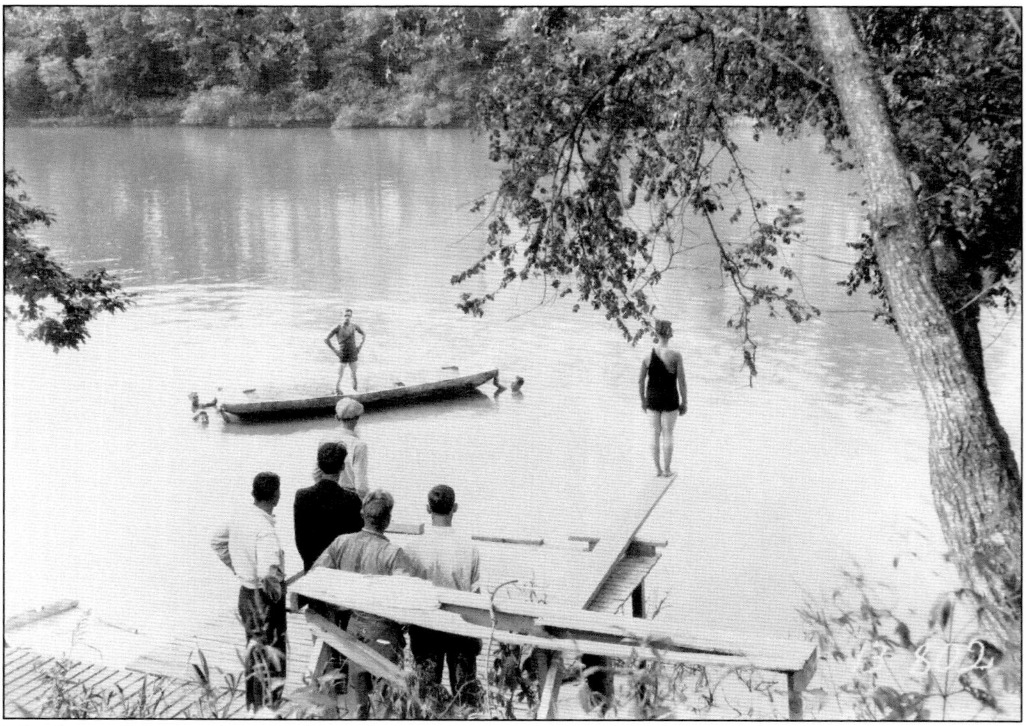

Members of Camp Crawford Civilian Conservation Corps Company 1512 enjoy a swim at the "old swimming hole" on the Little Kanawha River near what is now Sportsman Park in Elizabeth. Company 1512 was formed at Fort Knox, Kentucky, in October 1933 and arrived in Elizabeth on May 17, 1934, to build roads, plant trees, and stop soil erosion. The area continued to benefit from their conservation efforts until the camp closed in March 1939. (Courtesy of the West Virginia State Archives.)

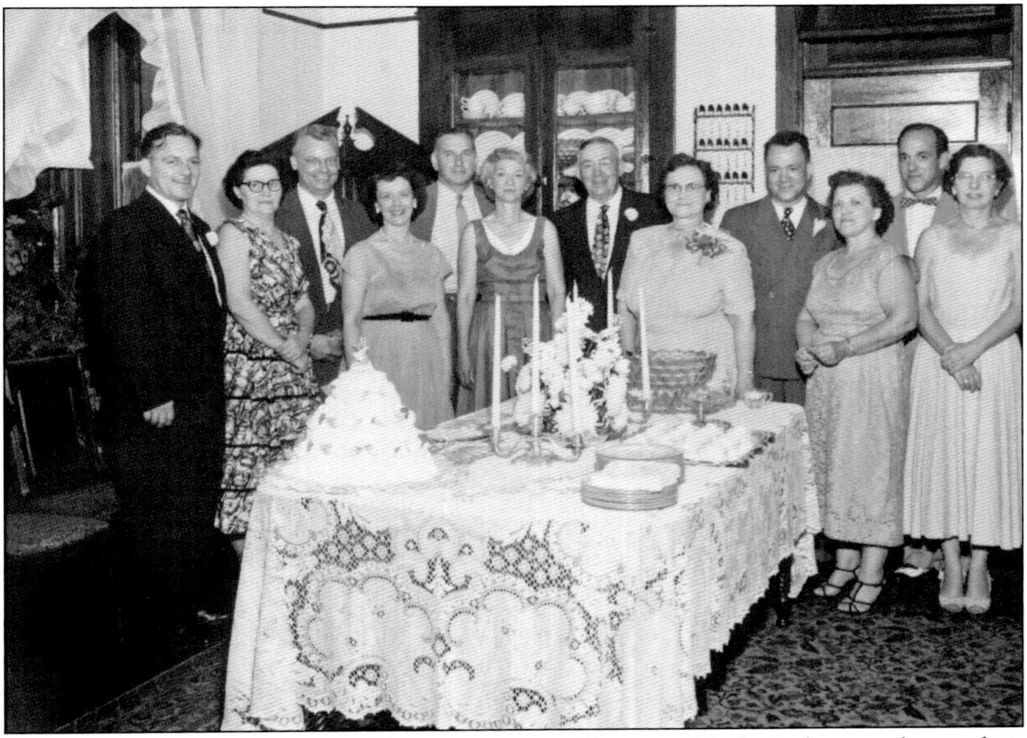

This photograph of the golden wedding anniversary of James and Lydia Parks was taken at their residence on Washington Street in Elizabeth. The Park home was converted into the Busch Funeral Home by Gregg and Mary Beth Busch in the mid-1980s. (Courtesy of the West Virginia State Archives.)

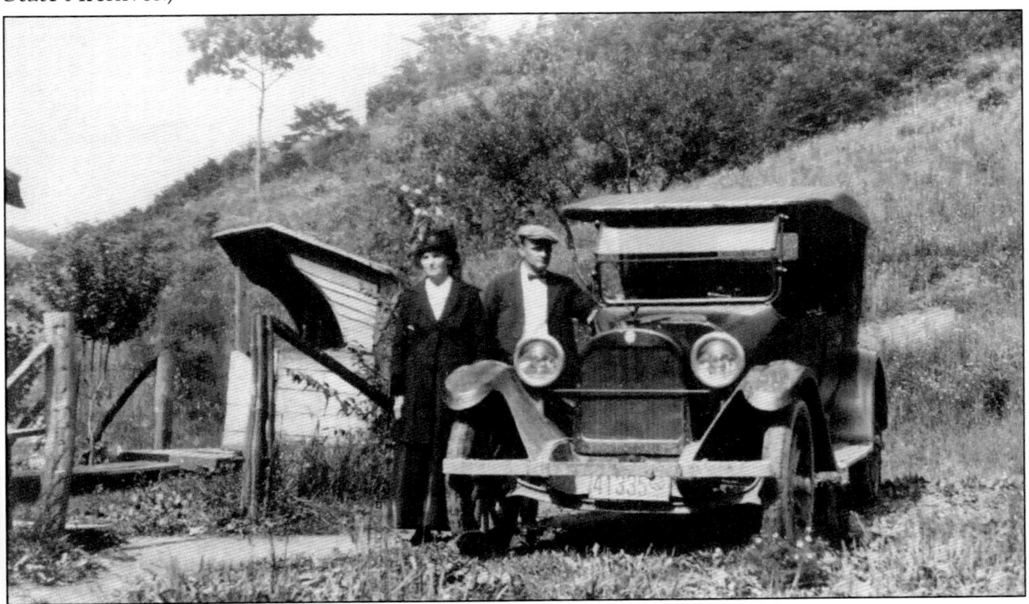

Sarah Ellen Cain and her son Sam posed for this photograph beside their Dodge in the early 1920s. (Courtesy of Carole Menefee.)

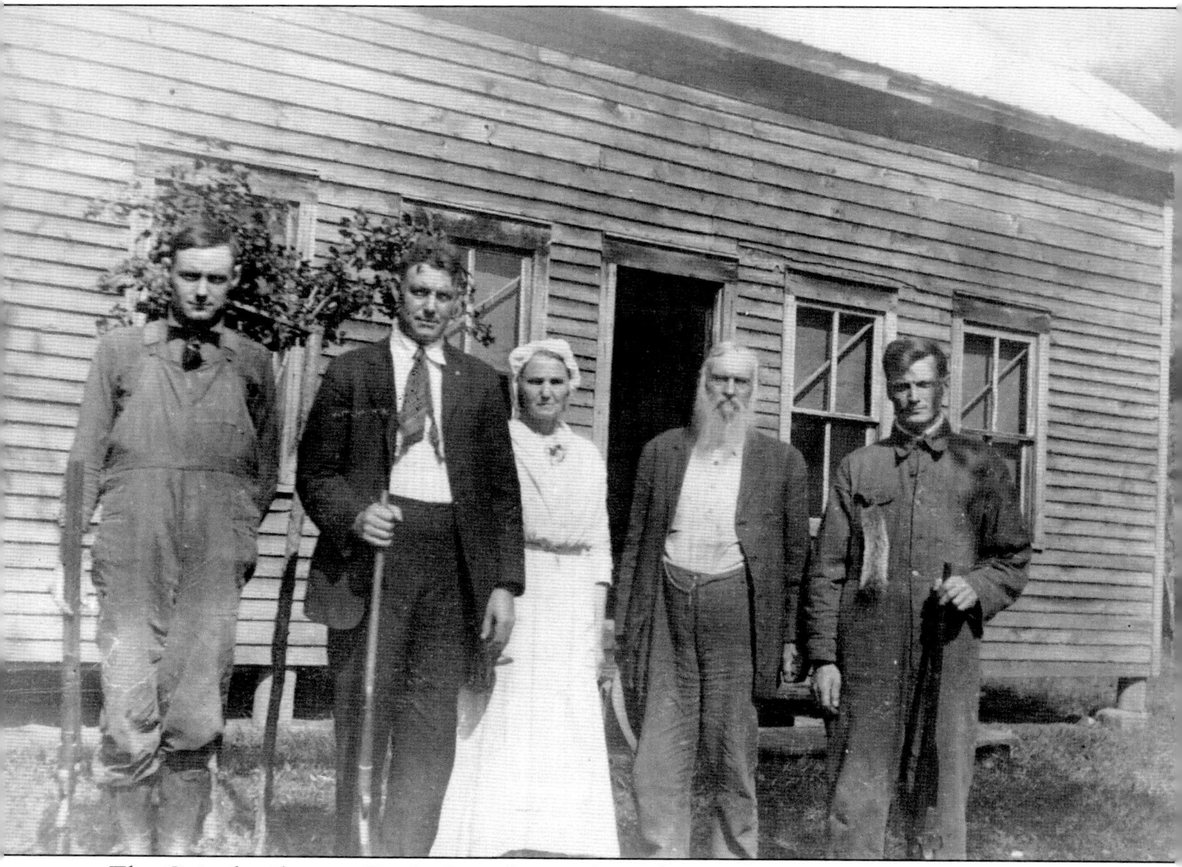

The Cain family proudly displays their right to bear arms. Pictured from left to right are George Cain Jr., Elmmer Cain, Sarah Ellen Cain, George Cain Sr., and Ben Cain. (Courtesy of Carol Menefee.)

Joe Webb is seen here leaving a speakeasy on Coal Bank near Creston with two pistols tucked in his belt and a couple of bottles of Braddock rye whiskey. His cousin, Albert Isaiah Curtis "Court" Cunningham, stands just inside the door. (Courtesy of Bob Lowe.)

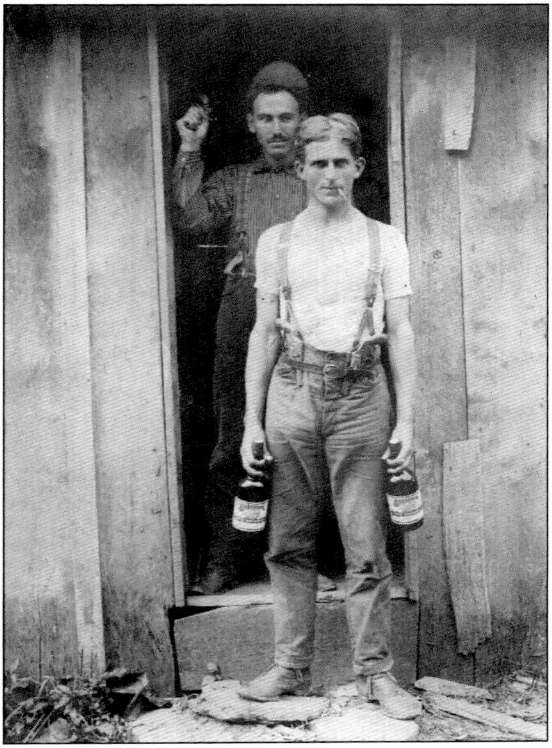

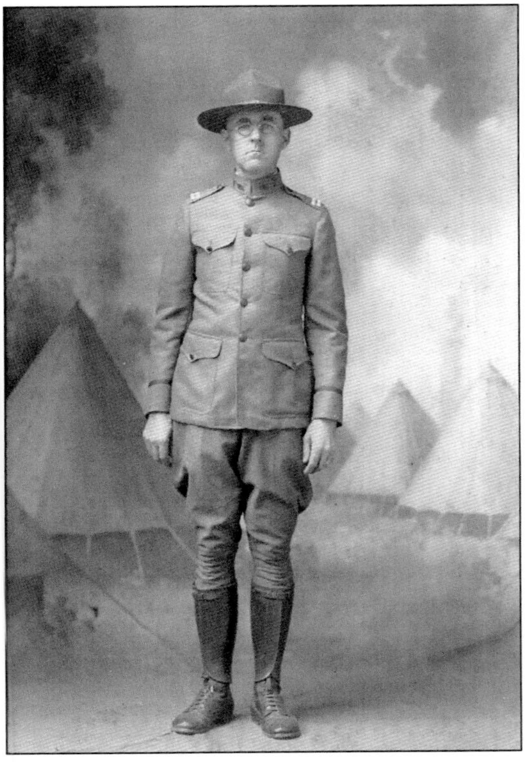

Dr. Park Walker McClung served his country as a captain in the Medical Corps in France during World War I. After completing his tour of duty, he returned to Wirt County to open a medical practice in a small, one-room, weather-boarded structure next to his residence on Market Street in Elizabeth. (Courtesy of Paula Licklider Smith.)

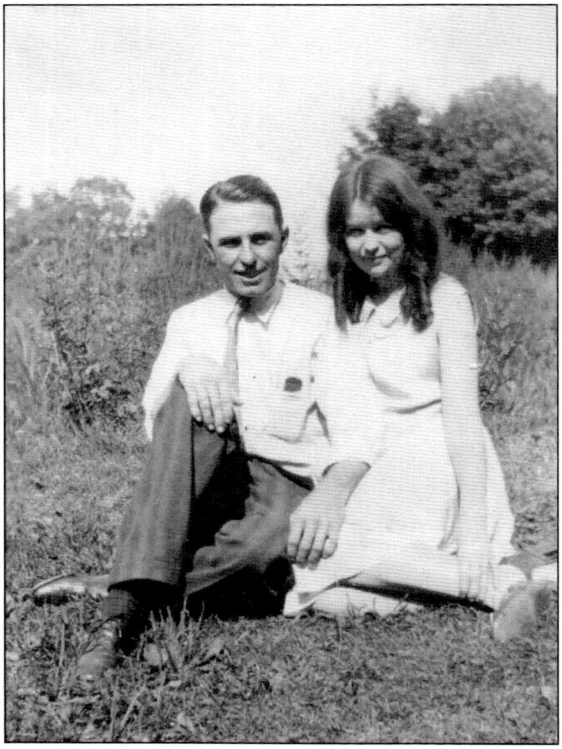

Claude and Inza Caltrider were longtime residents of Wirt County. They married on July 1, 1929, and began housekeeping in a two-story farmhouse just outside of Elizabeth, where they raised their six children.

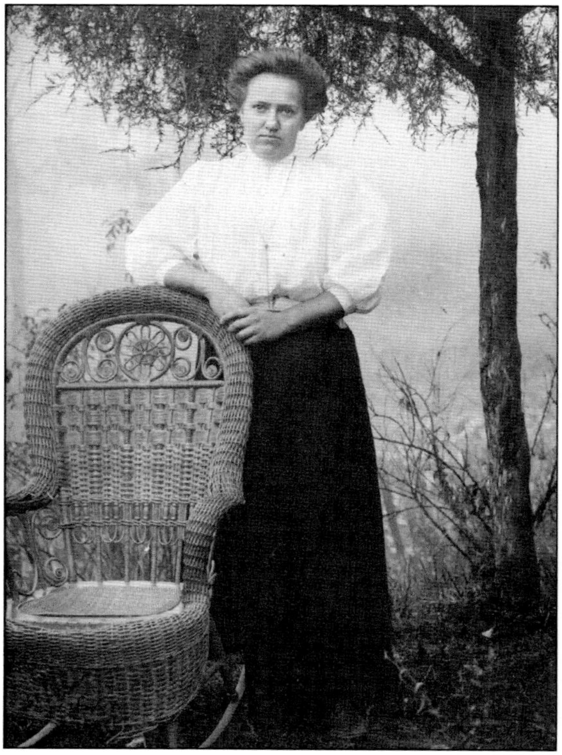

Mae Wilson Rexroad and her husband, Wheeler Rexroad, lived on the corner of Market and Mulberry Streets in Elizabeth. Following Mae's death, her son Raymond remained in the homestead until his death. Although the house is no longer standing, several will surely remember Raymond speaking to them as they walked by the "old Rexroad house."

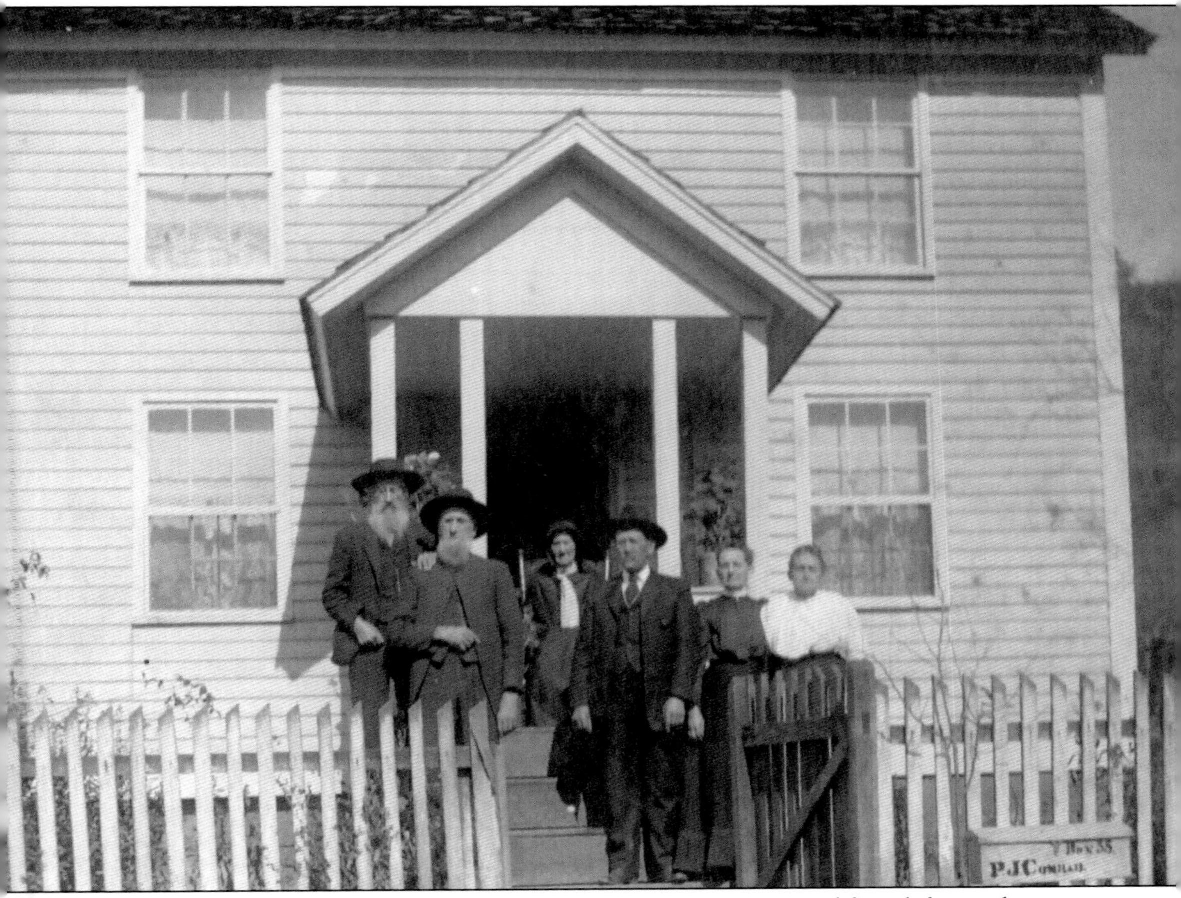

Peter Conrad's home was built on acreage located at Conrad Run. Pictured from left to right are Jacob Conrad, John Conrad, Eliza Cain (seated), Peter Conrad Jr., Clementine "Clemmie" Conrad, and Susan Conrad Dalrymple. After Peter's death, Clemmie sold the family home to George A. Dye Jr. Ownership changed again in 1965, when the West Virginia Pulp and Paper Company bought the property to harvest its timber supply. (Courtesy of the DAP.)

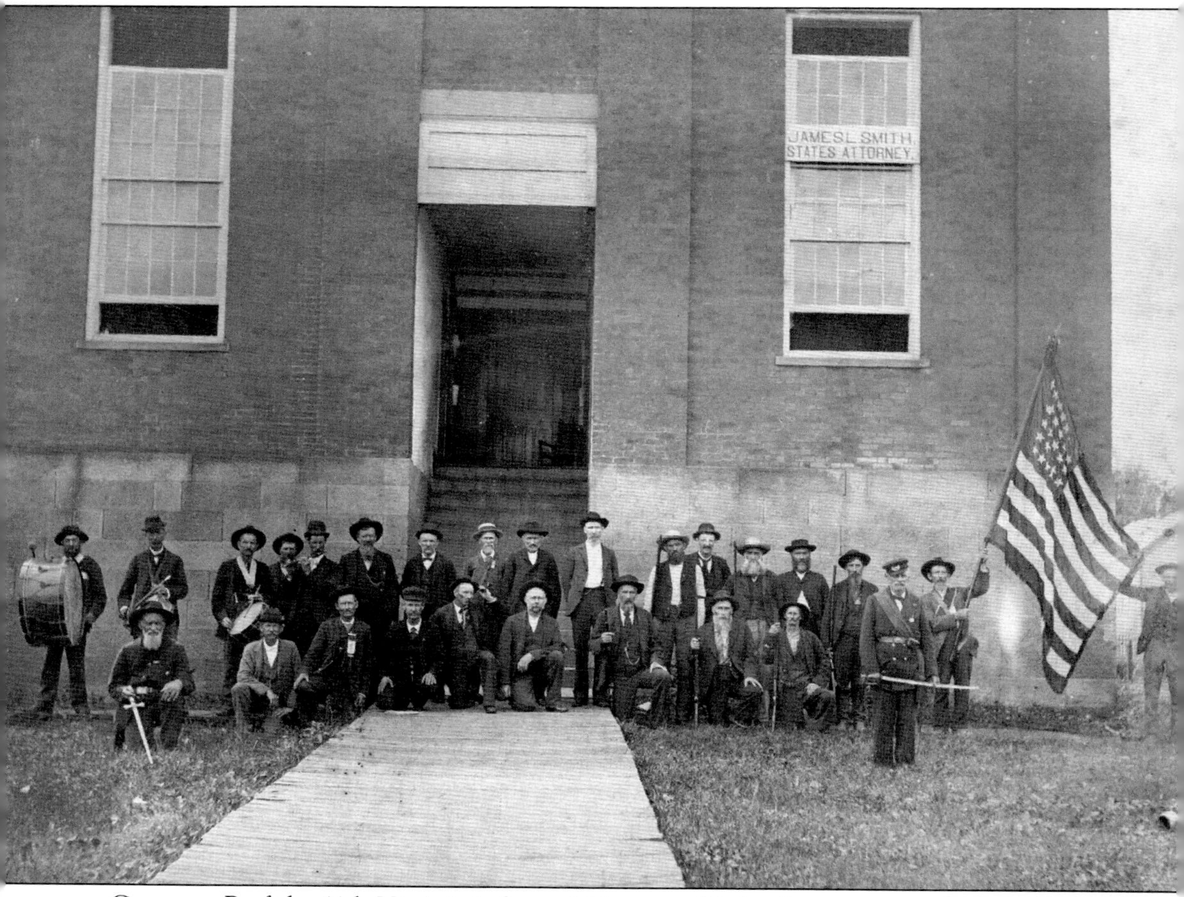

Company B of the 11th Virginia Infantry Volunteers (Federal) was organized in October and November 1861 at Burning Springs. Pictured from left to right are (kneeling) George Cain, Rufe Weaver, Billy Hall, George Riddle, Martin Willett, Smith Day, Abe Hickman, George Copen, and ? Yonkins; (standing) Jay Martin, John Showalter, Joe Stewart, unidentified, William Meredith, Henry Boyles, Charley Reeder, unidentified, Sam Harris, Ed Shiflett, ? Martin, F. T. Lockhart, three unidentified, Capt. Sam Rathbone, C. P. Townsend, and Caleb Lott. (Courtesy of the DAP.)

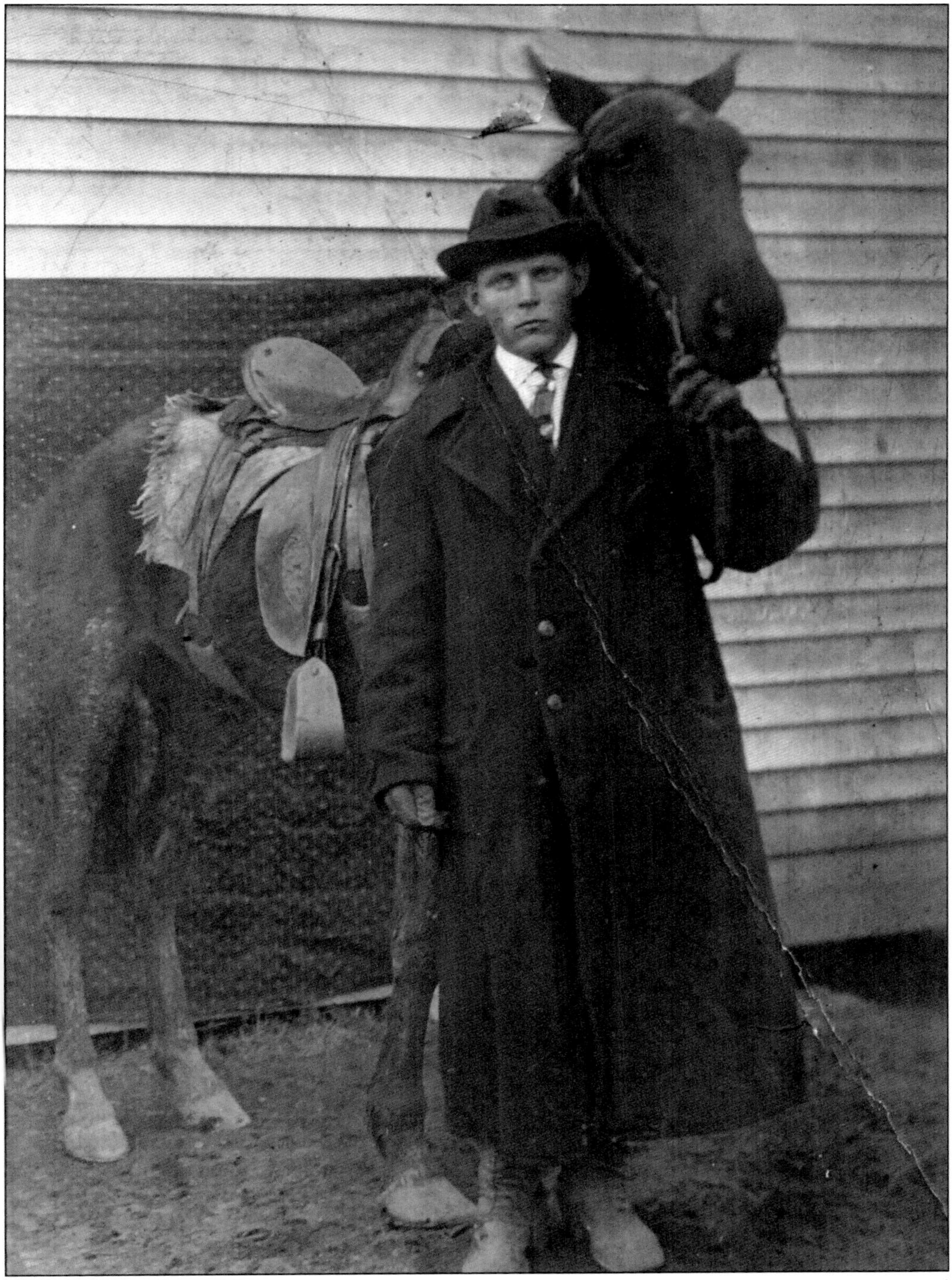

This photograph of Enoch R. Thorn, age 19, and his horse Dan was taken at Lynn Camp around 1916. Enoch was born on June 29, 1897, and died on September 25, 1962. (Courtesy of Waneta Thorn Lawrence.)

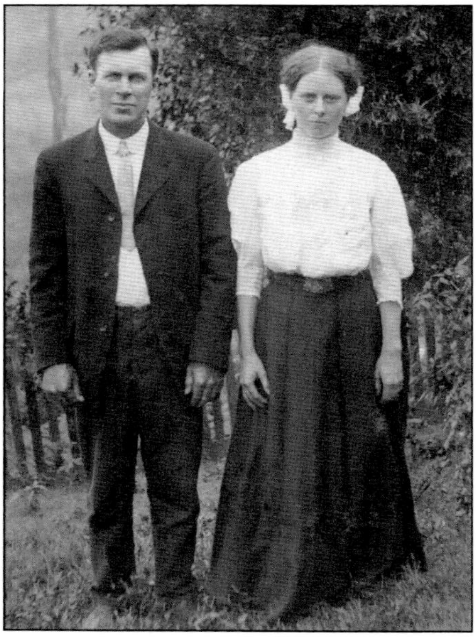

This early photograph is of Okley Ott and his wife, Effie Caltrider Ott. The couple lived in downtown Palestine. In later years, Effie moved to a small house at the entrance to the Knights of Pythias Cemetery in Elizabeth. (Courtesy of Gayle Lowe.)

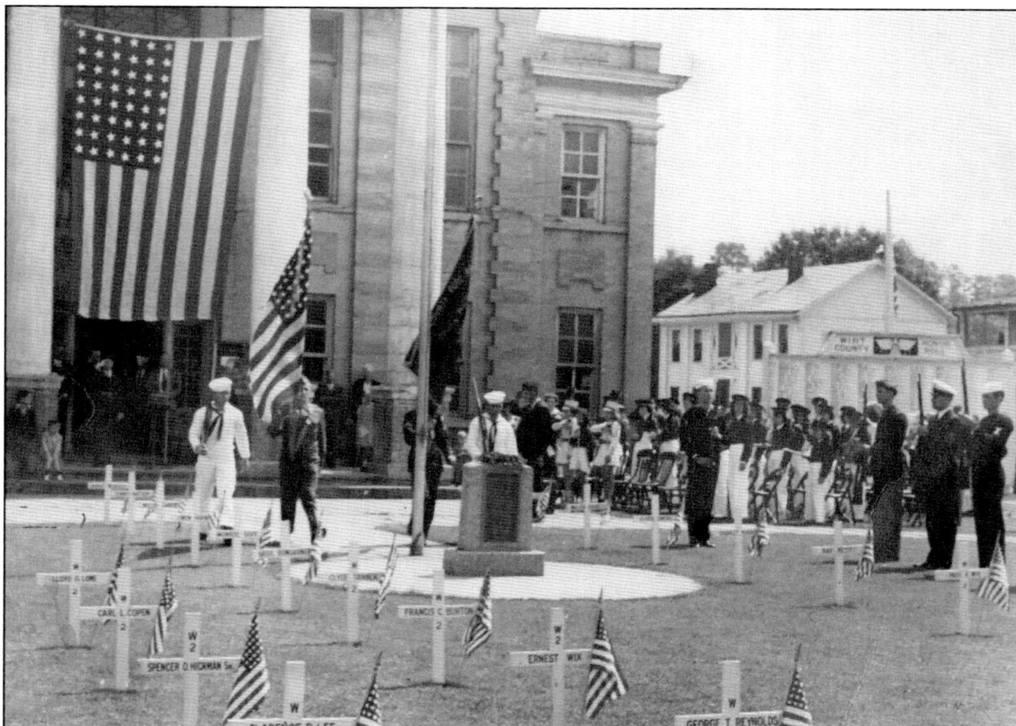

This Memorial Day ceremony was organized by Wirt County Post No. 55 of the American Legion and held on the front lawn of the Wirt County Courthouse in 1946. The monument in the center of Court Square was erected by the citizens of Wirt County in 1941 and honors the following men who lost their lives during World War I: Basil Bumgarner, Owen Hopkins, Charley Kidder, Monroe Goff, Shirley McCauley, Ira Haught, Towny Matson, Oliver Owens, Willie Davis, Frank Lee, Walter Trickett, and Ray Pettit. (Courtesy of Betty Thorn.)

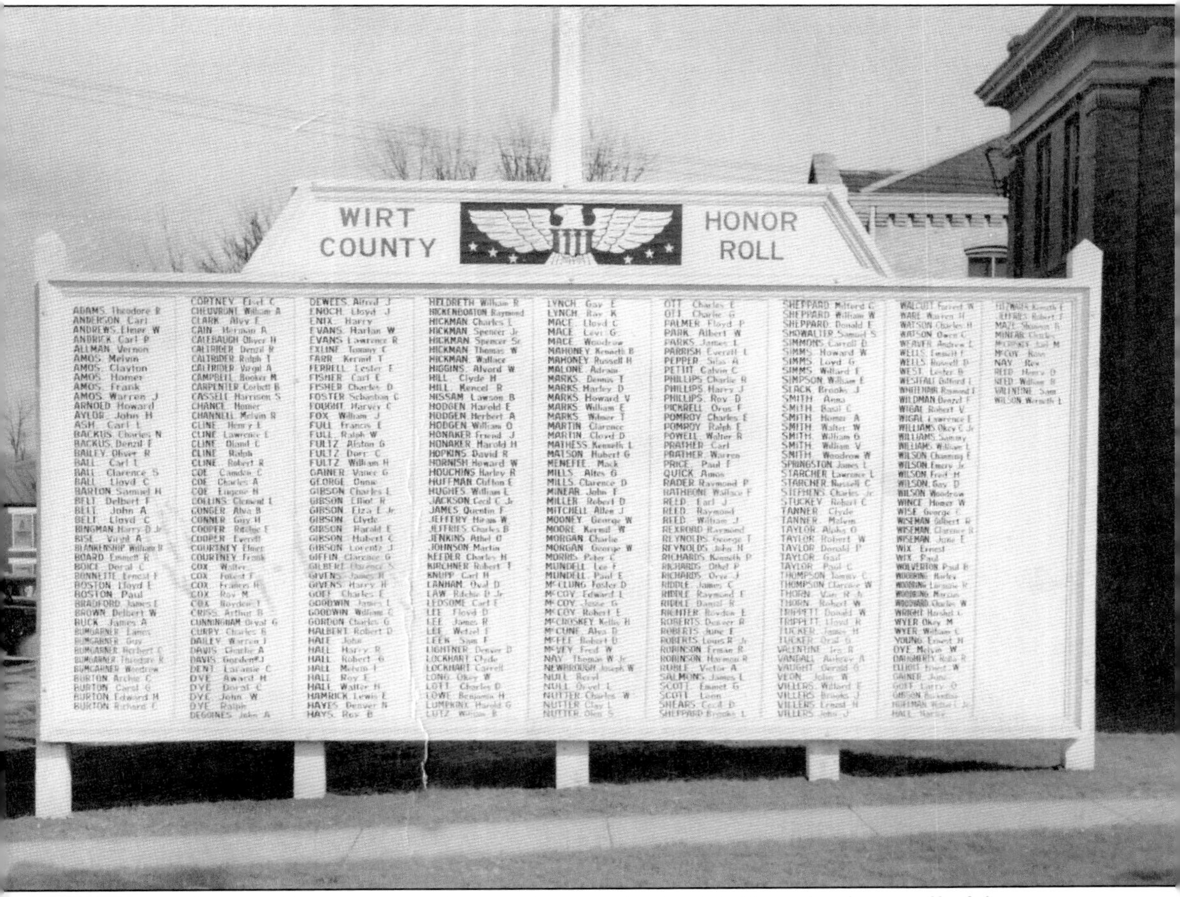

Wirt County Post No. 55 of the American Legion provided this billboard to honor all of the men and women who were inducted into the service in World War II. It stood on the courthouse lawn in their honor until 1949. (Courtesy of Linda Sams.)

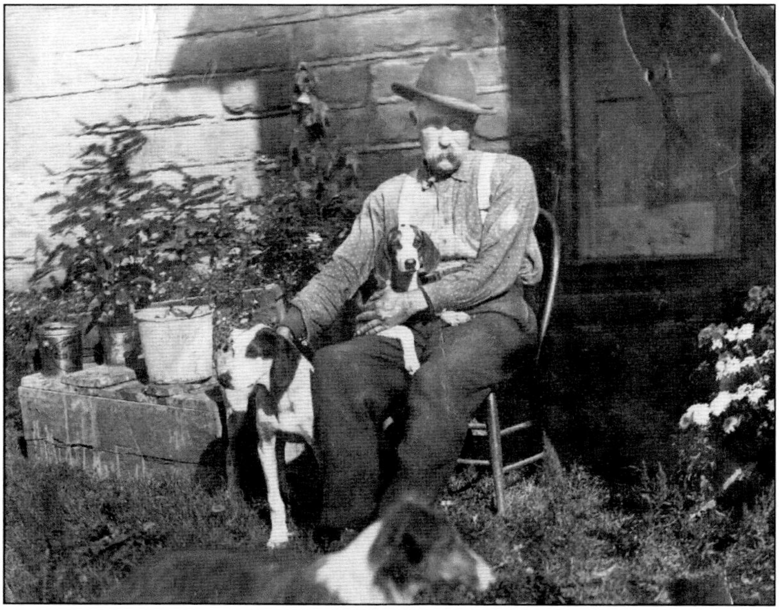

Local Creston blacksmith Al Blankenship takes a break from his shop to enjoy his three dogs. (Courtesy of Sherry R. Smith.)

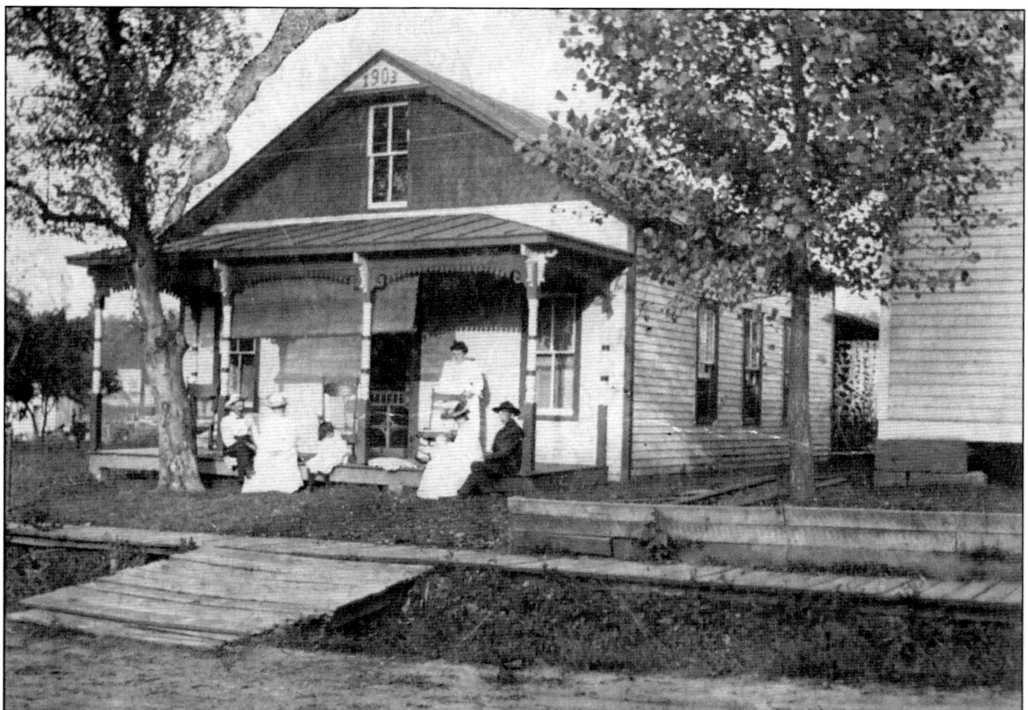

This photograph of Harry and Rosa Reed's house, built in 1903 on Court Street in Elizabeth, is from before the road was paved and when wooden-plank sidewalks were fashionable. The building to the right was the South Methodist Church. (Courtesy of Sherry R. Smith.)

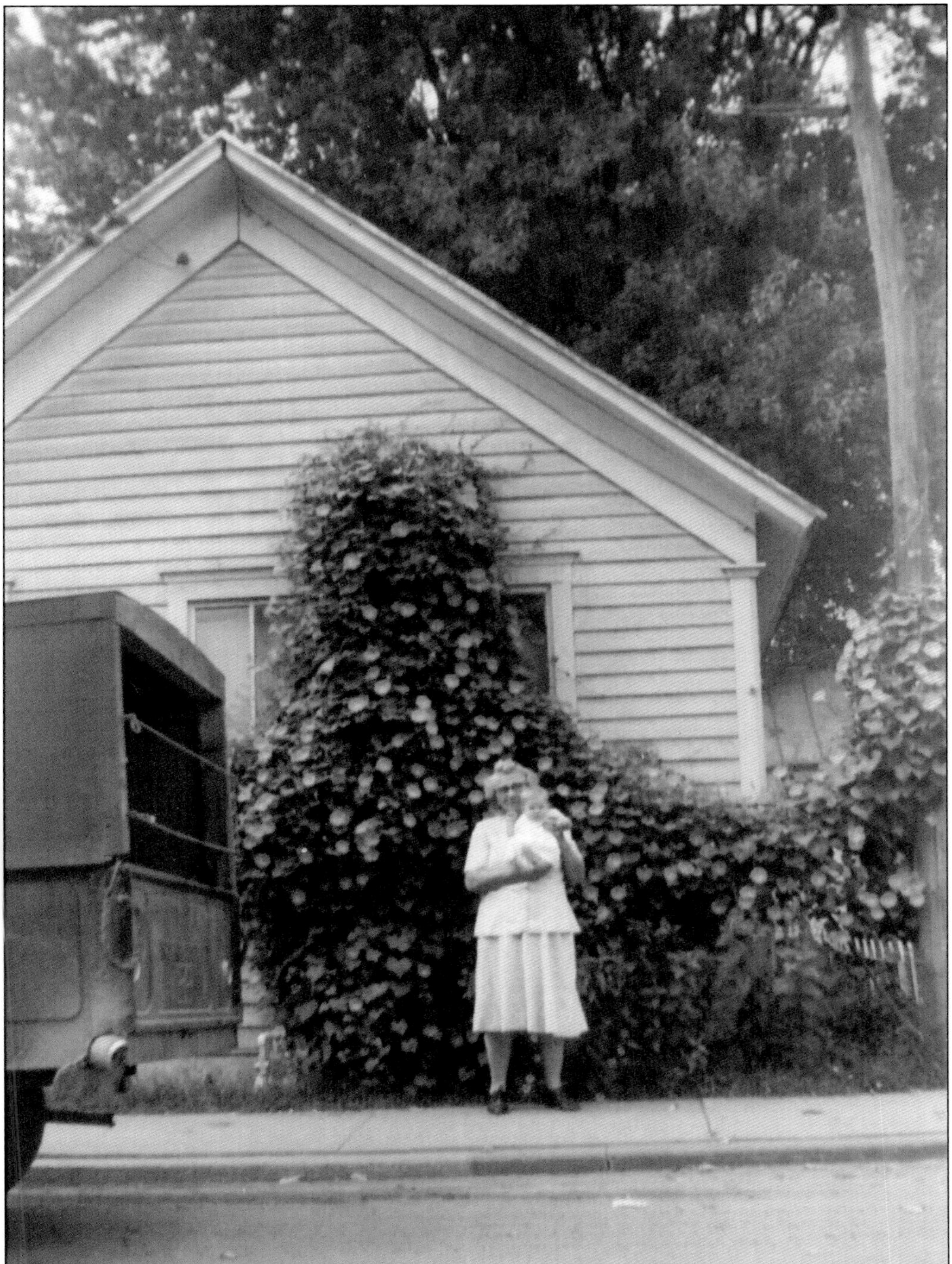

Elizabeth resident Adah Springston posed for this picture in 1951. She is standing in front of her home on Court Street holding her granddaughter Kathy Springston. (Courtesy of Sherry R. Smith.)

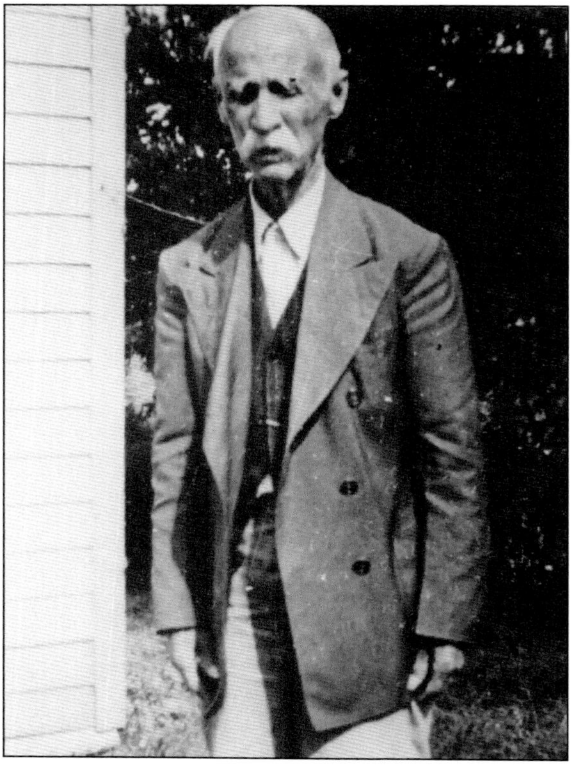

Dr. David S. Stewart was a longtime country doctor in the Creston area. He also was the druggist and operated a drugstore out of the Creston General Store. Dr. Stewart lived to be 105 years old. (Courtesy of Russ Snyder.)

This World War I service roll of honor was presented to Jess Merrill for his service to his country. (Courtesy of Carole Menefee.)

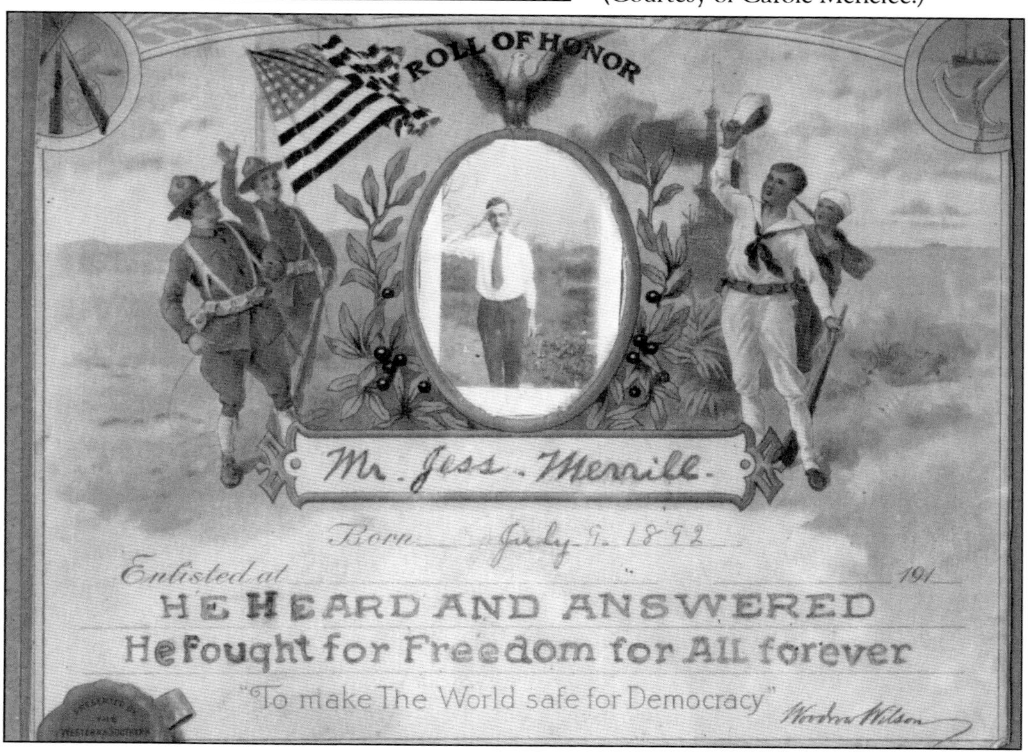

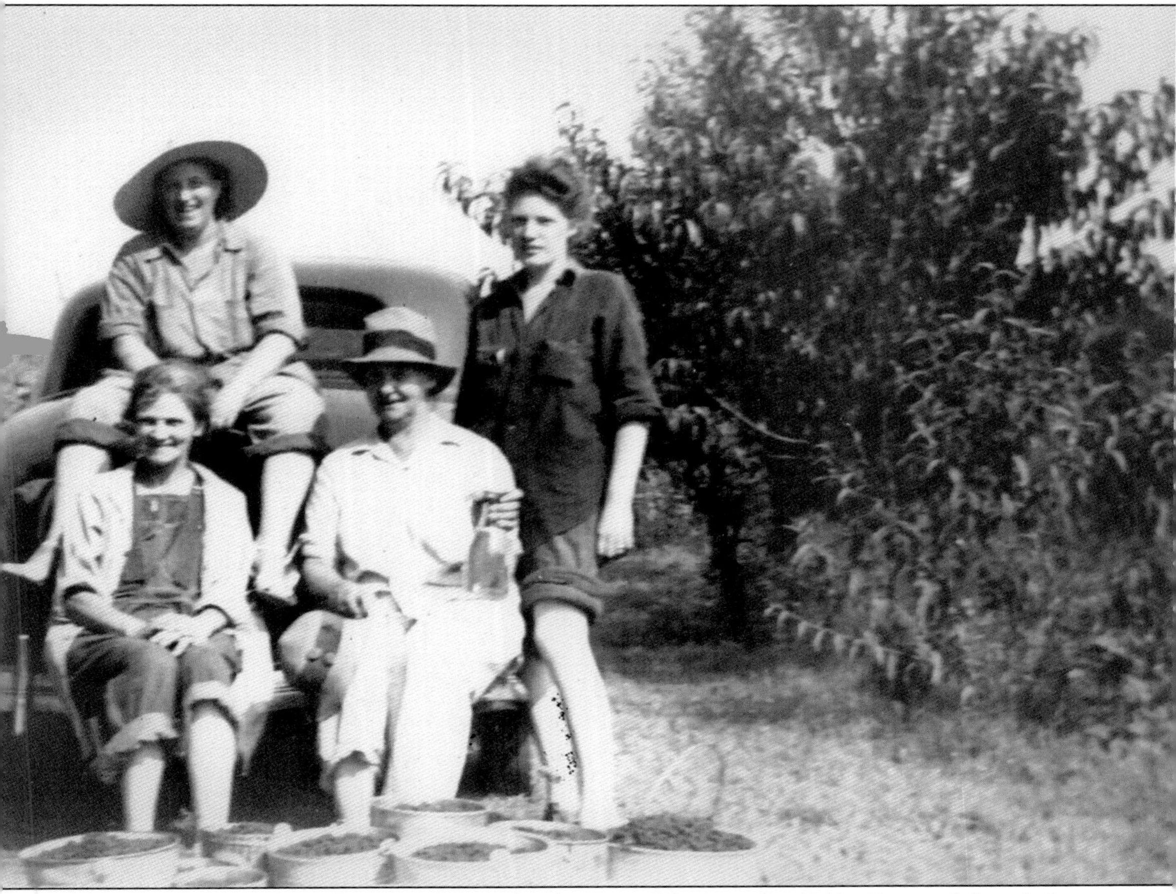

Picking blackberries was a favorite pastime for these neighbors in the 1940s. Pictured from left to right are (first row) Olive Smith and Frances Hayes; (second row) Nettie Hetzel and Tabitha Wilson. (Courtesy of Linda Sams.)

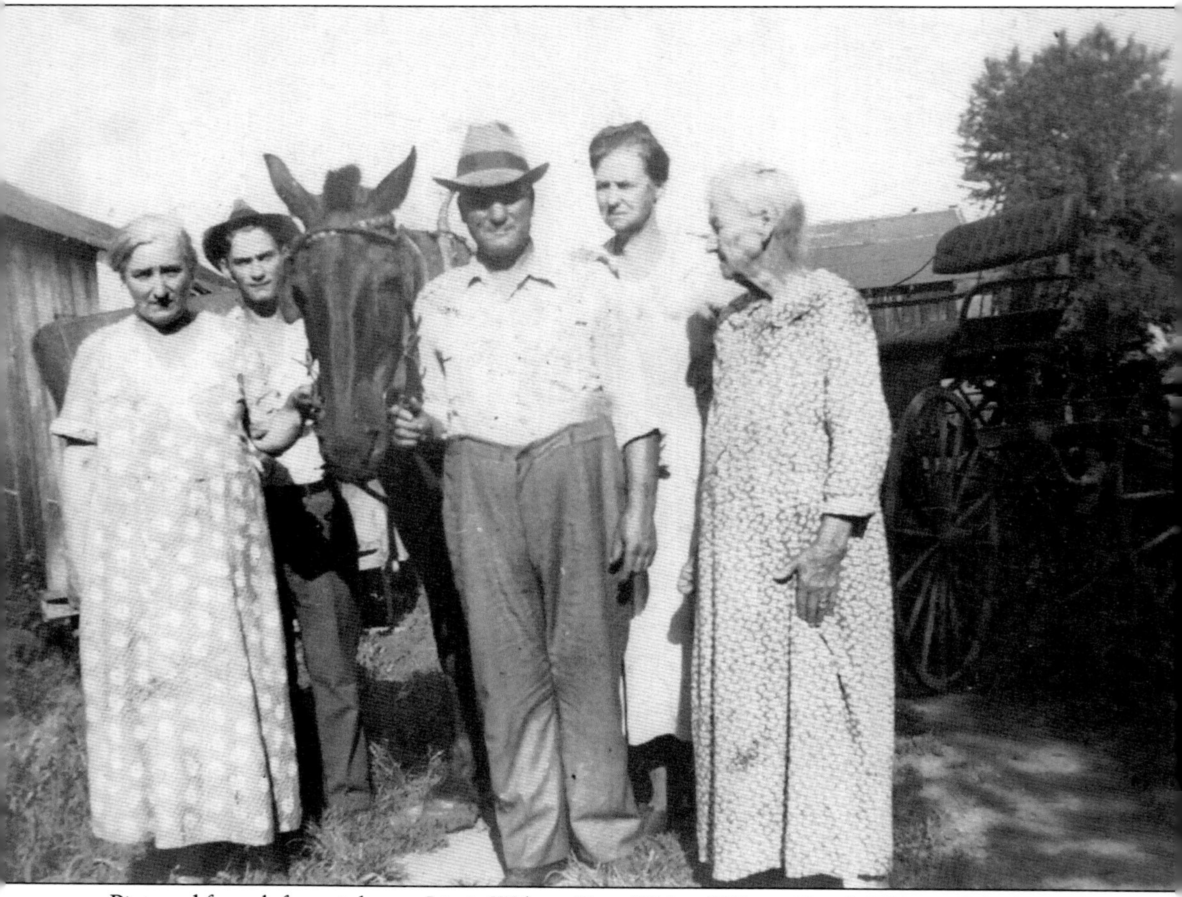

Pictured from left to right are Lizzie Wilson Fint, Walter Wilson, Frank Wilson, Tabitha Wilson, and Violet Wilson with their horse and buggy on Bee Alley (now Churchill Street) down by the Little Kanawha River in Elizabeth. (Courtesy of Linda Sams.)

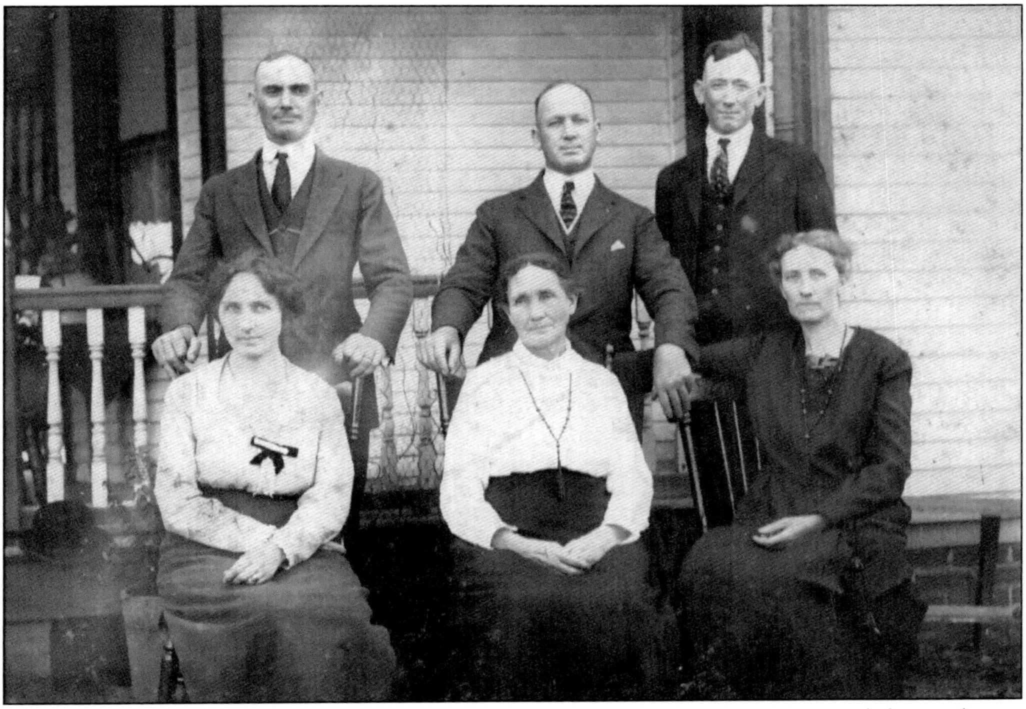

Members of the James family from Tucker Creek posed for this photograph. From left to right are (first row) Clara James Guinn, Eliza Jenny Cumberledge James, and Annie James Gant; (second row) Ottobein James, Charles James, and Harry James. Harry James later served as Wirt County sheriff from 1953 to 1957. (Courtesy of Randall D. James.)

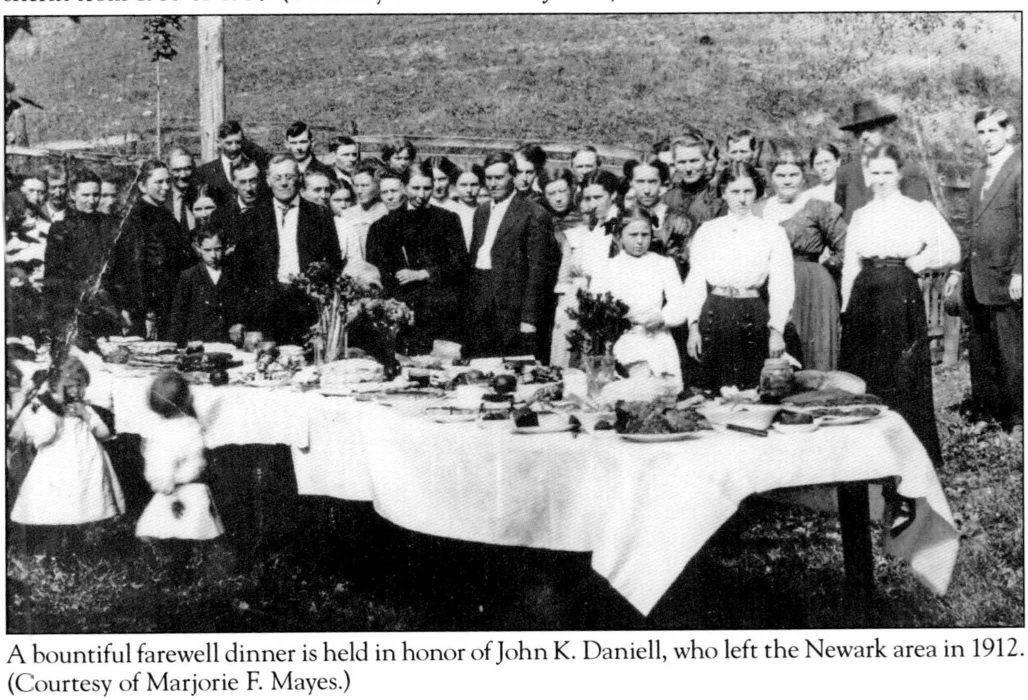

A bountiful farewell dinner is held in honor of John K. Daniell, who left the Newark area in 1912. (Courtesy of Marjorie F. Mayes.)

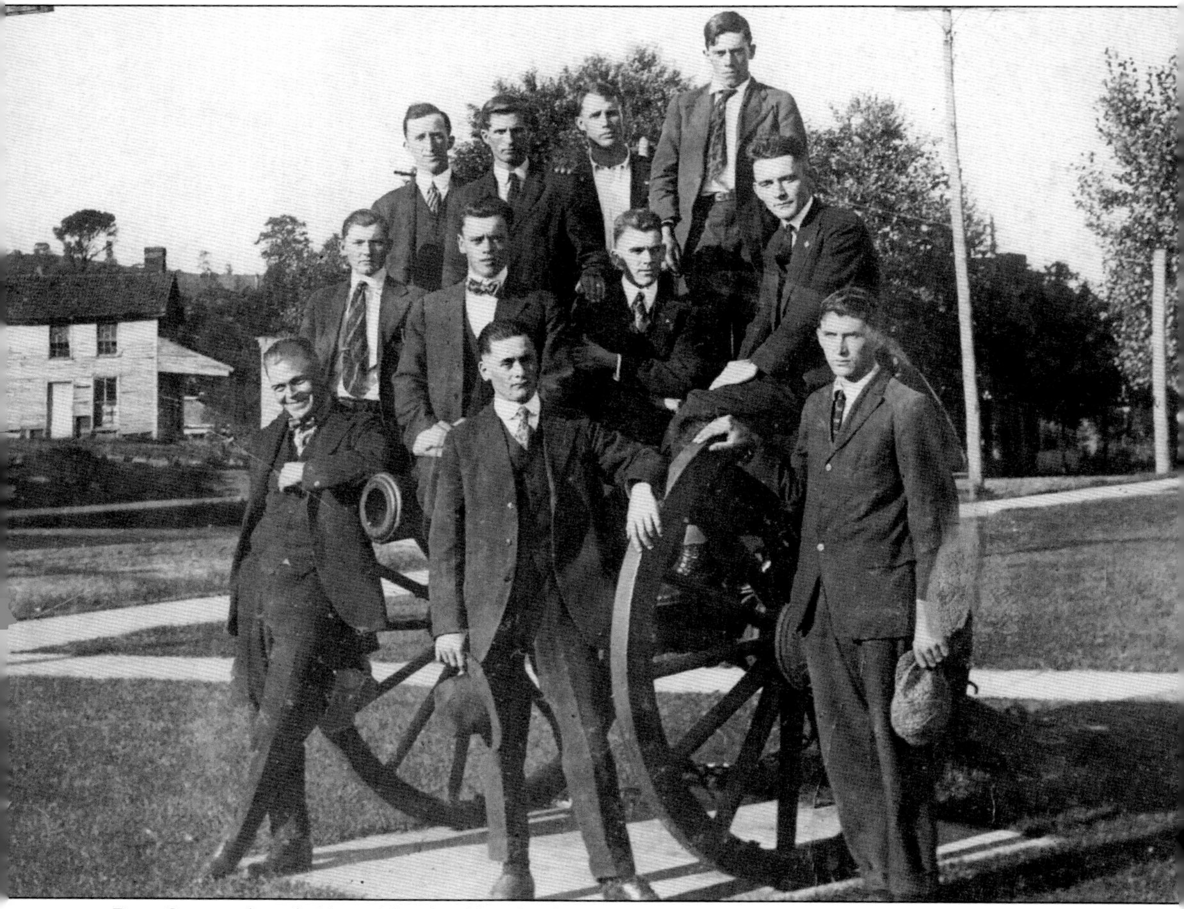

Ben Owens (top left) and his buddies had their picture taken beside one of the cannons on the front lawn of the Wirt County Courthouse shortly before heading off to serve their country in World War I. (Courtesy of Sherry R. Smith.)

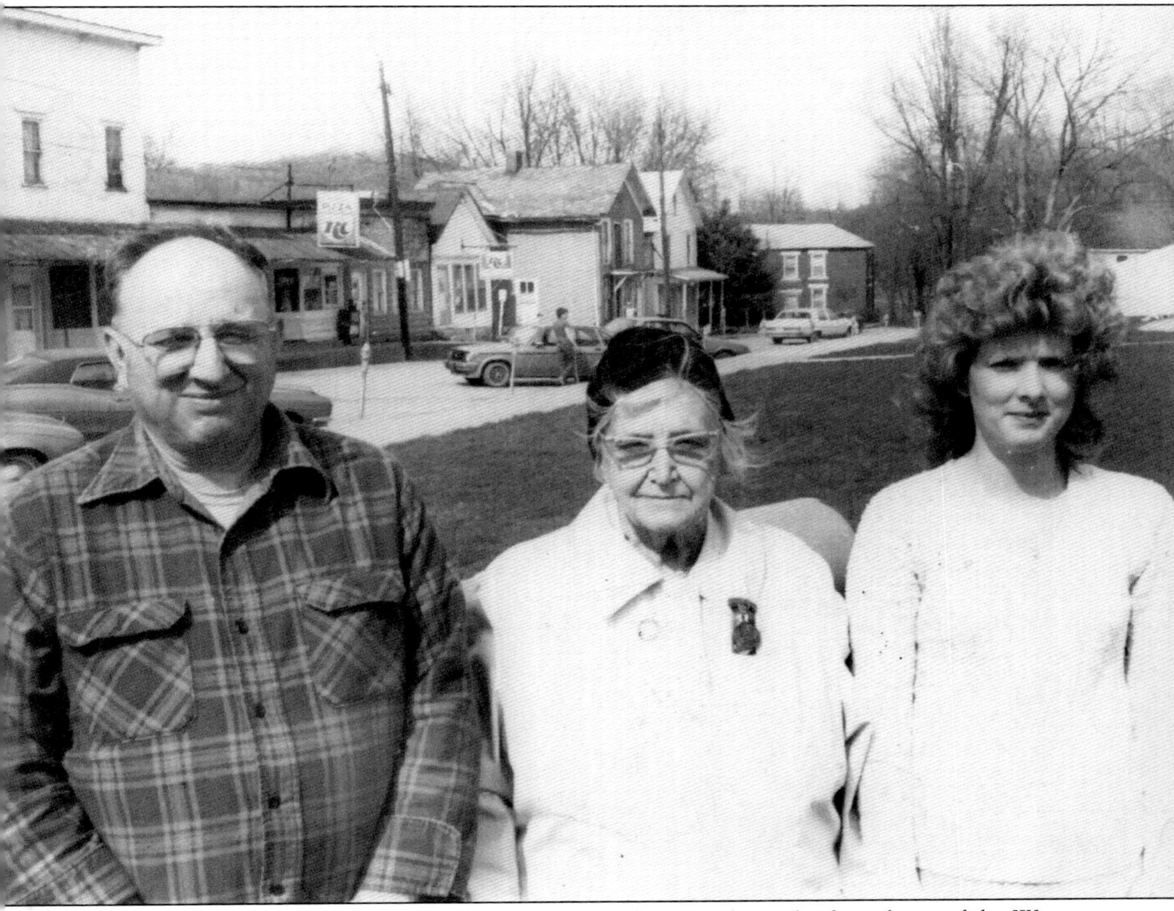

Three generations of the Ludwig family posed for this photograph on the front lawn of the Wirt County Courthouse in the 1980s. Pictured from left to right are Chester Ludwig, Genevieve Ludwig, and Suellen Ludwig Calebaugh. (Courtesy of the Ludwig family.)

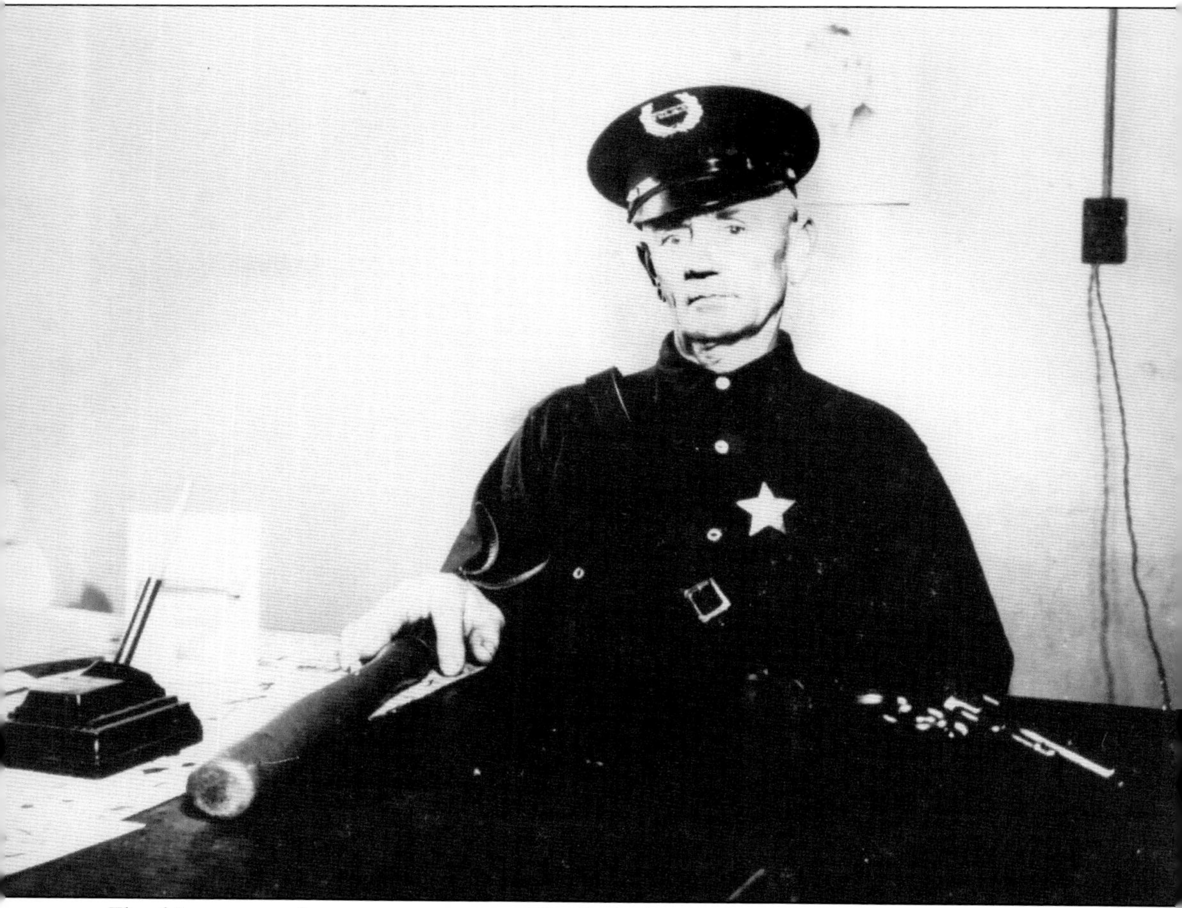

Floyd Lowe was the town sergeant in Elizabeth during the 1940s. This publicity photograph was taken in the office of J. Henry Smith, prosecuting attorney. The picture on the wall in the background was of Pres. Franklin Delano Roosevelt. (Courtesy of Bob Lowe.)

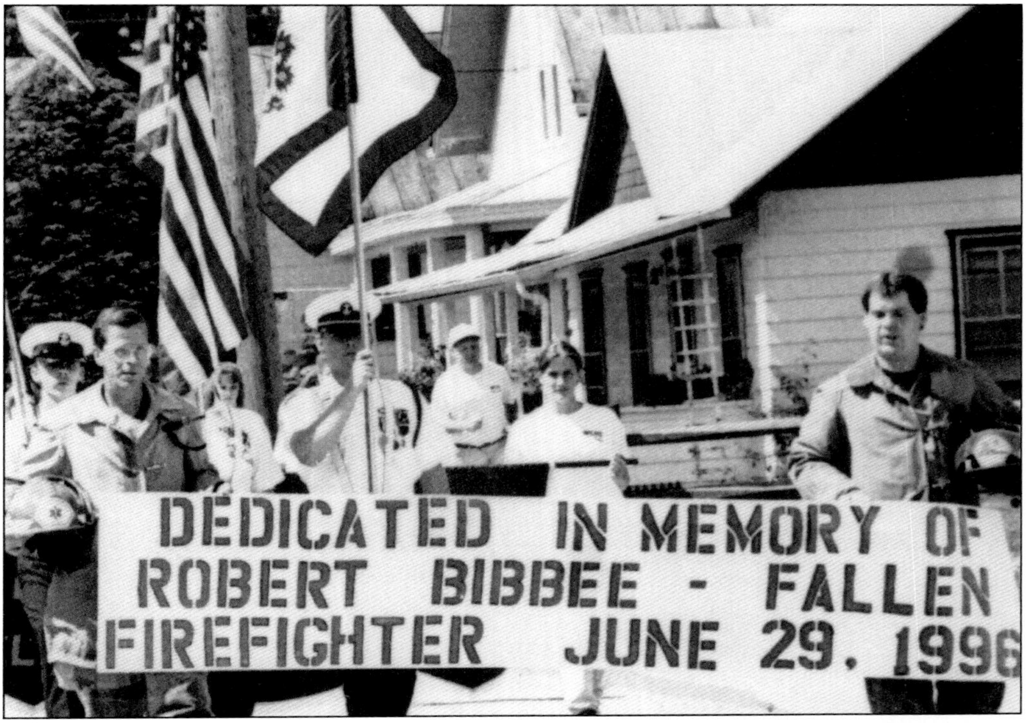

Firemen Bob Hickman (left) and Kurt Starcher (right) are shown participating in the Fireman's Fourth of July Parade carrying a banner in honor of fallen firefighter Robert Bibbee, who died in the line of duty on June 29, 1996. (Courtesy of the Elizabeth-Wirt VFD.)

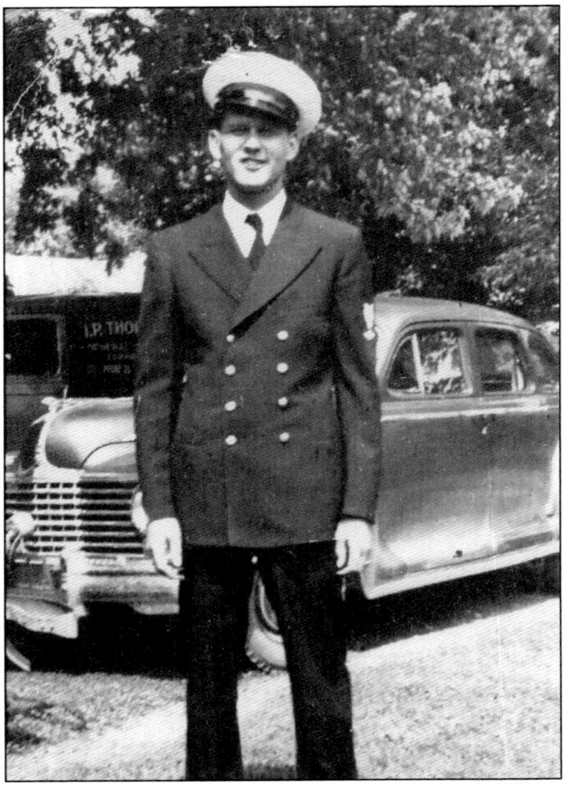

Richard "Dick" Thorn posed for this photograph in his navy uniform. The I. P. Thorn Store delivery truck can be seen in the background. (Courtesy of Betty Thorn.)

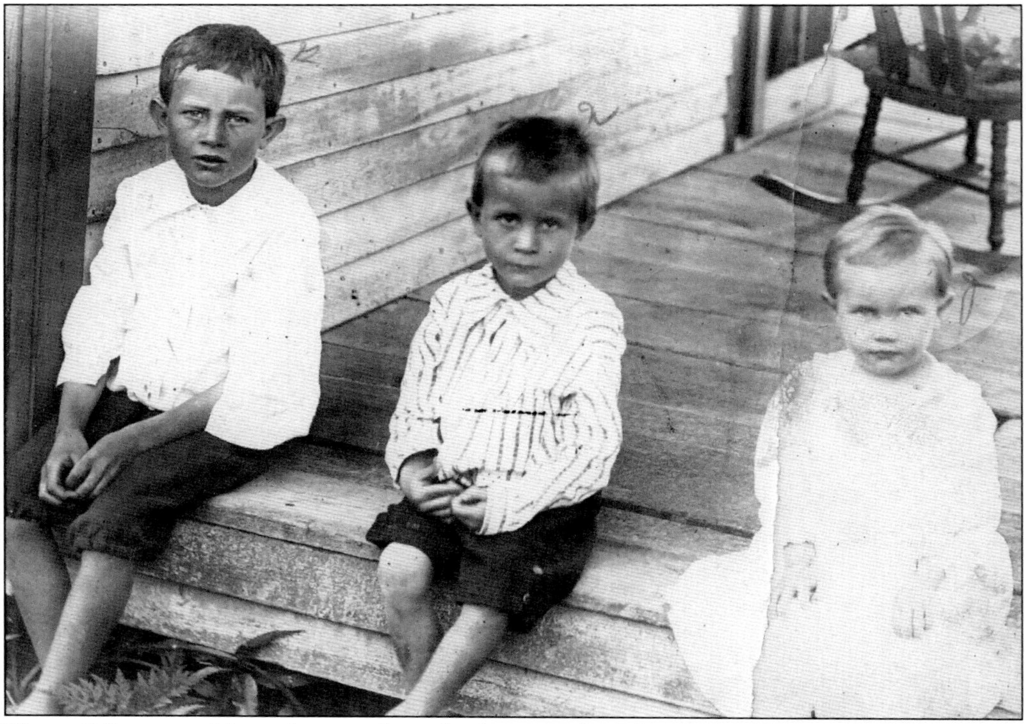

These siblings posed for a photograph on the front porch of their home (the property now referred to as the Matheny Farm) on State Route 14. Pictured from left to right are Gerald Levi Mace, Woody Mace, and Juanita Mace. (Courtesy of James Matheny.)

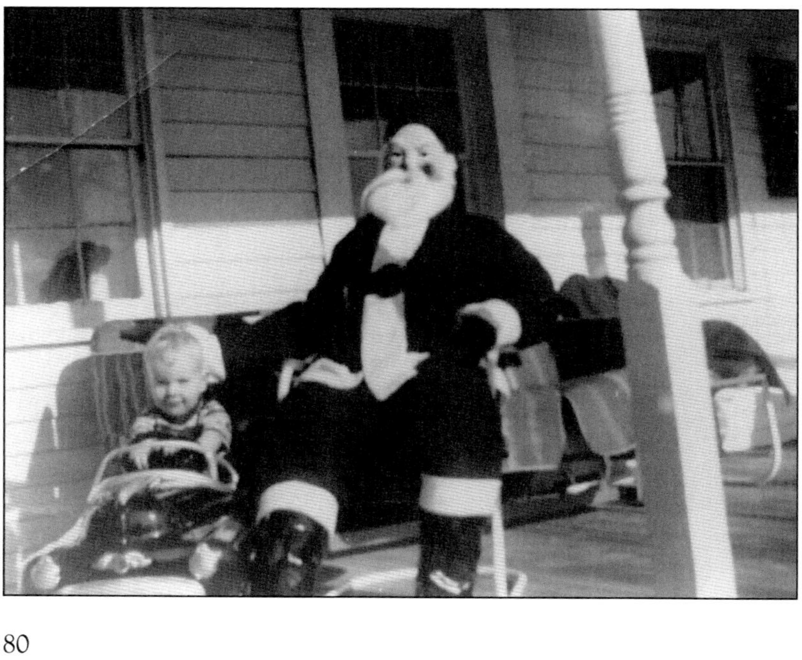

James Matheny drives on his front porch in the new convertible he received as a Christmas present from Santa in 1948. (Courtesy of James Matheny.)

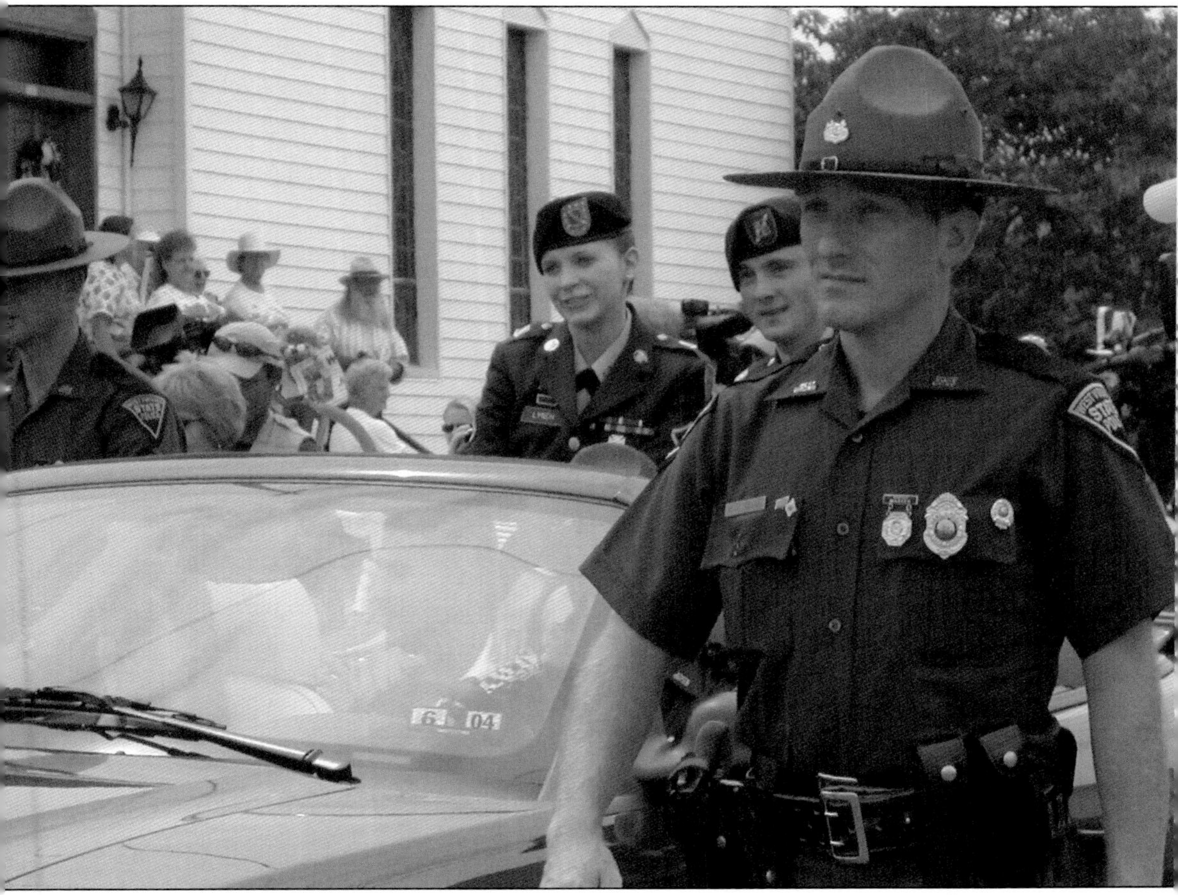

Pvt. Jessica Lynch of Palestine was in the 507th Maintenance Company convoy when it was ambushed on March 23 near the Iraqi city of Nasiriyah in an attack that killed 11 soldiers. U.S. forces rescued Lynch at a Nasiriyah hospital on April 1, 2003, while five other captured 507th soldiers were rescued on April 13, 2003. Her historic homecoming celebration back to Wirt County took place on July 22, 2003. Lynch's service in the army was recognized with the Bronze Star, Purple Heart, Prisoner of War Medal, and the Army Service Ribbon. (Courtesy of Diane Ludwig.)

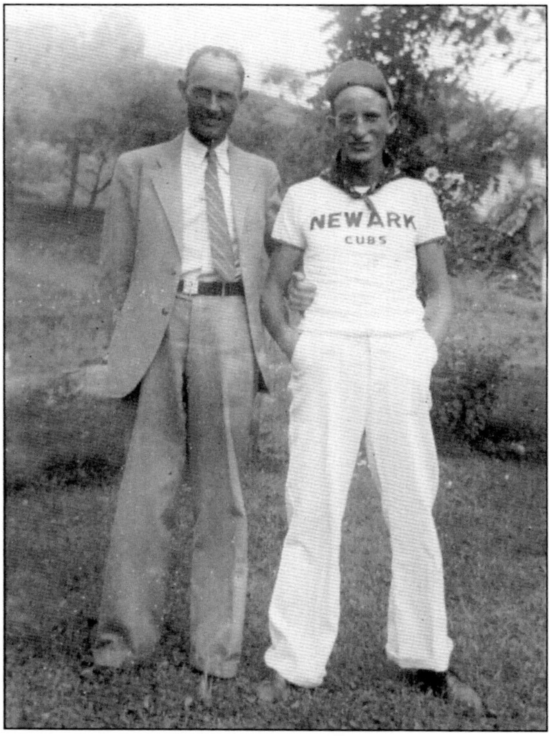

Woody Mace (right) is seen wearing his Newark Cubs baseball jersey alongside his brother Gerald Levi Mace. (Courtesy of James Matheny.)

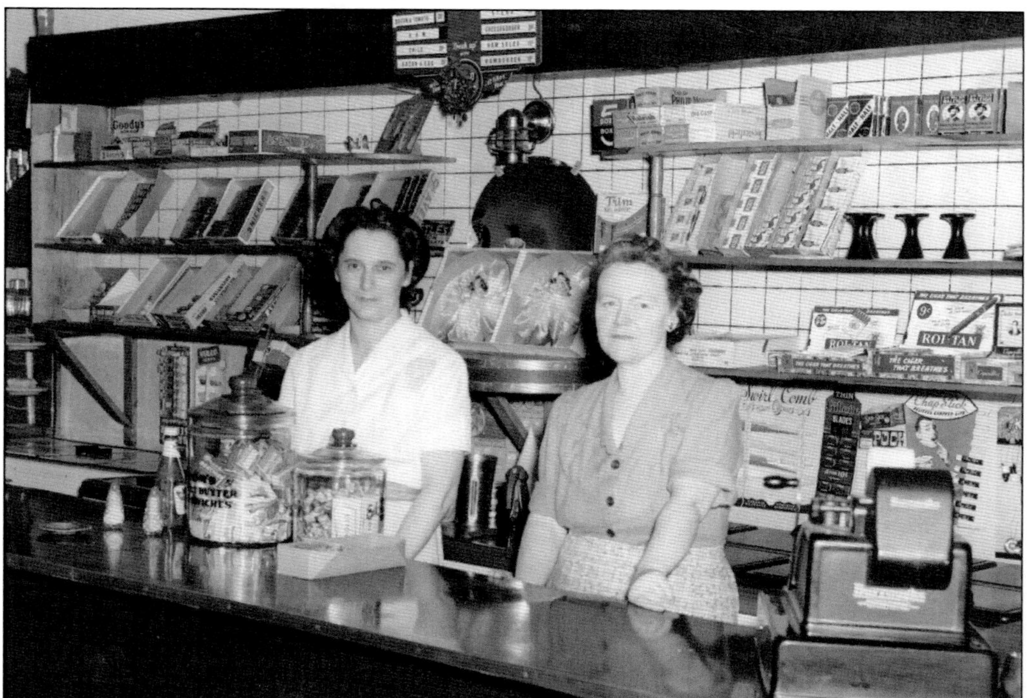

Mary Cooper (left) and Lona Gibson were employed as cooks at the Theater Restaurant in Elizabeth during the 1950s.

Lifelong Wirt County resident Robert Lowe served as a private first class in the U.S. Army's 40th Antiaircraft Artillery Brigade during Korean War. Robert was stationed in Hyoshi, Japan, in 1951. (Courtesy of Gayle Lowe.)

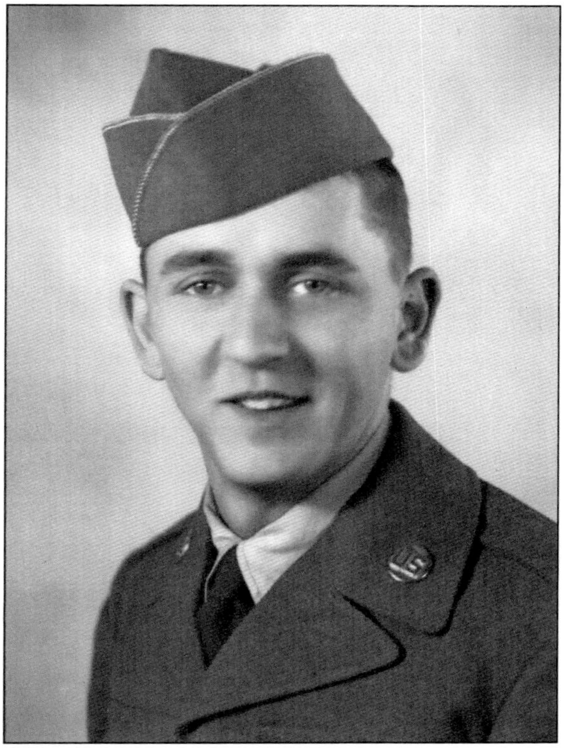

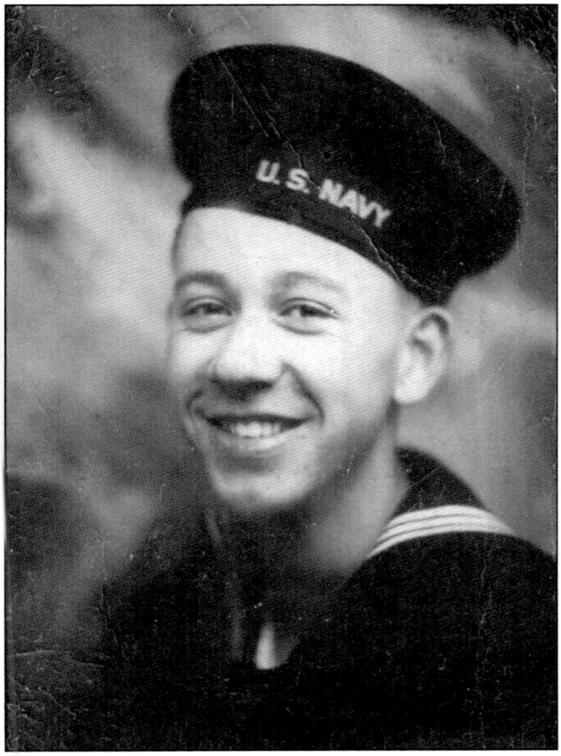

Floyd "Mutt" Lowe was photographed in his navy uniform before heading off to the South Pacific in the late 1940s to serve his country during the war. (Courtesy of Bob Lowe.)

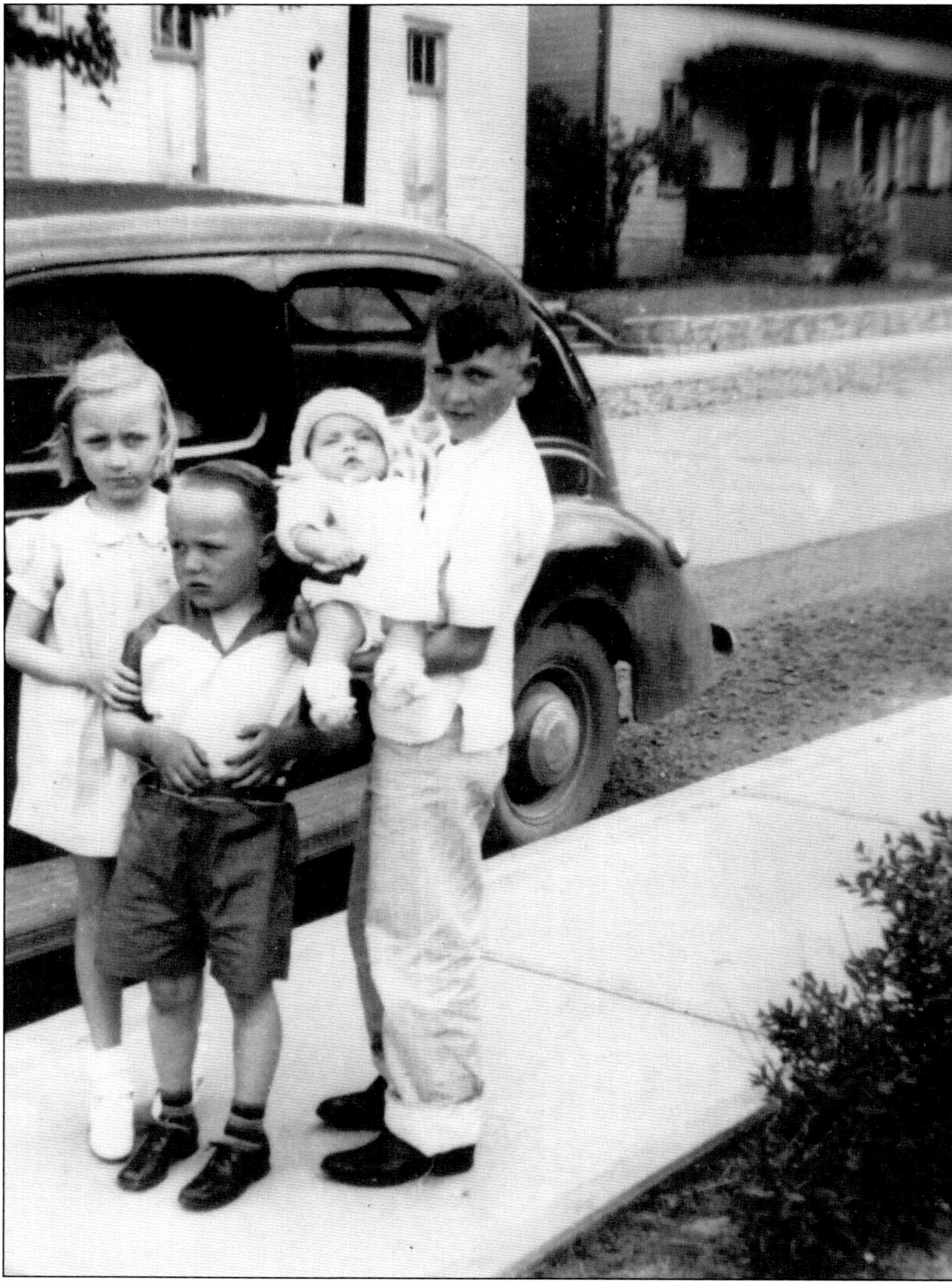

This early-1940s photograph was taken on Court Street in Elizabeth. From left to right are Gathalea Lowe, William "Bill" Higgins, and Bob Lowe holding his niece, Rosalee Higgins. The structure in the background is the South Methodist Church, and just up the street is the home of Lona Gibson. (Courtesy of Bob Lowe.)

Six

Farming and Recreation

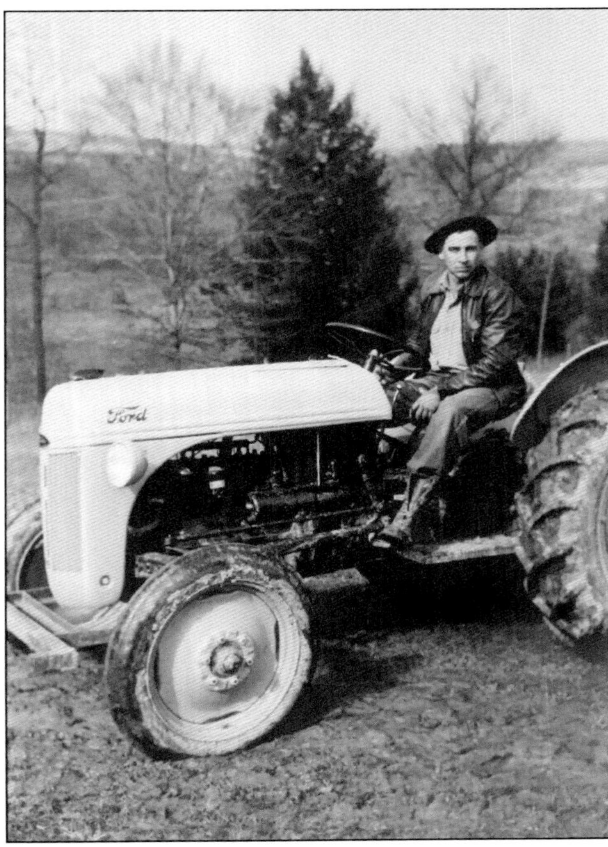

Robert G. Hall of Spring Creek is shown here on his new Ford tractor around 1949. Farm tractors of its kind featured a 30-horsepower, 4-cylinder engine with rubber tires and were manufactured in Dearborn, Michigan. (Courtesy of the West Virginia State Archives.)

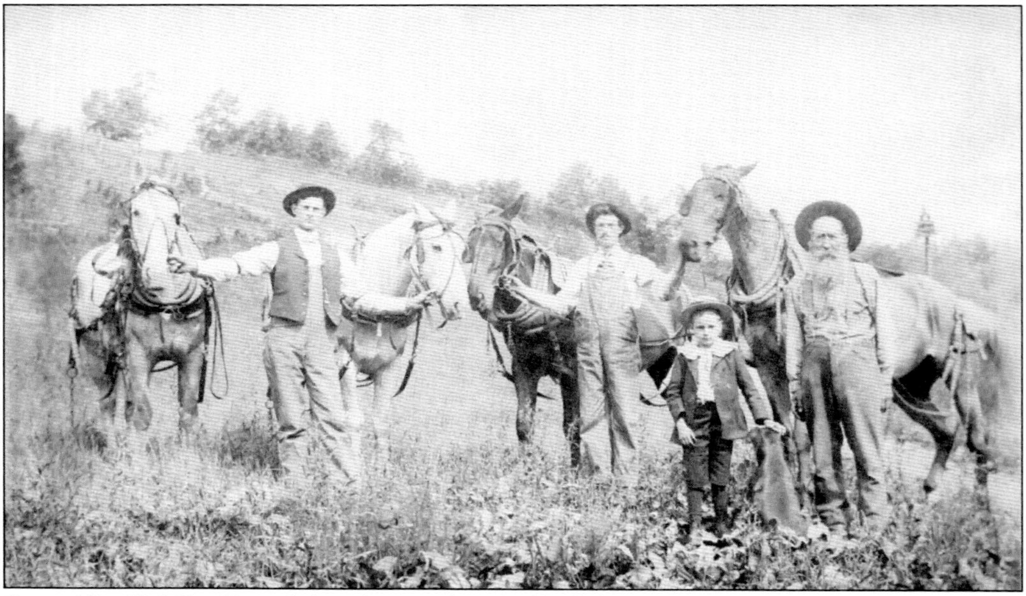

Samuel Ford McFee (far right) and an unidentified little boy stand in front of two teams of horses and their drivers in this *c.* 1900 photograph. (Courtesy of the West Virginia State Archives.)

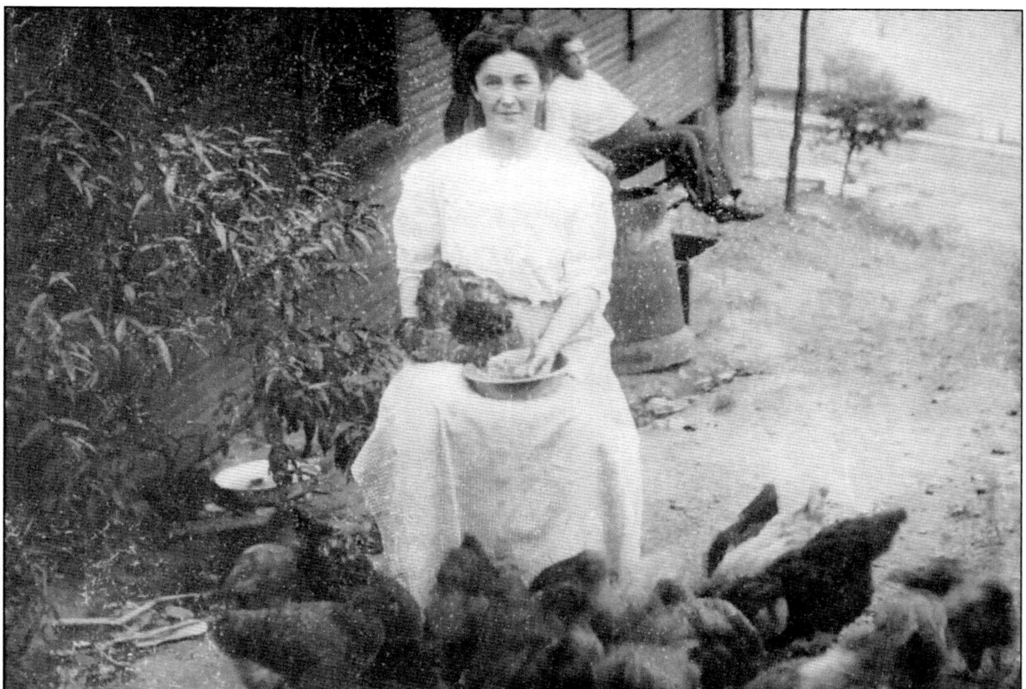

Harriet "Hattie" Windland Ellyson Lee Markley feeds her chickens around 1874. (Courtesy of the West Virginia State Archives.)

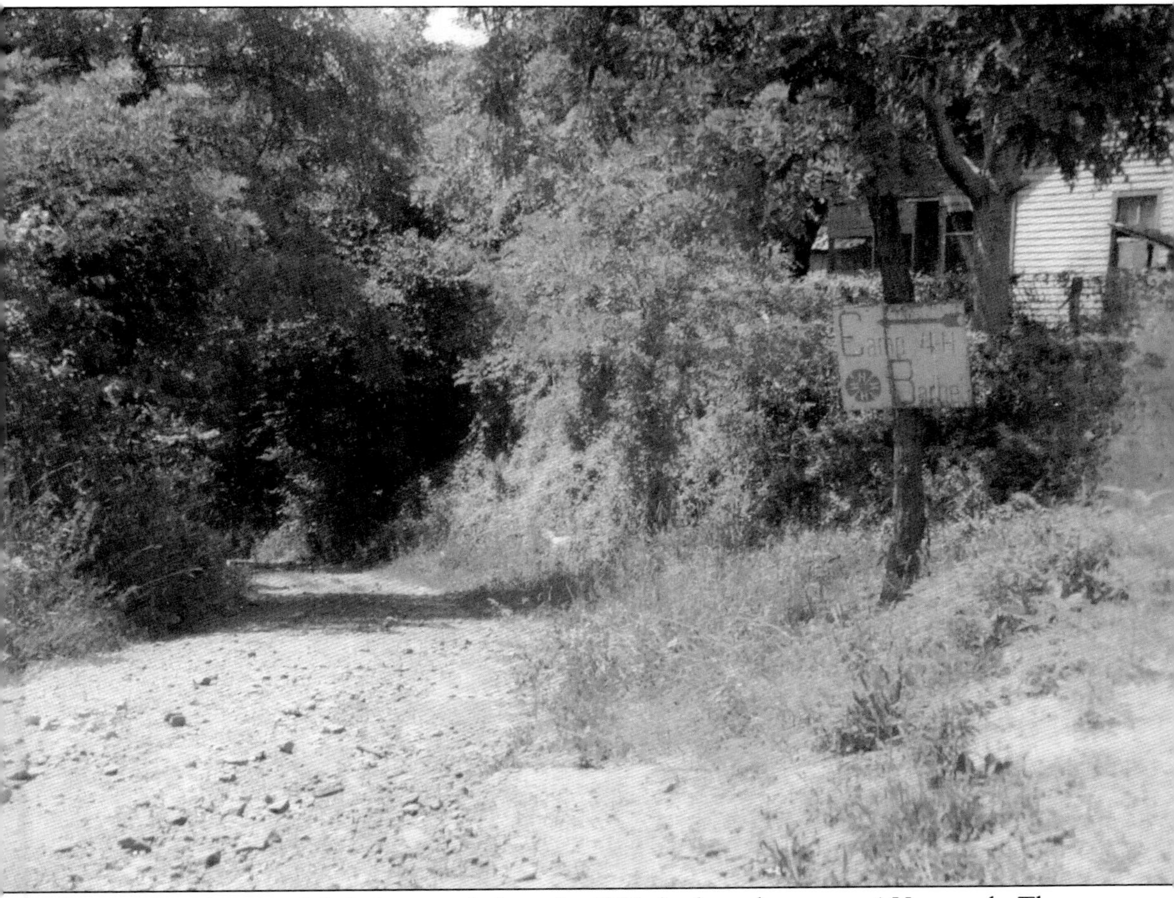

The gravel road in this faded photograph from the 1930s leads to the county 4-H grounds. The 58-acre tract of land was purchased on June 19, 1931, and serves as a meeting place for the county's 4-H clubs and the home to the Wirt County Fair. The camp was previously named Cabin Range and was the summer home of Waitman T. Barbe and his wife, Clara. Barbe was an early educator and noted author who attended both Harvard and Oxford Universities. (Courtesy of Gayle Lowe.)

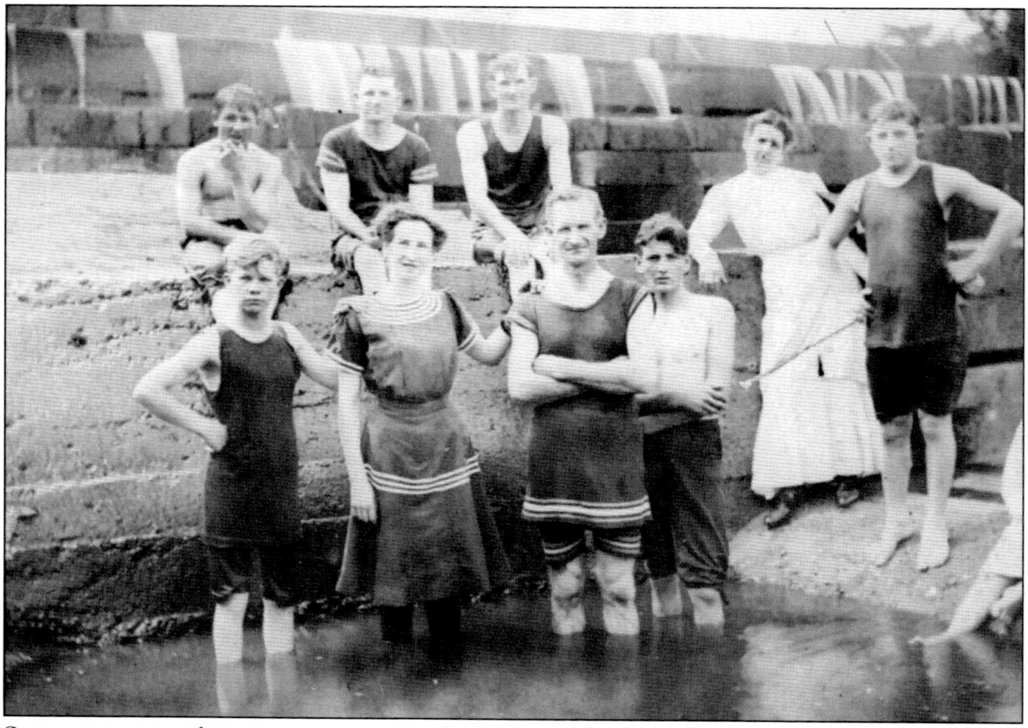

Swimming was a favorite pastime at Lock and Dam No. 5 on the Little Kanawha River above Burning Springs. (Courtesy of the DAP.)

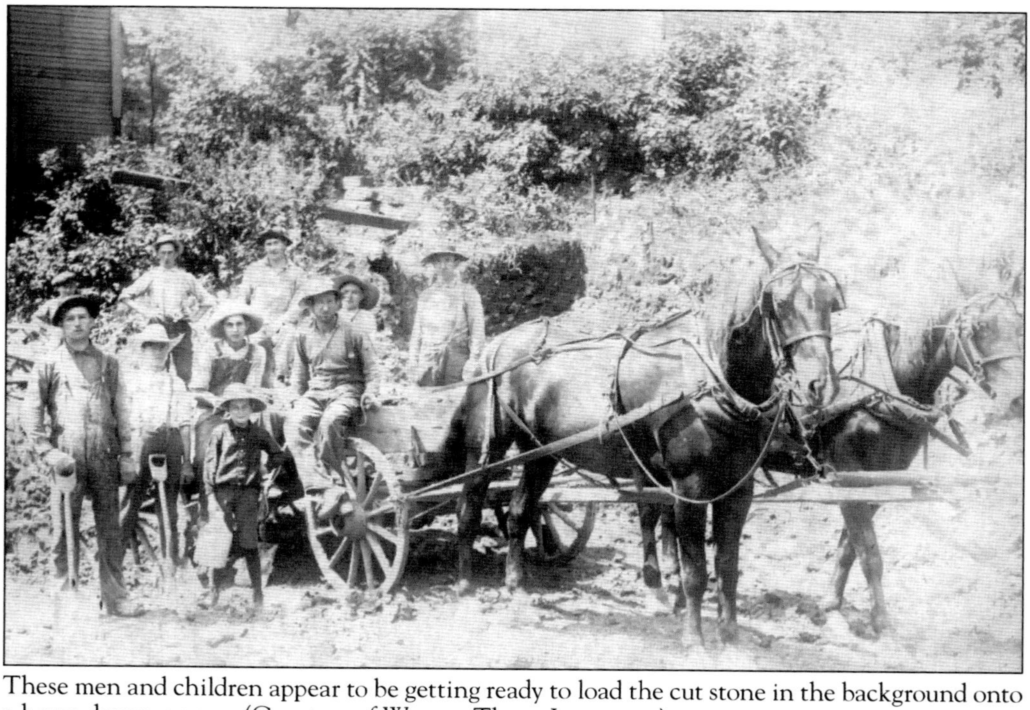

These men and children appear to be getting ready to load the cut stone in the background onto a horse-drawn wagon. (Courtesy of Waneta Thorn Lawrence.)

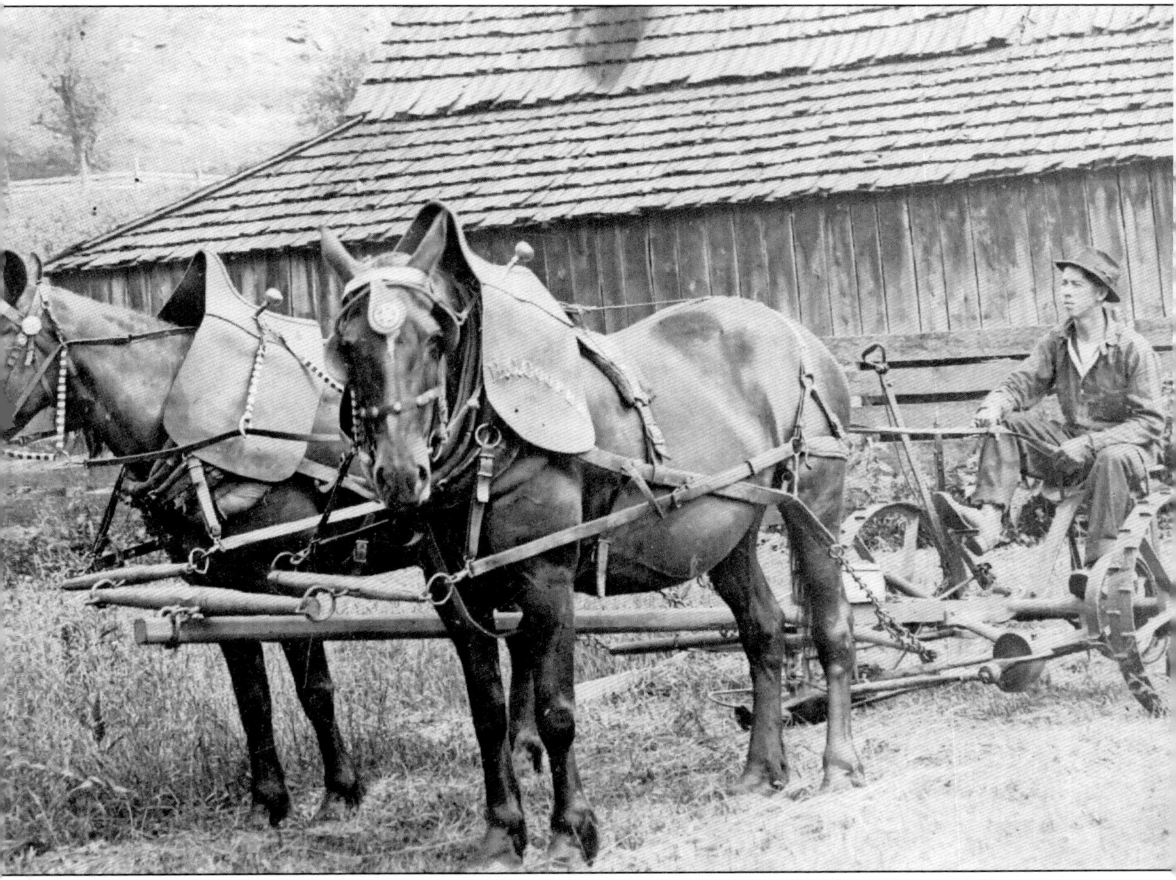

Many improvements have been made in farming equipment since the days Howard Cooper tended crops on a horse-drawn sulky plow. Following the Civil War, slower, hand-operated farm equipment was replaced with modern equipment such as sulky plows, cultivators, binders, and reapers. With these mechanical and technical advances in farming equipment, Howard was able to provide farming services to the people in the Creston community. Howard and his wife, Jane, lived on Little Creek near Creston. (Courtesy of Sherry R. Smith.)

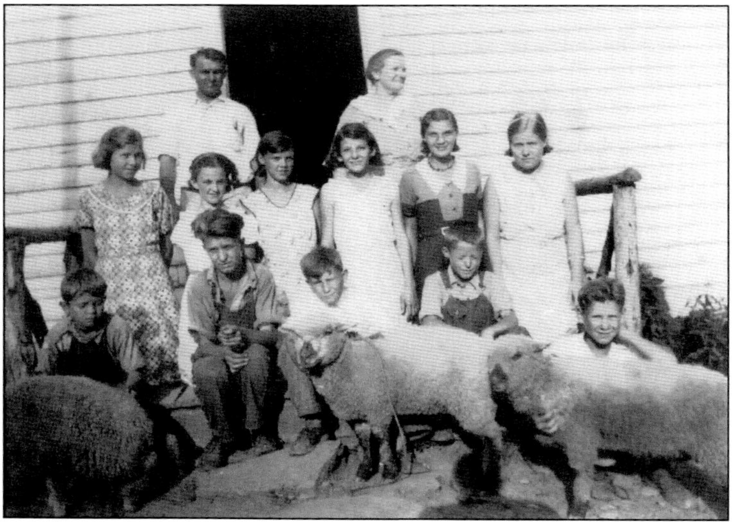

Local teacher Val Sayre Hammond is seen here in the early 1930s with her 4-H club at the Parrish Fork School. Hammond taught school in Wirt County for 33 years. She later organized the Elizabeth Beauchamp Chapter of the Daughters of the American Pioneers to preserve Wirt County's rich history. (Courtesy of Linda Sams.)

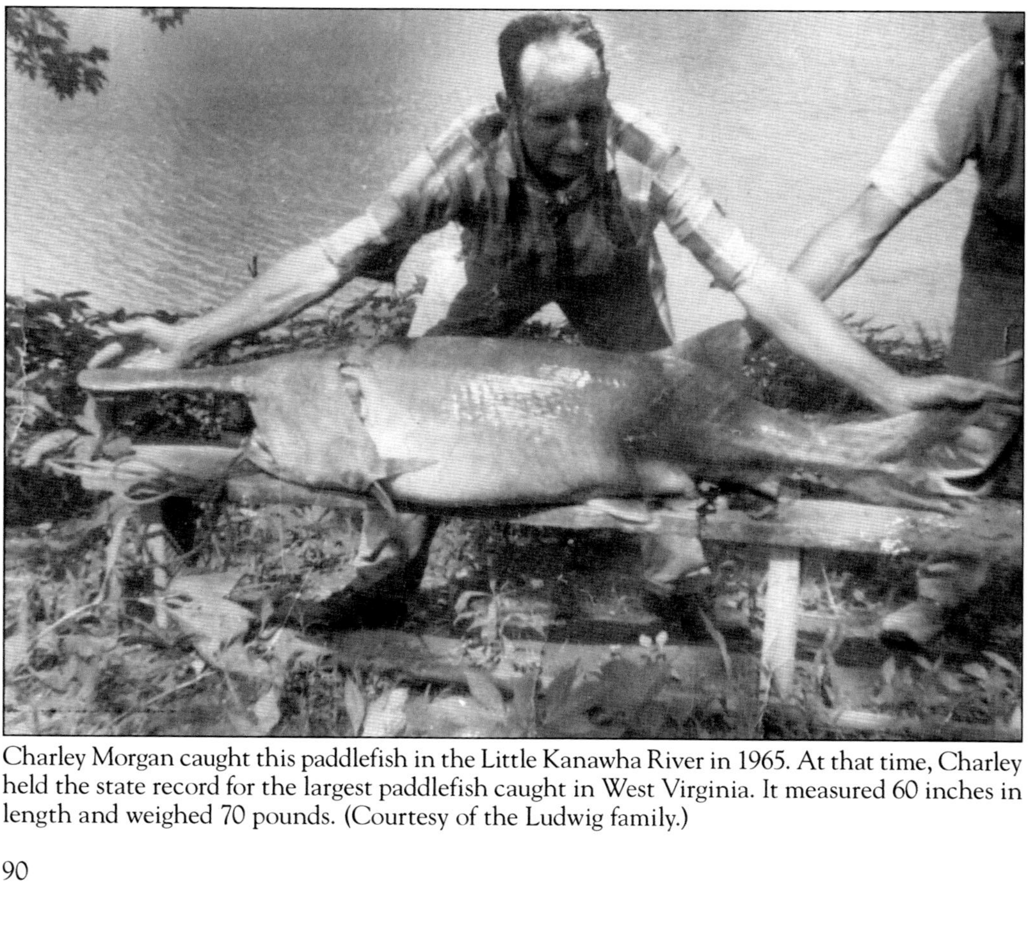

Charley Morgan caught this paddlefish in the Little Kanawha River in 1965. At that time, Charley held the state record for the largest paddlefish caught in West Virginia. It measured 60 inches in length and weighed 70 pounds. (Courtesy of the Ludwig family.)

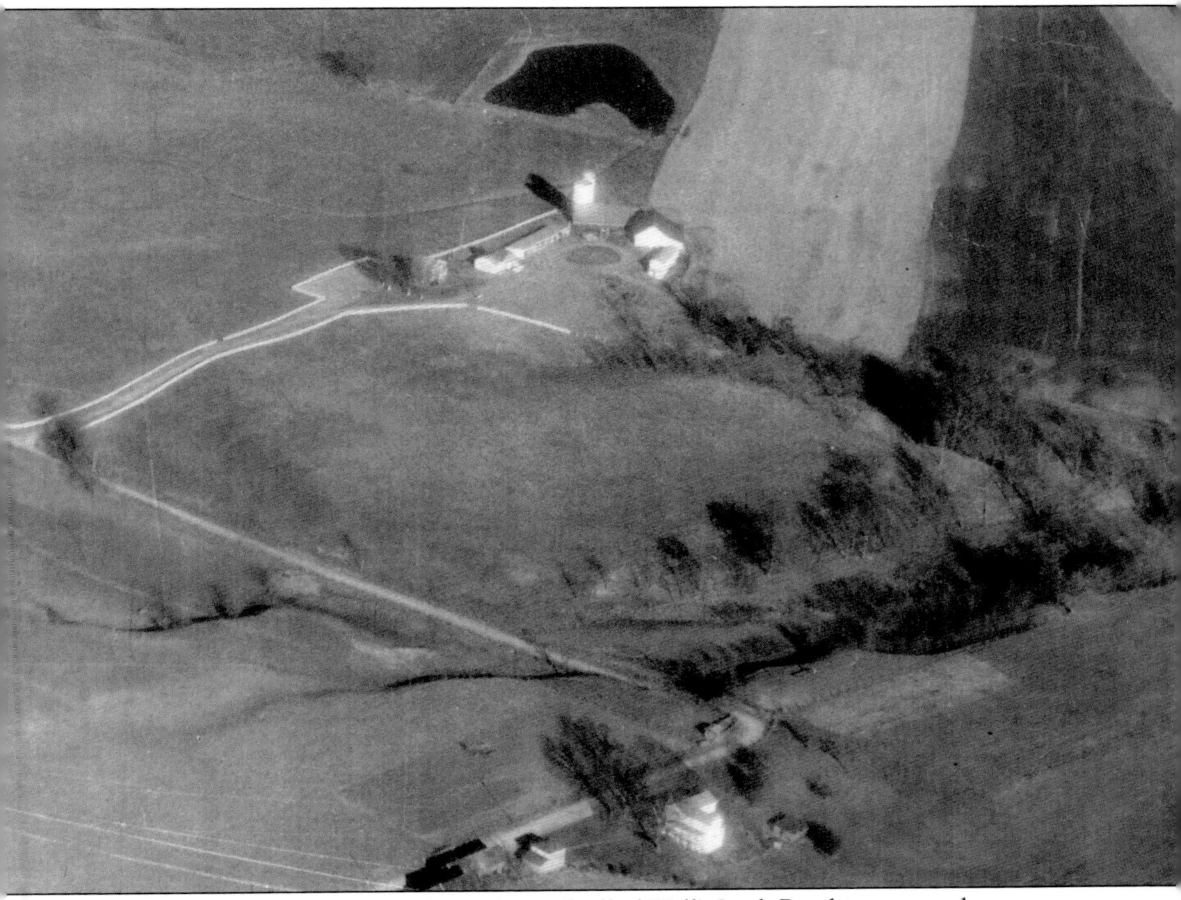

This aerial view of the Cale Dairy Farm, located off of Well's Lock Road in an area known as Mingo Bottom, was photographed in 1970. Clyde Cale purchased this 325-acre farm from his father in 1951. By 1957, he added a milking parlor to the farm and switched from a beef cattle operation to a dairy operation. In recent years, the farm has been converted into the Mingo Bottom Golf Club. (Courtesy of Ann Cale Boyce.)

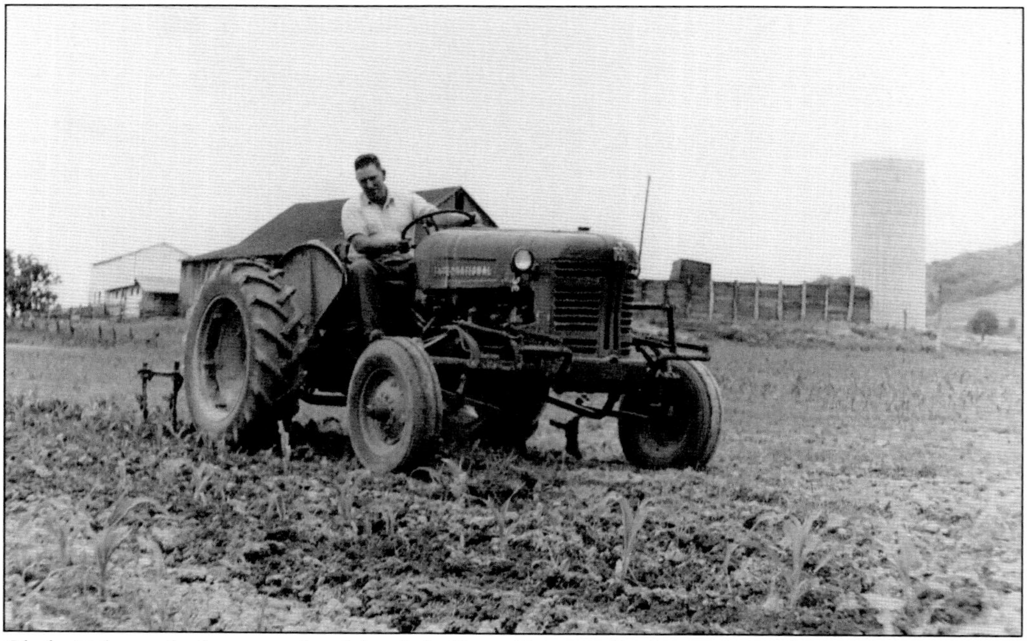

Clyde Cale tends the grounds of the Cale Dairy Farm on his International Harvester. (Courtesy of Ann Cale Boyce.)

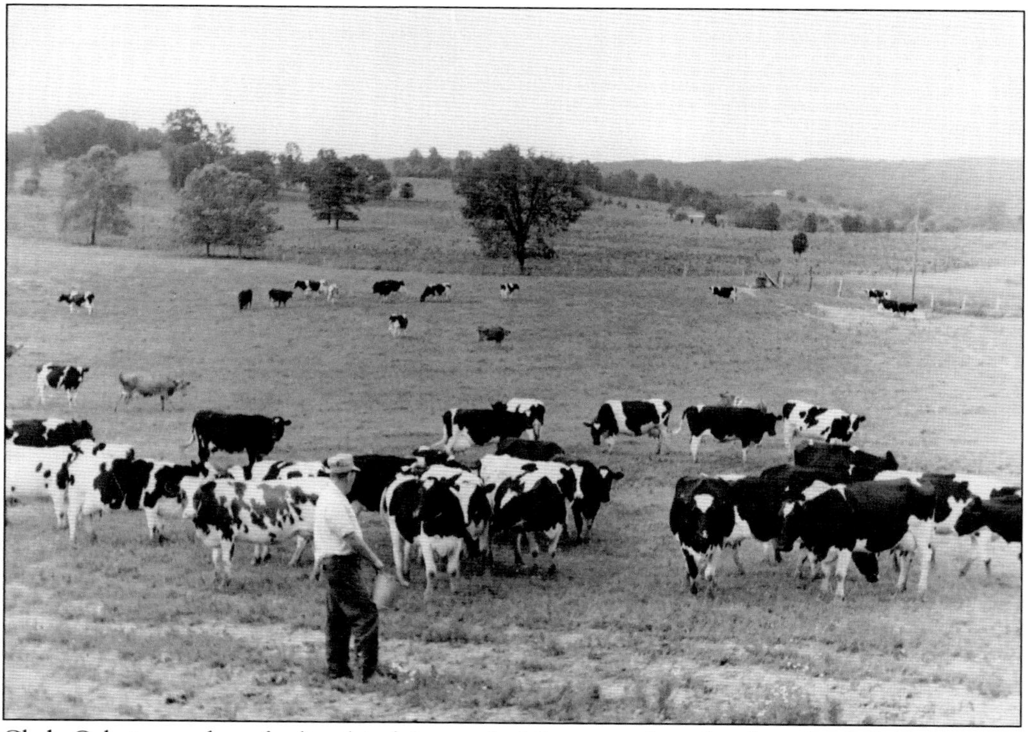

Clyde Cale is seen here feeding his dairy cattle. Like many dairy families, the Cale Dairy Farm supplied milk to distributors in order to meet growing consumer demand for dairy products. (Courtesy of Ann Cale Boyce.)

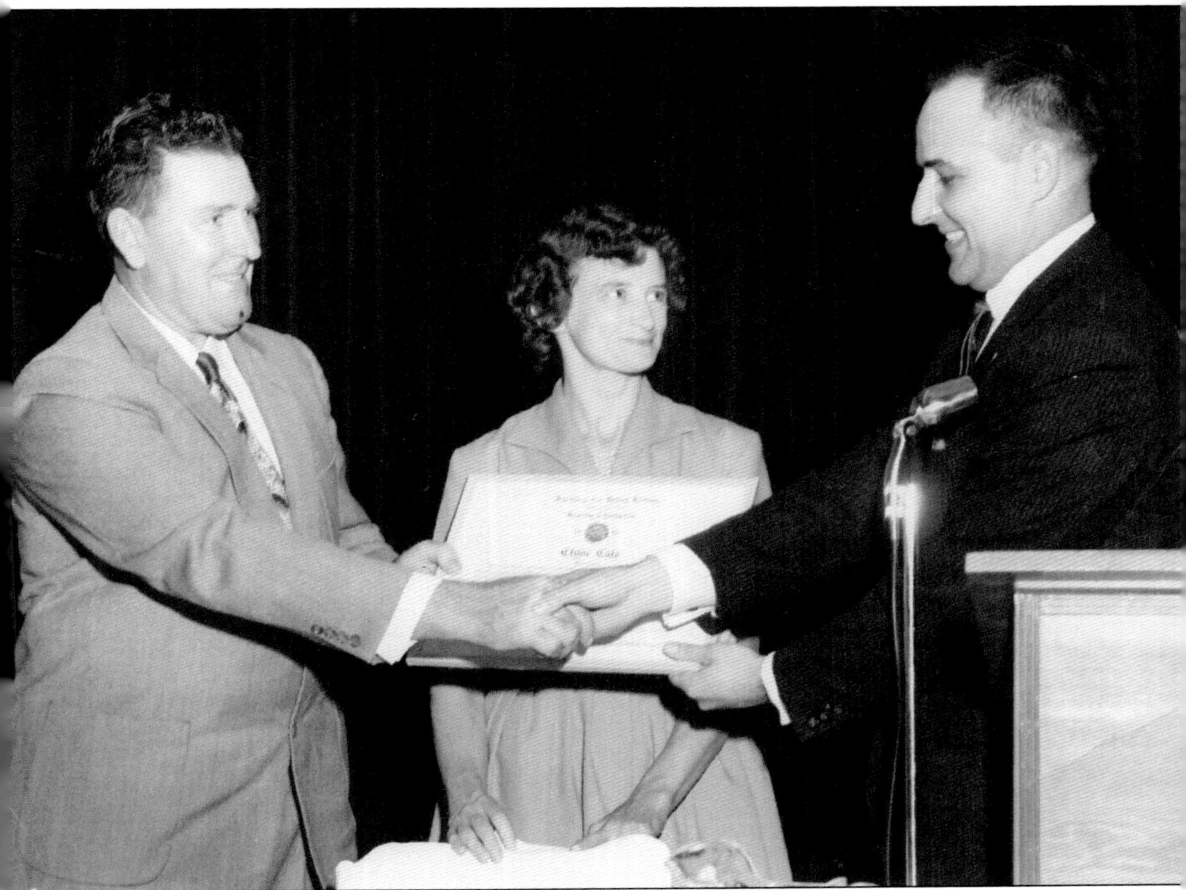

Clyde Cale, with his wife, Virginia, looking on, received the Farming for Better Living Award for becoming the regional champion of the Little Kanawha area on January 14, 1961. (Courtesy of Ann Cale Boyce.)

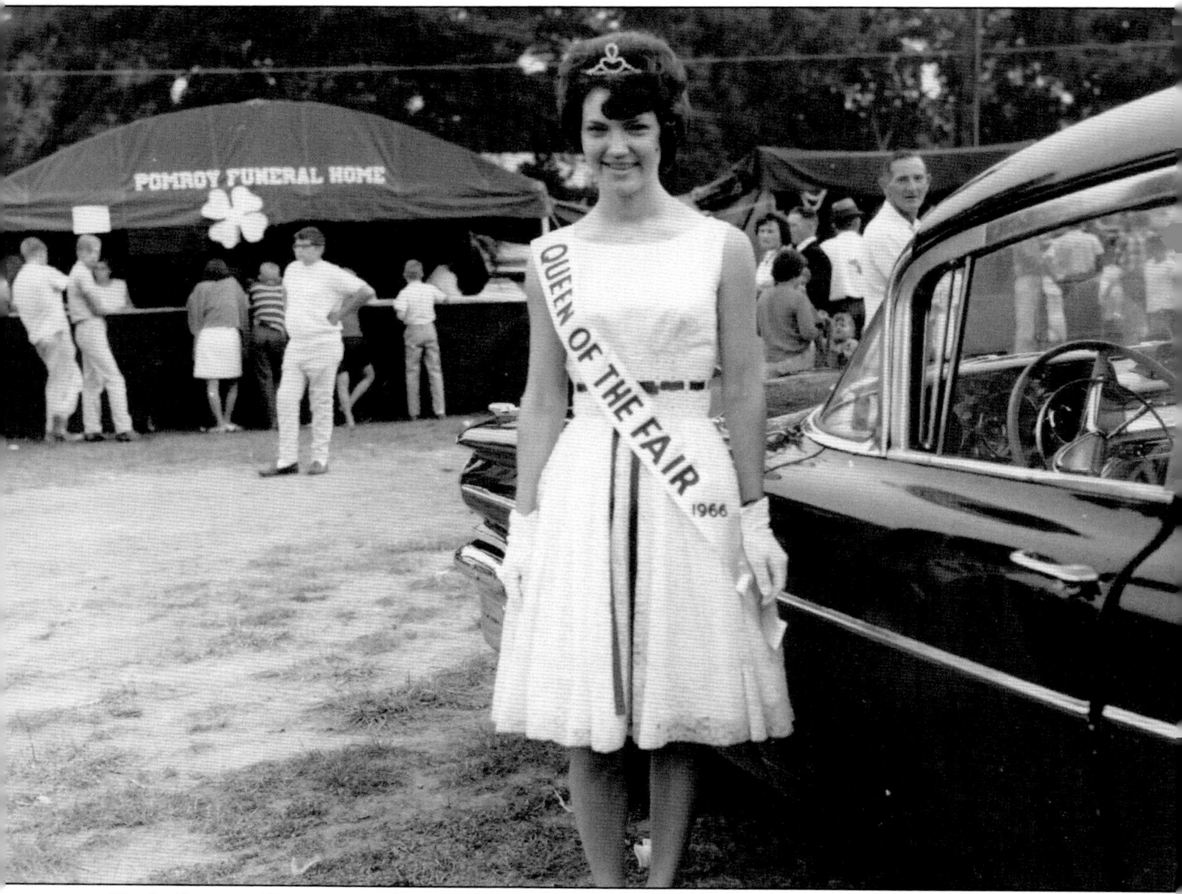

Doris Somerville poses in front of Denzil Sims's car after being crowned the 1966 Wirt County Fair Queen. Just before the photograph was taken, Woody Wilson of the *Wirt County Journal* placed a pack of chewing gum underneath Somerville's tiara to hold it in place while he took this photograph. (Courtesy of the Wirt County Fair Association.)

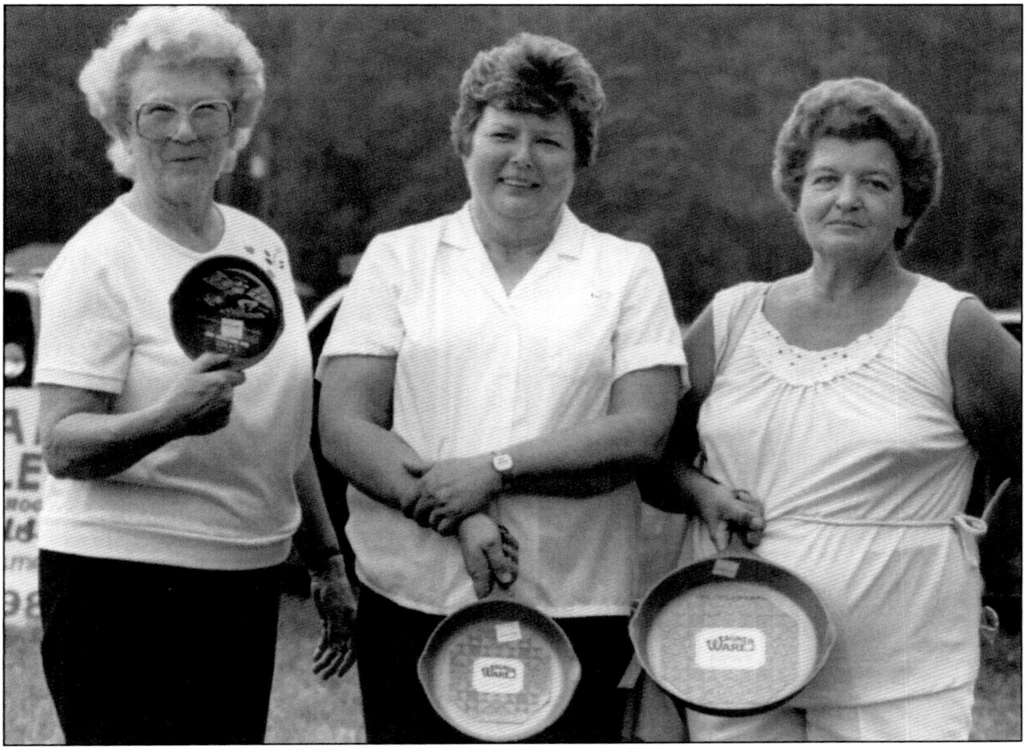

Winners of the skillet toss at the Wirt County Fair are, from left to right, Clarice Sheppard, Juanita Coakley, and Joyce Edwards. (Courtesy of the Wirt County Fair Association.)

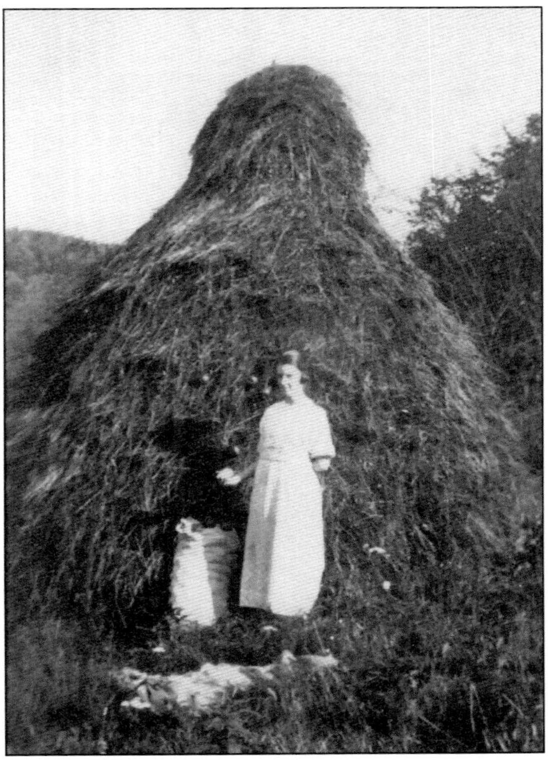

Sarah Ellen Cain Merrill prepares apples for winter storage by placing them in the center of a haystack. Root cellars eventually replaced this early food storage method. (Courtesy of Carole Menefee.)

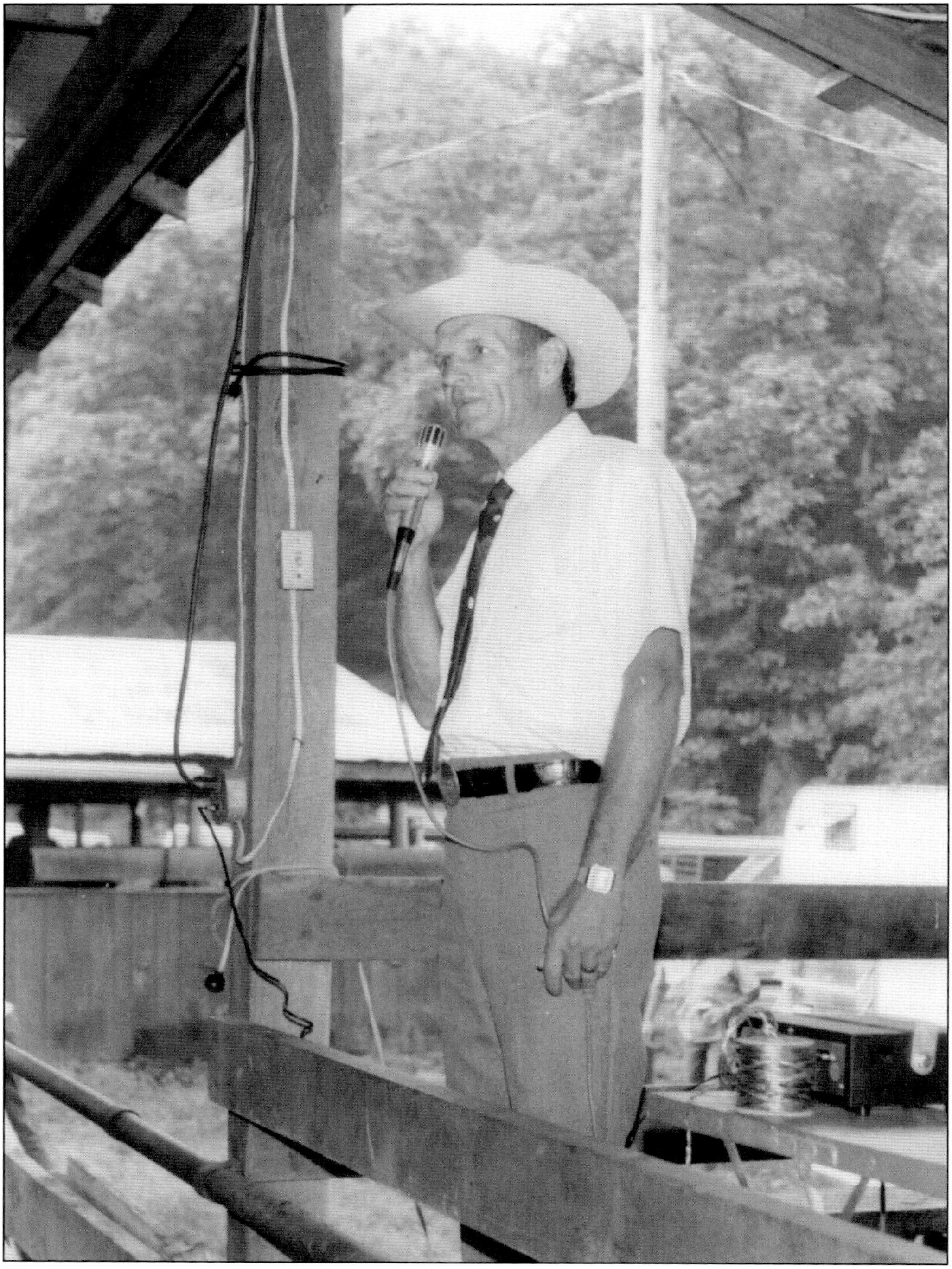

West Virginia commissioner of agriculture Gus Douglas is shown addressing fairgoers at the Wirt County Fair's 4-H and FFA livestock sale. (Courtesy of the Wirt County Fair Association.)

Lee Young is seen here waiting for the livestock sale to begin at the Wirt County Fair. (Courtesy of the Wirt County Fair Association.)

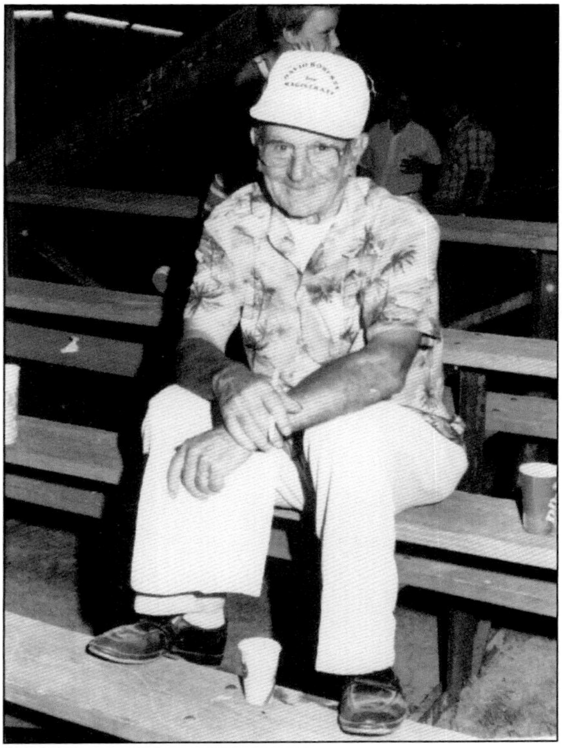

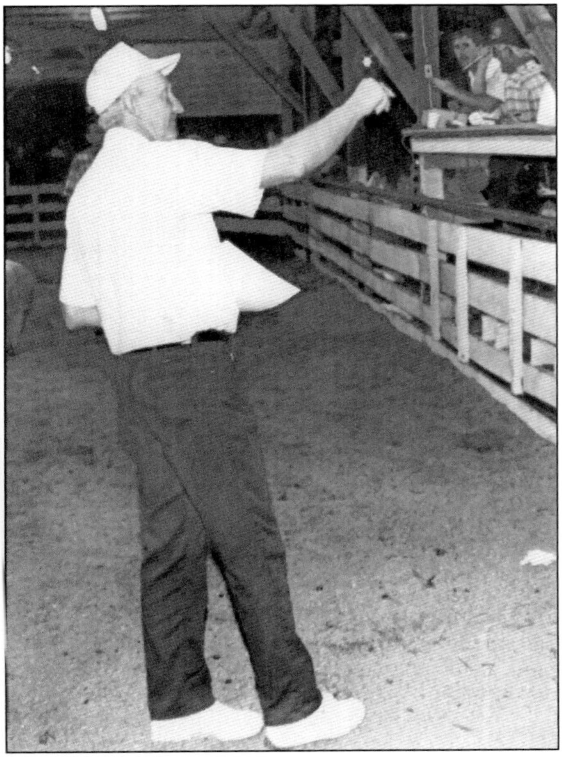

Cam Campbell can be seen at left volunteering during the livestock sale at the Wirt County Fair. (Courtesy of the Wirt County Fair Association.)

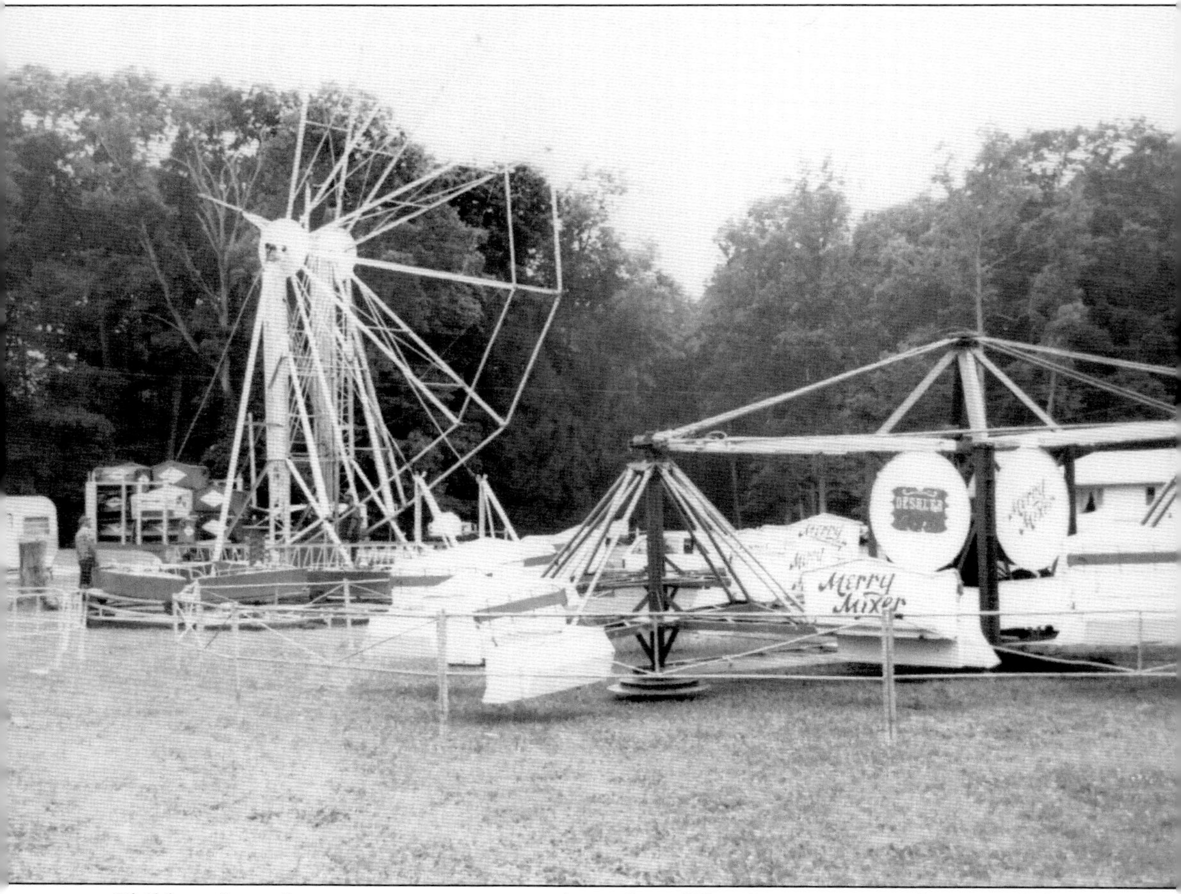

Children from the various communities throughout Wirt County anxiously awaited the Wirt County Fair. This annual event offers a variety of amusement rides, as seen here. (Courtesy of the Wirt County Fair Association.)

Billy Wells is pictured with his steer in the cattle barn at the Wirt County Fair. (Courtesy of the Wirt County Fair Association.)

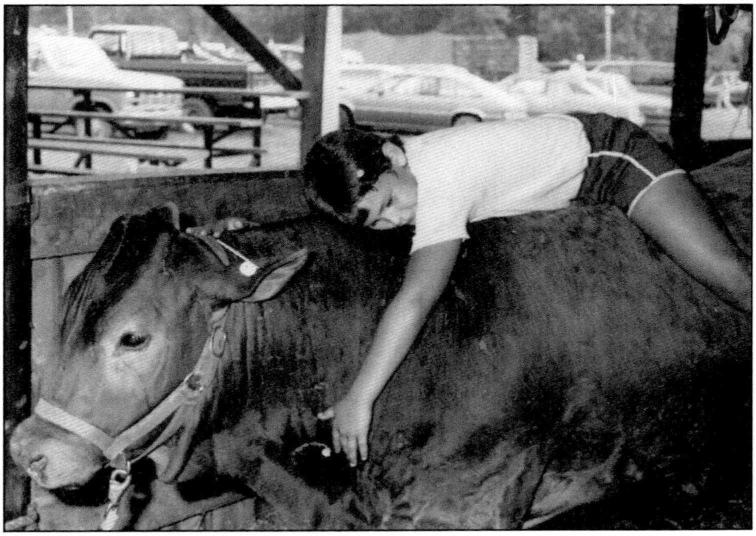

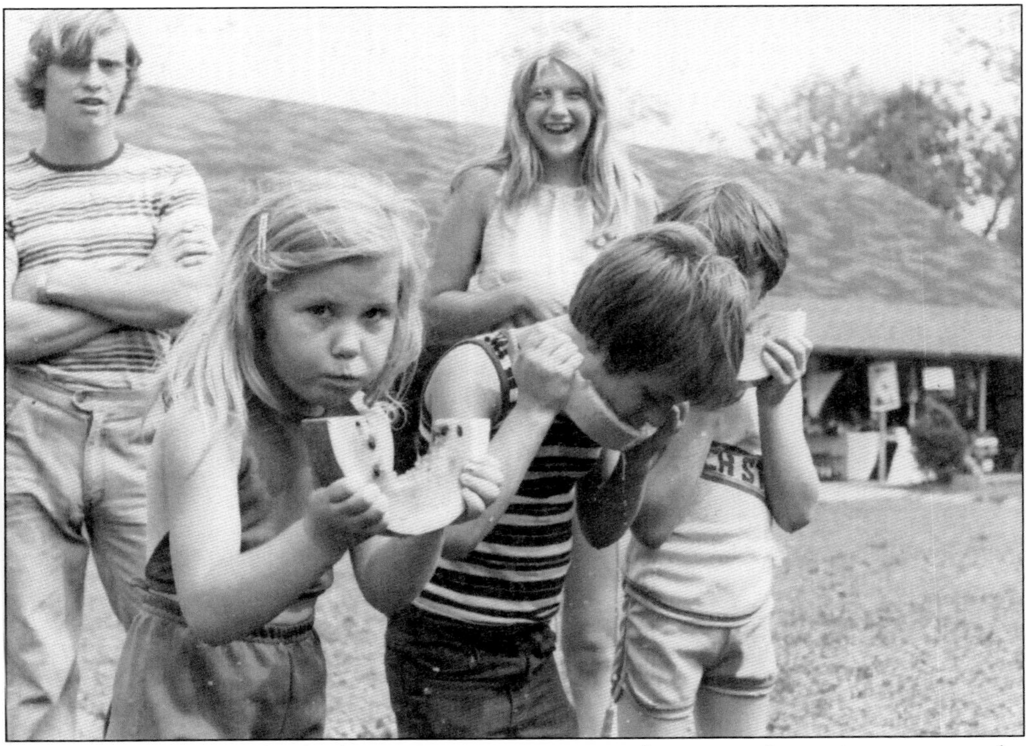

Mary Ellison watches as her little sister Juanna competes in the watermelon-eating contest at the Wirt County Fair. (Courtesy of the Wirt County Fair Association.)

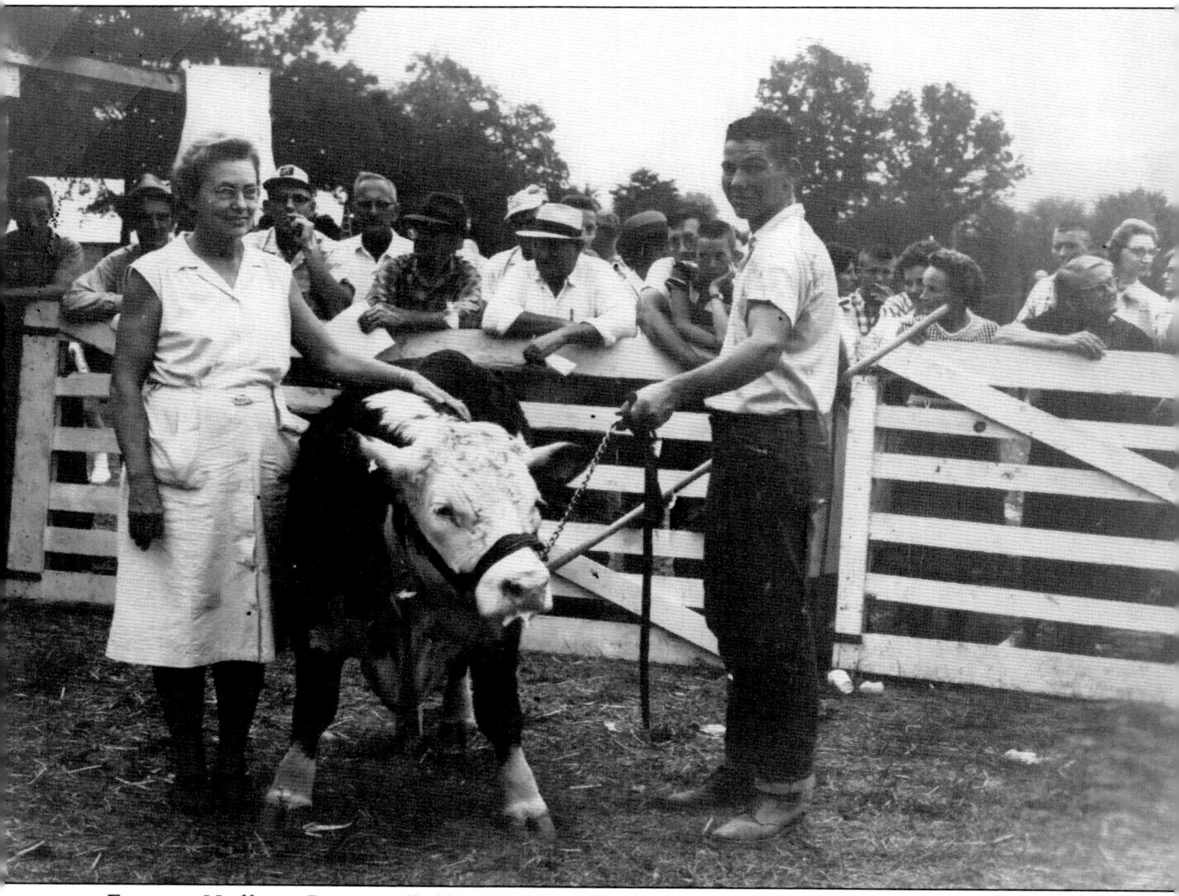

Faustine Huffman Bauman (left) and Mike Sims (right) are shown at the Wirt County Fair with a livestock entry. (Courtesy of the Ludwig family.)

Seven

Traveling Wirt County

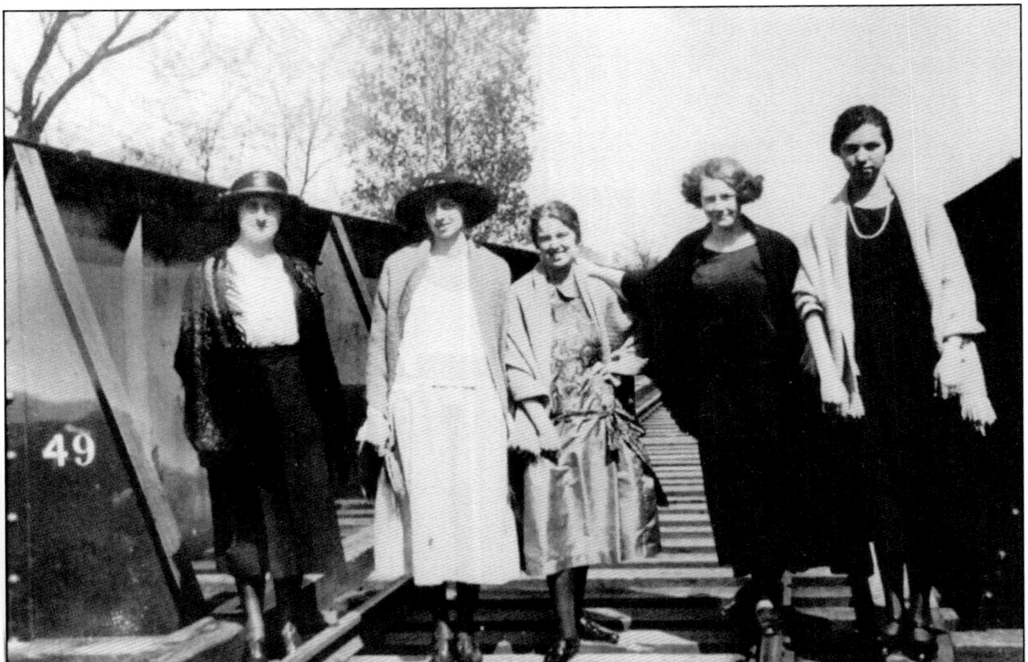

These early educators gathered to have their photograph taken at the railroad bridge across Tucker Creek. Pictured from left to right are Amanda Wilson, teacher (class of 1923); Beulah Woodyard, stenographer (class of 1923); Frank Huffman, teacher (class of 1922); Ethel Seaton Cheuvront, teacher (class of 1923); and Edith Gibson, teacher (class of 1924). (Courtesy of the Ludwig family.)

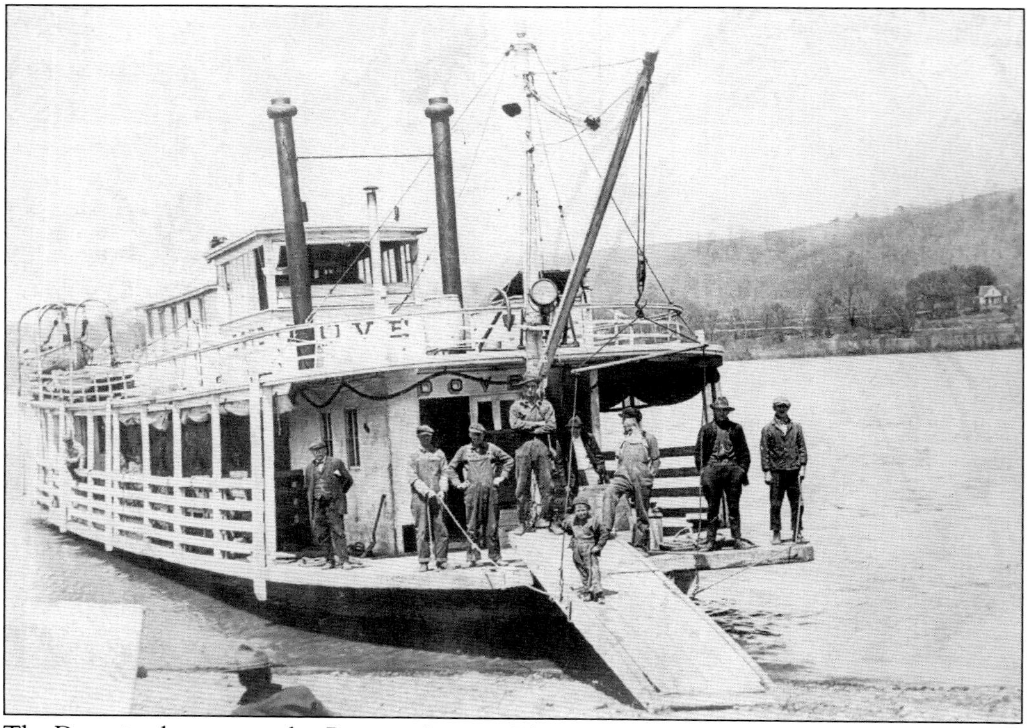

The *Dove* riverboat moored at Burning Springs. The *Dove* was owned by the Gibson family. This gasoline-powered riverboat was one of the fastest of its time. (Courtesy of Sue Douglas.)

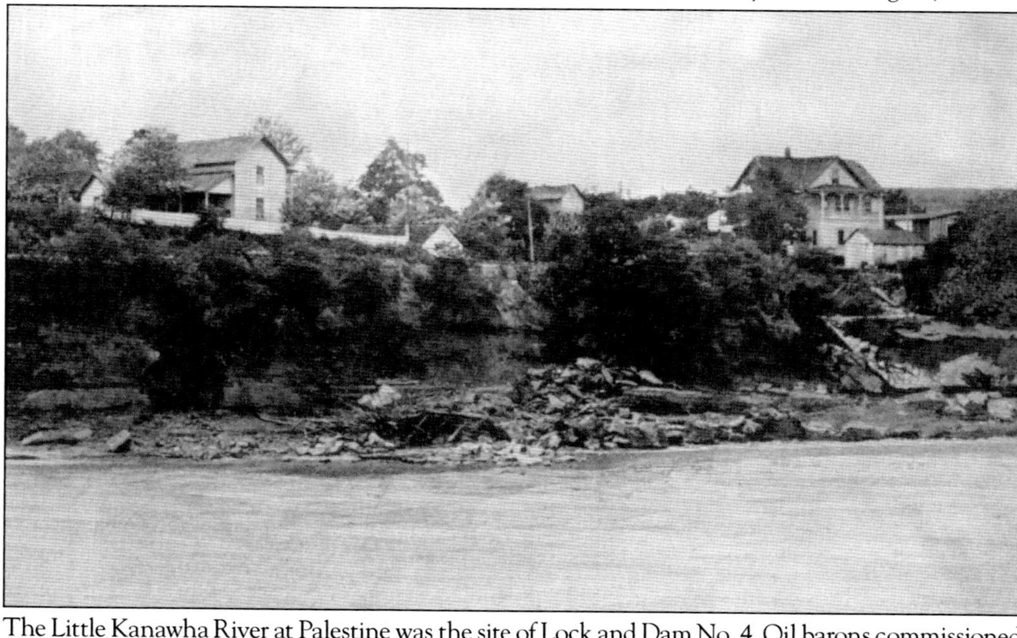

The Little Kanawha River at Palestine was the site of Lock and Dam No. 4. Oil barons commissioned the lock and dam, built in 1871, in order to transport oil to Parkersburg. The old hotel at the top of the hill was one of three hotels in the Palestine community that offered refuge to travelers whose journey was often preempted when the river was not navigable. (Courtesy of Diane Ludwig.)

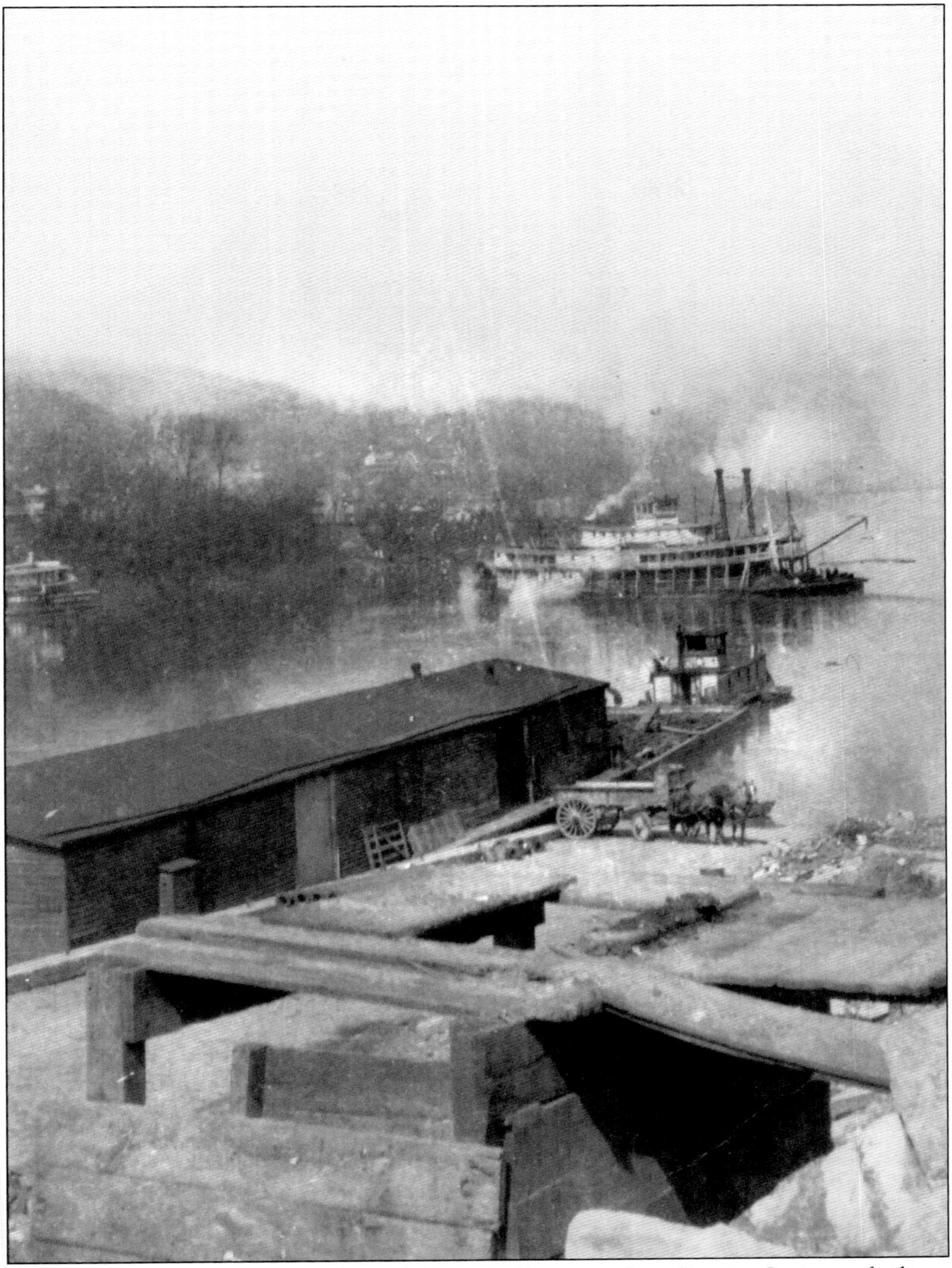

Lock and Dam No. 5 was built on the Little Kanawha River just above Burning Springs to facilitate river traffic. Construction of the lock and dam was completed in 1891 and made it possible for gas- and steam-powered riverboats and barges to haul coal, carbon black, railroad ties, oil, lumber, grain, and salt up and down the river. (Courtesy of the DAP.)

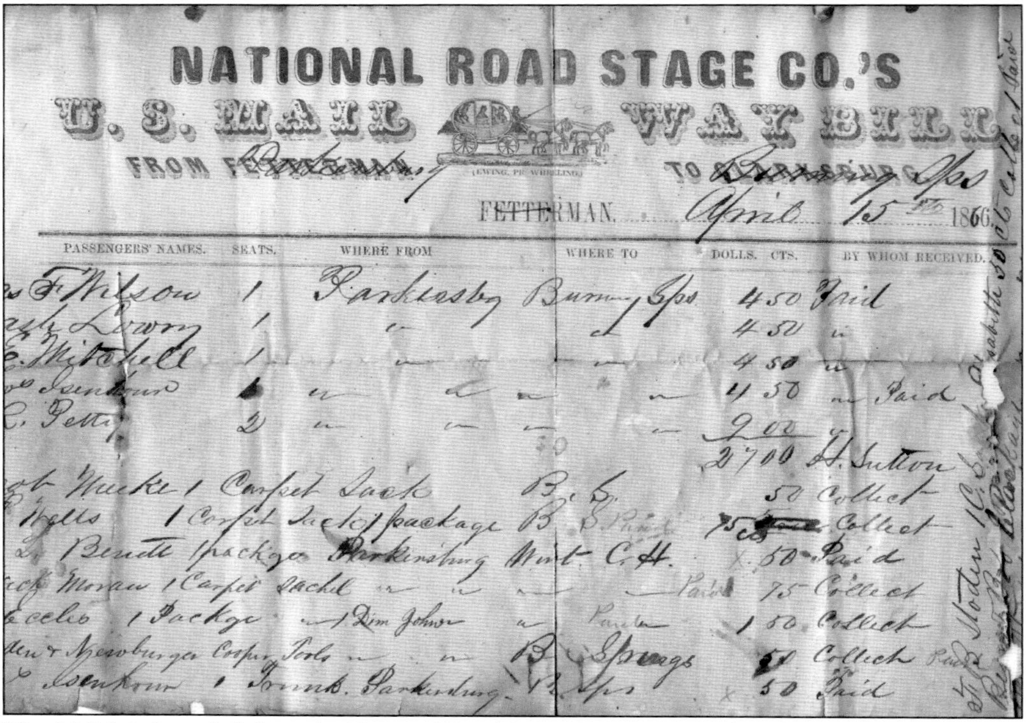
NATIONAL ROAD STAGE CO.'S
U. S. MAIL WAY BILL
FROM Parkersburg TO Burning Spgs
(EWING, PR. WHEELING)
FETTERMAN. April 15th 1866.

PASSENGERS' NAMES.	SEATS.	WHERE FROM	WHERE TO	DOLLS. CTS.	BY WHOM RECEIVED.

This U.S. Mail way bill from the National Road Stage Company was found in the attic of Richard Lowe's house, built by attorney Robert A. Brown before the Civil War. It lists the cost of travel from Parkersburg to Burning Springs as $4.50 in April 1866.

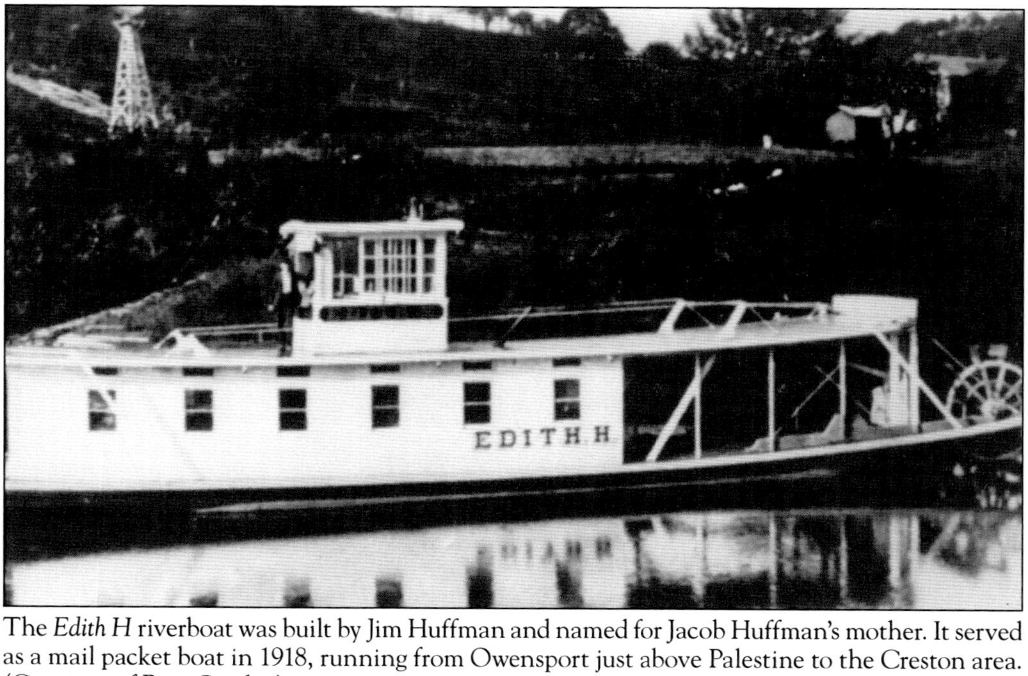

The *Edith H* riverboat was built by Jim Huffman and named for Jacob Huffman's mother. It served as a mail packet boat in 1918, running from Owensport just above Palestine to the Creston area. (Courtesy of Russ Snyder.)

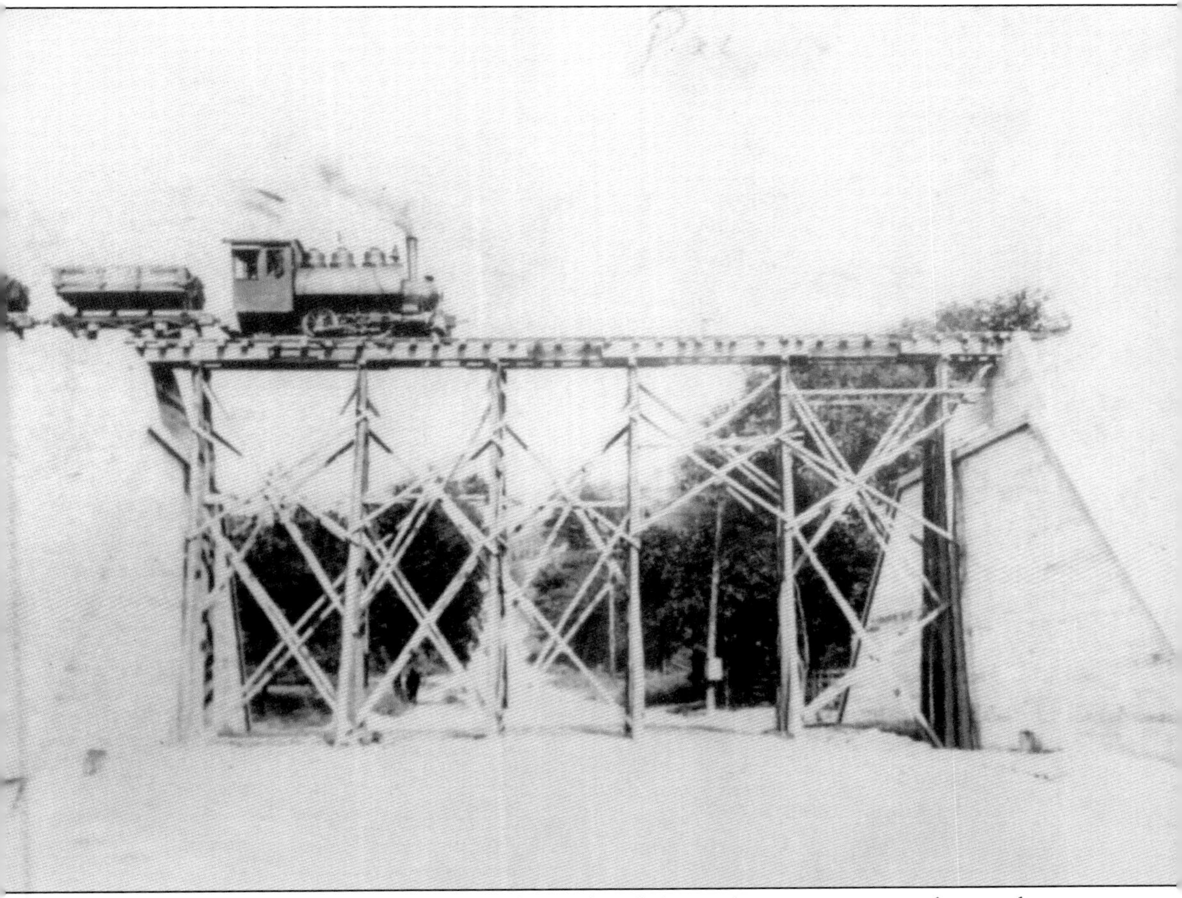

This early photograph of the Little Kanawha Railroad shows the train crossing the trestle at Palestine during one of two daily round-trips from Parkersburg to Palestine. The train made its last run on October 10, 1933. (Courtesy of the Ludwig family.)

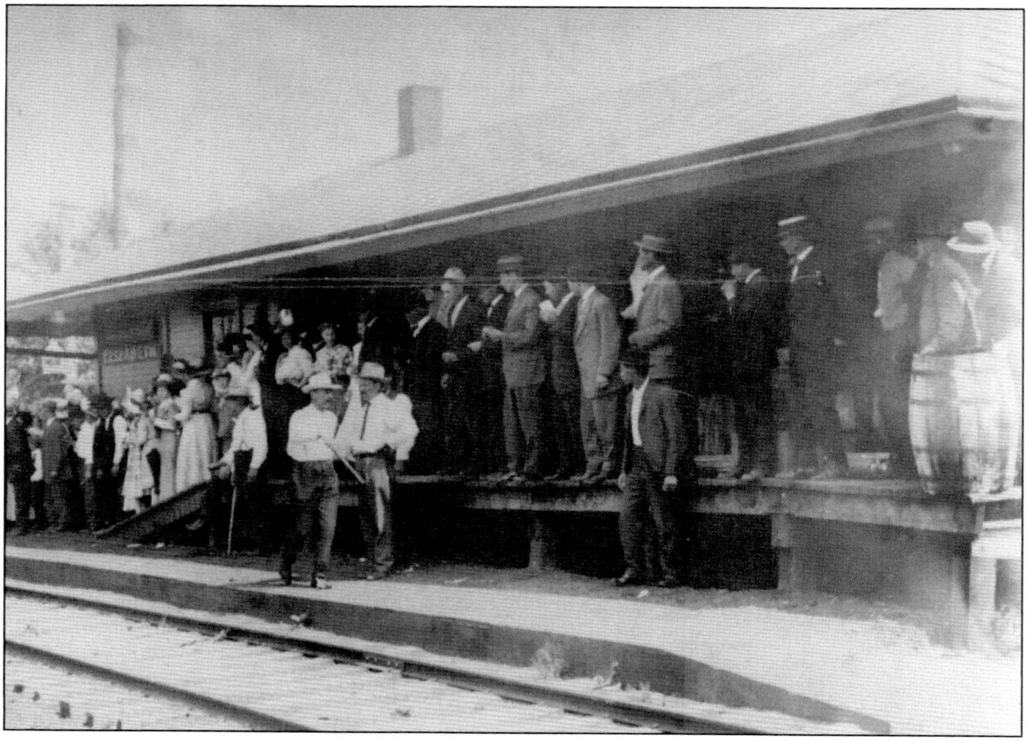

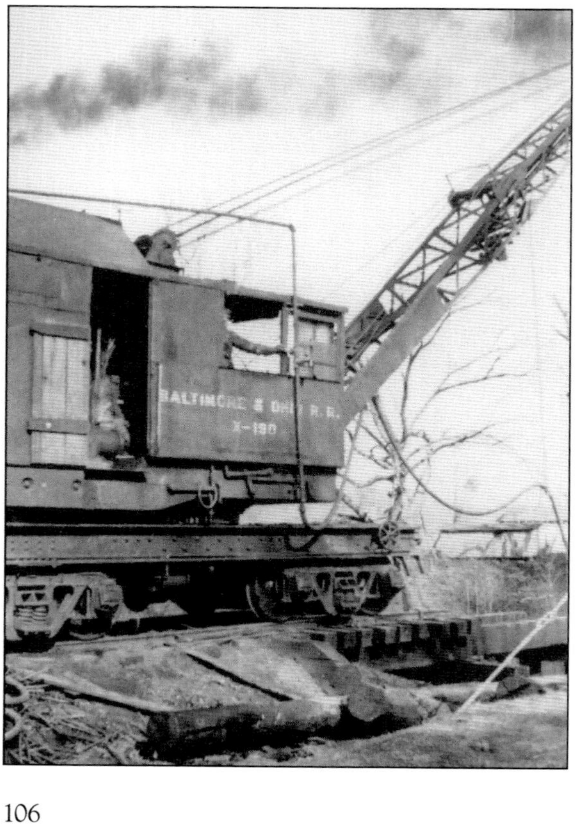

A crowd awaits the arrival of a train at the Elizabeth Depot. At the time this photograph was taken, the railroad was the modern mode of transportation, making two round-trips a day from Parkersburg to Owensport, near Palestine. The old train depot is now home to Mom's Place Restaurant. (Courtesy of Helen Burns.)

In 1897 and 1898, the Little Kanawha Railroad laid nearly 30 miles of track from Parkersburg to Owensport, near Palestine. The railroad opened the area to commerce and provided speedy transportation to and from Parkersburg for over 35 years. As new highways were developed in the 1930s, the railroad became obsolete. An employee of the Baltimore and Ohio Railroad is seen here removing the tracks in Wirt County. (Courtesy of the DAP.)

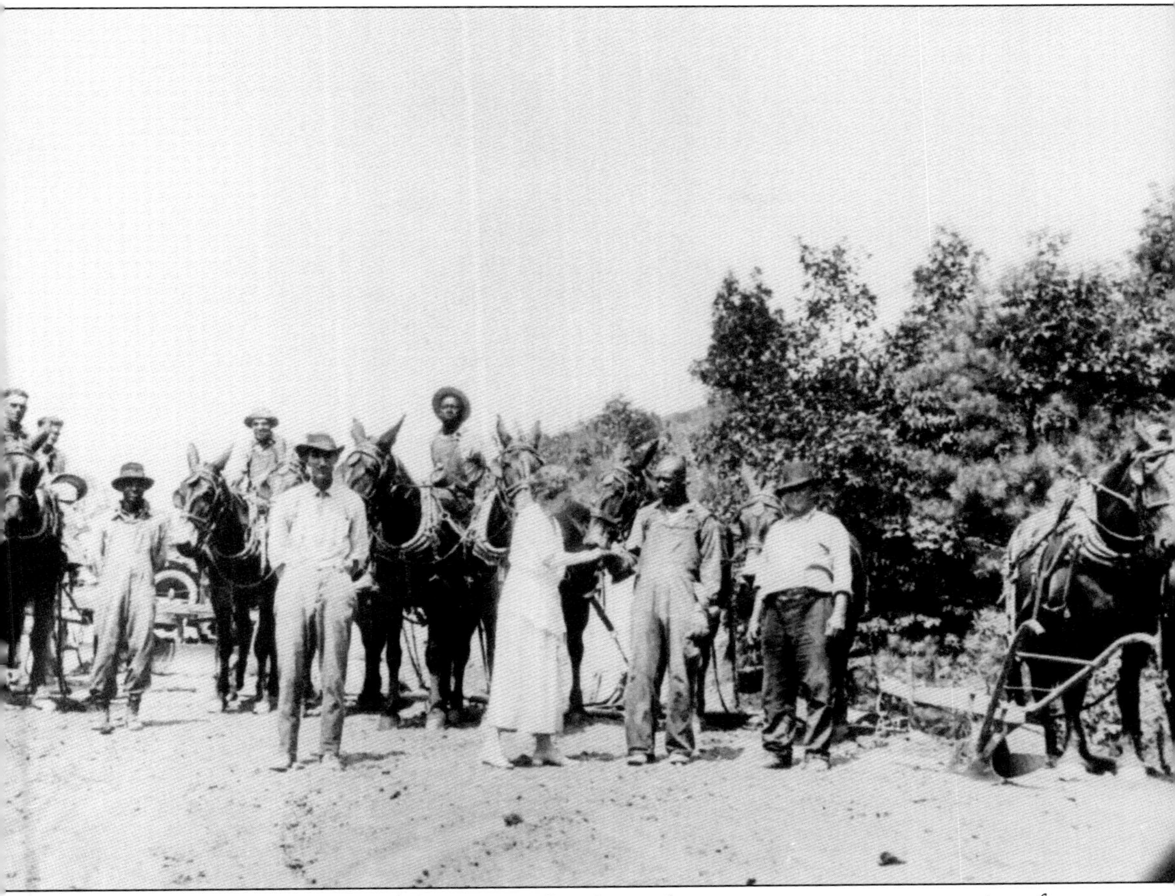

In the early 1920s, the State Road Commission hired a road crew to commence construction of a portion of State Route 14 leading into Elizabeth. (Courtesy of the West Virginia State Archives.)

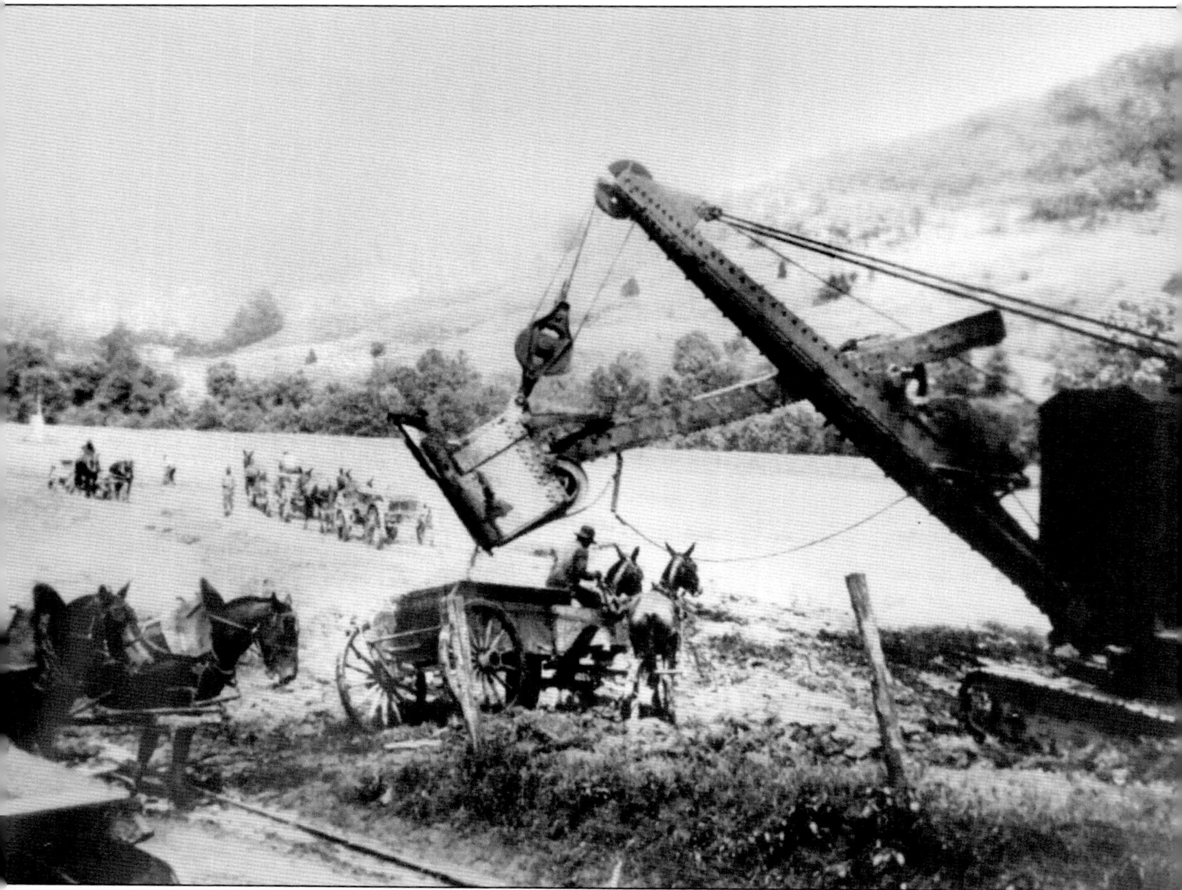

Construction of State Route 14 was a slow process that was accomplished during the years 1923–1926 with the assistance of mule teams and steam-powered dump shovels filled with coal. Mules were preferred over horses because of their ability to climb steep, rugged terrain. (Courtesy of the West Virginia State Archives.)

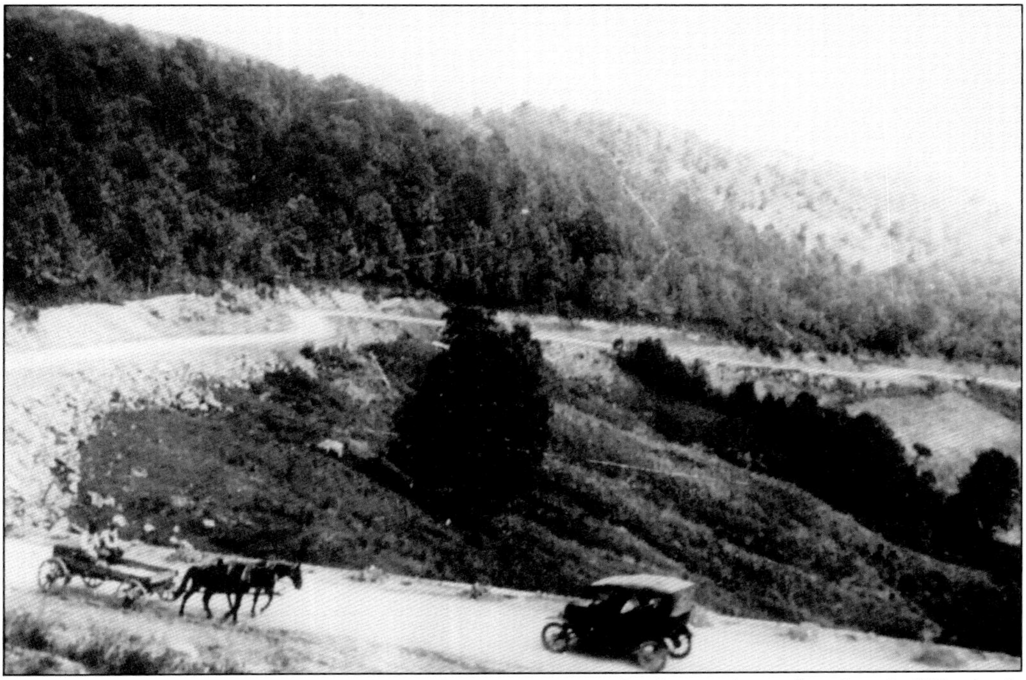

An early-1920s automobile passes a horse-drawn wagon on the famous horseshoe bend of Elizabeth Hill. Prior to its construction, travel to Parkersburg and back could take as much as a day or two depending on the road conditions. This section of Elizabeth Hill was eventually bypassed in the late 1990s. (Courtesy of the Ludwig family.)

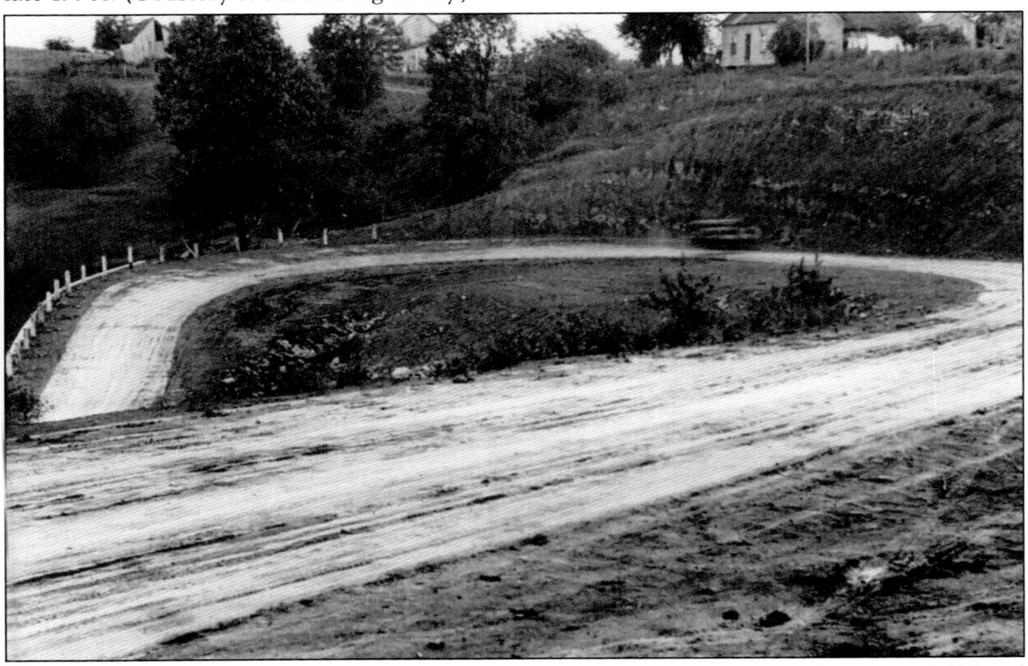

This photograph of the horseshoe bend on Elizabeth Hill shows the road before Rose Hill Road was built. (Courtesy of the Ludwig family.)

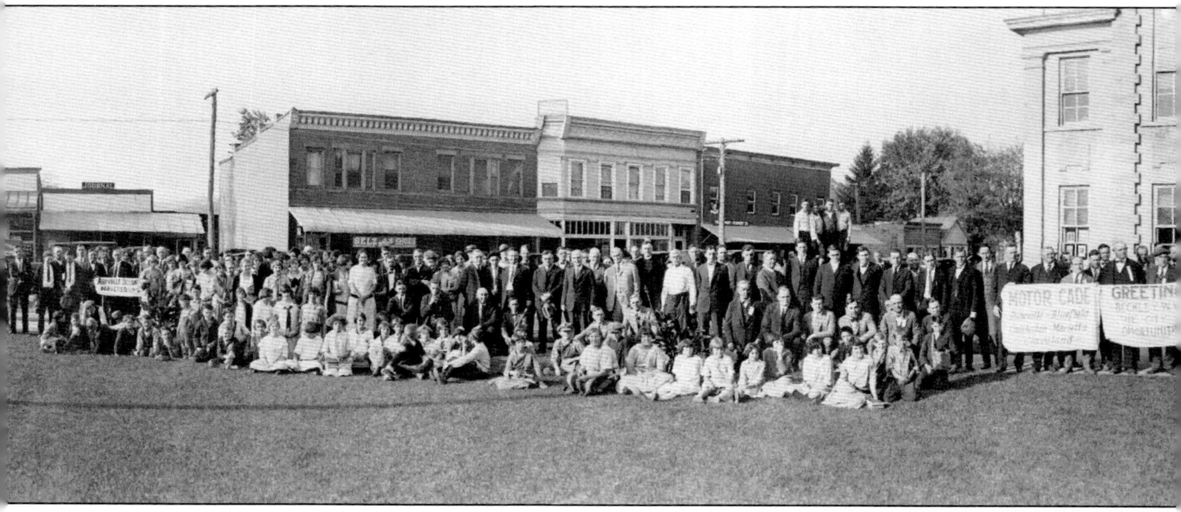

A motorcade of representatives from Charleston, Bluefield, Marietta, Asheville, Parkersburg, Beckley, Williamston, and Cleveland stopped by the Wirt County Courthouse in Elizabeth on September 24, 1926, to celebrate the opening of the first paved road from Parkersburg to Charleston.

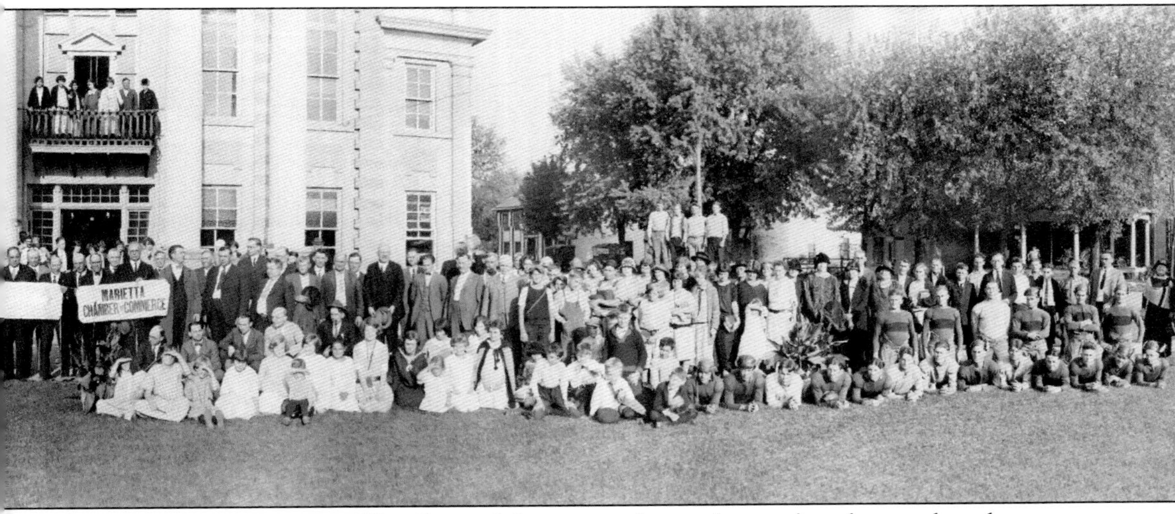

This was an exciting time in Wirt County's history, as the newly paved road opened up the area for progressive development and commerce. (Courtesy of the West Virginia State Archives.)

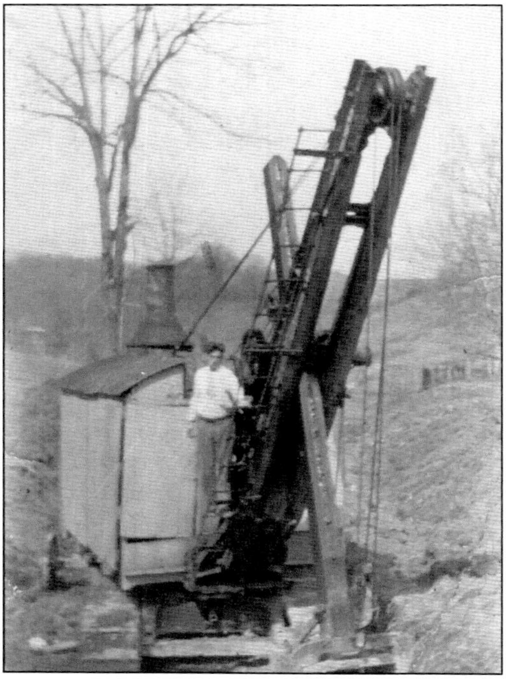

Steam shovel operator Ernest Duncan is pictured working to build a portion of State Route 5 at Cherry near Burning Springs. (Courtesy of Mildred Kirby.)

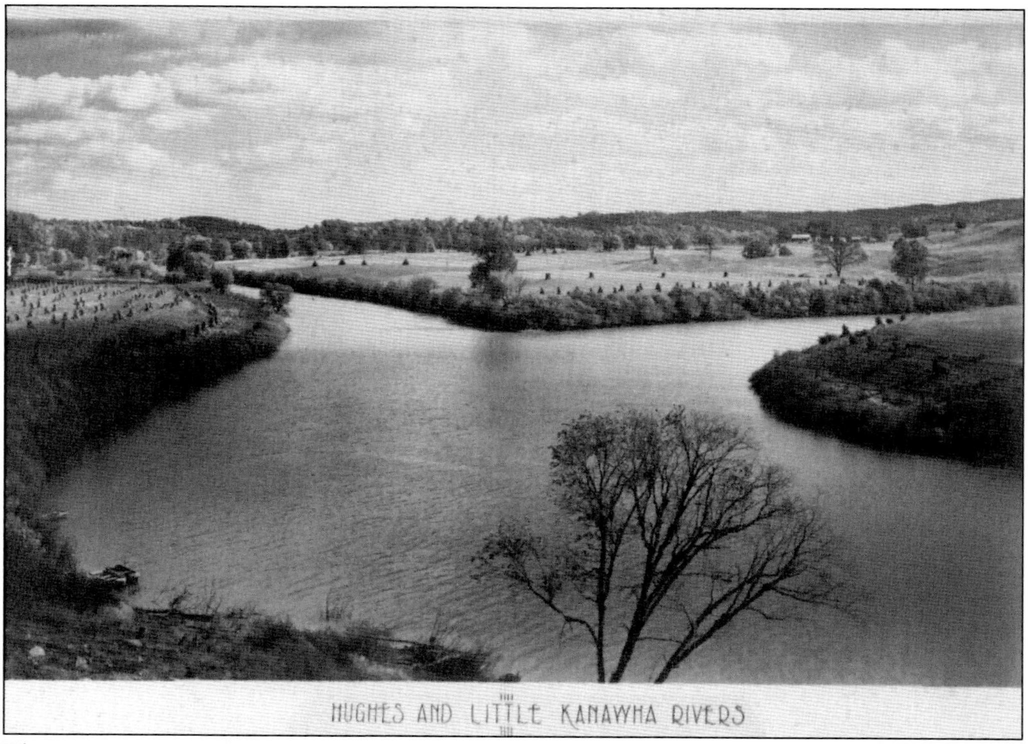

This picture postcard features the point where the Little Kanawha and Hughes Rivers meet. In earlier years, both rivers were bustling with riverboat traffic; now they are largely recognized by the community for their recreational value. (Courtesy of the DAP.)

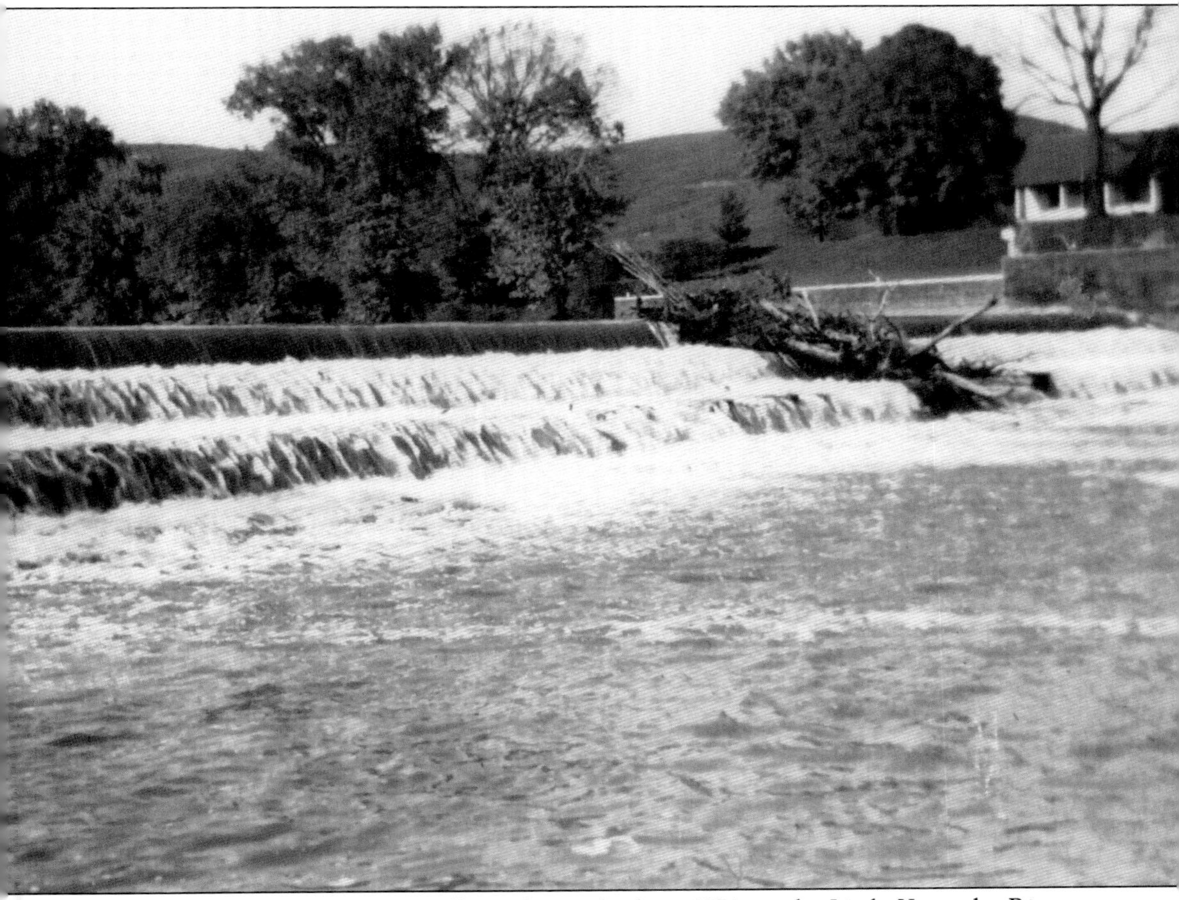

Lock and Dam No. 3, known as Wells Lock, was built in 1874 on the Little Kanawha River some 25 miles from Parkersburg. It is the last remaining lock and dam structure along the river. (Courtesy of Linda Sams.)

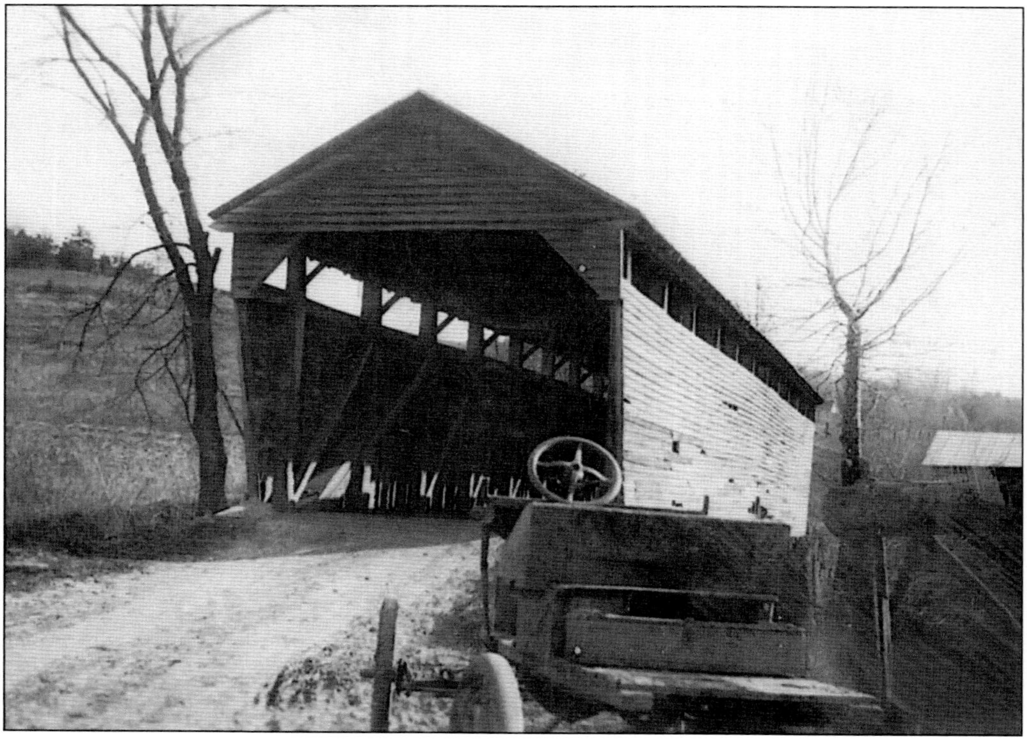

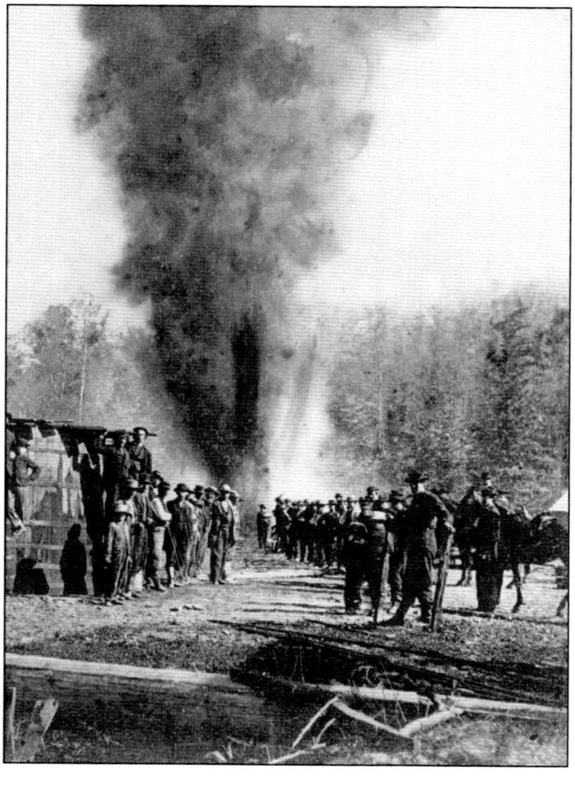

This covered bridge at Freeport crosses Goose Creek where it empties into the Hughes River. This bridge was part of the Staunton Pike, which connected Parkersburg, West Virginia, to Staunton, Virginia. (Courtesy of Marjorie F. Mayes.)

This early photograph shows one of many oil wells discovered in the Burning Springs area during the mid-1860s. (Courtesy of the Ludwig family.)

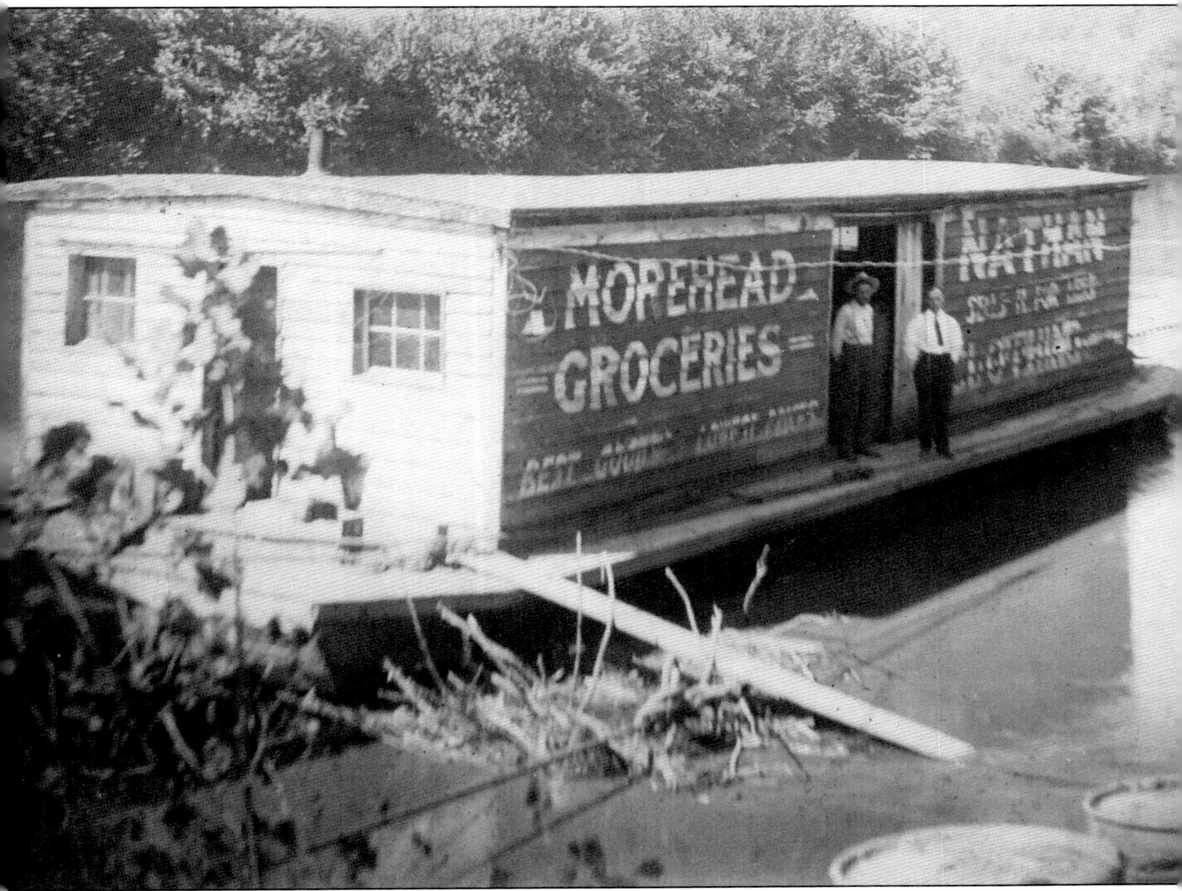

Junk boats traveled the waters of the Little Kanawha River, making several stops in small communities throughout Wirt County in order to peddle their wares. It was common for the junk boats to offer different items each month. This particular junk boat features Morehead Groceries and Nathan Clothing. (Courtesy of Annabelle Snider.)

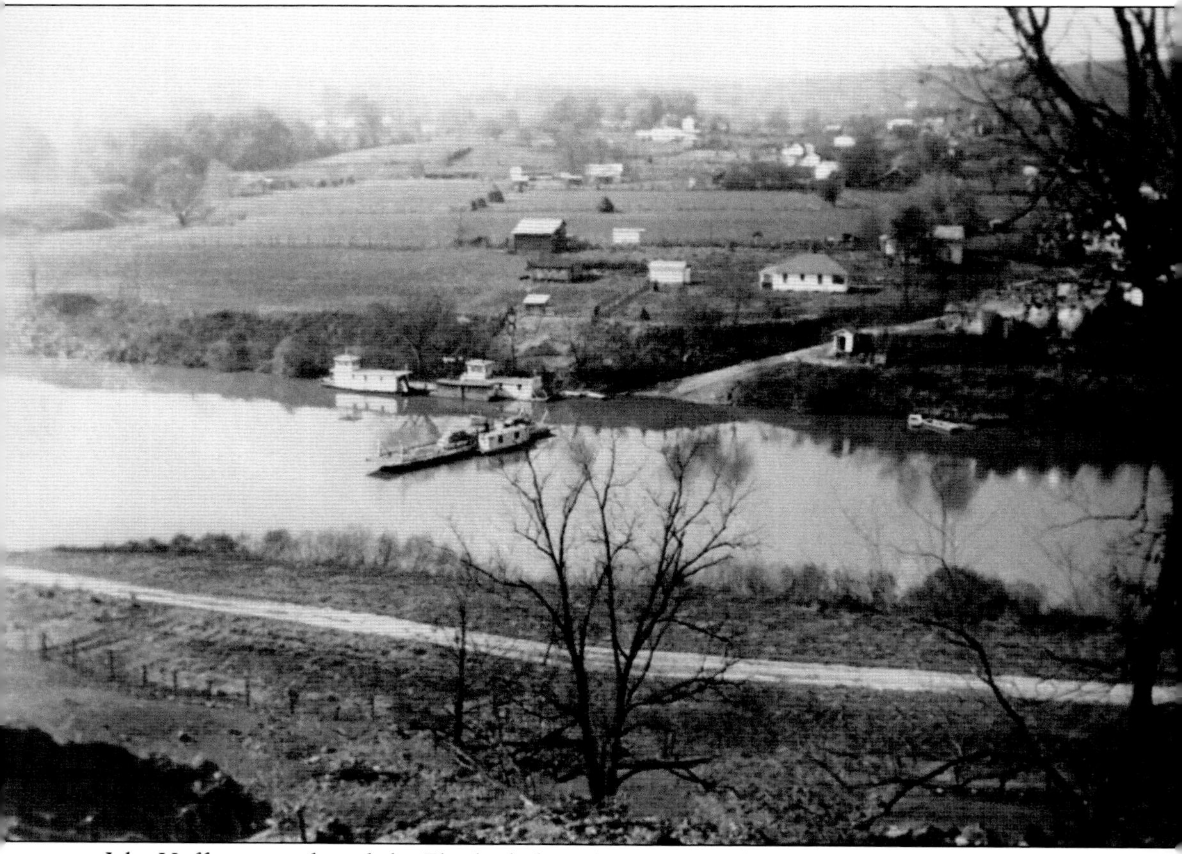

Jake Huffman purchased the Elizabeth ferry from W. L. Gibson around 1918. He operated the upper ferry at the end of Washington Street in Elizabeth until the new bridge on State Route 5 opened on December 1, 1949. River Road can be seen in the forefront of this photograph. (Courtesy of the DAP.)

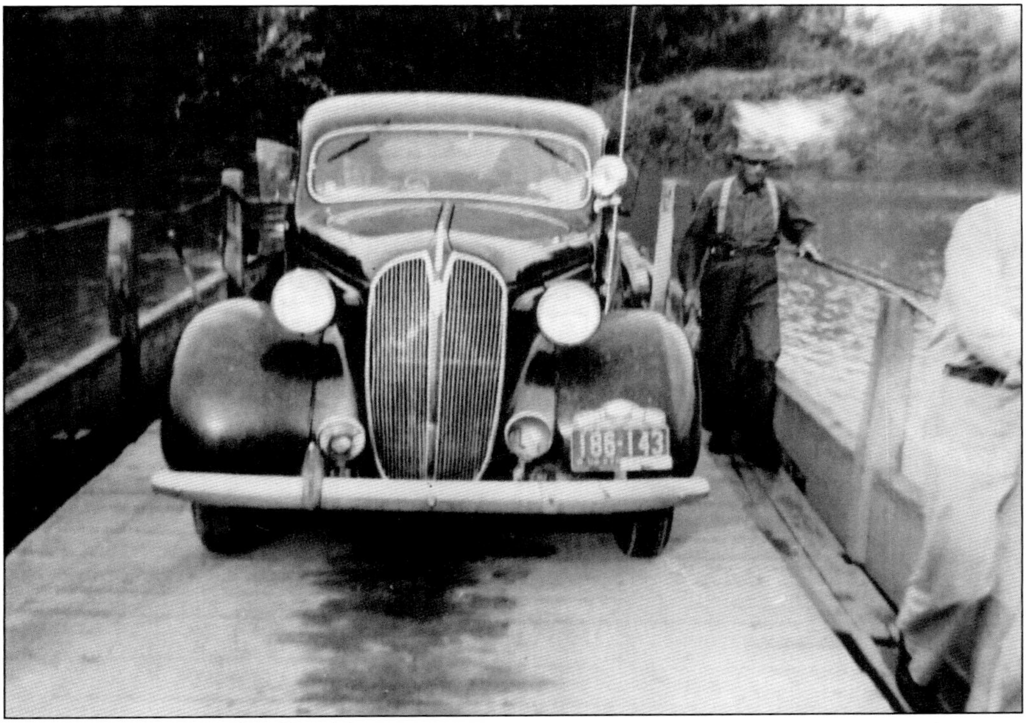

Newark ferryman Arthur Franklin is seen transporting a car across the river. The fare for a one-way trip was 25¢ for wagons and automobiles and 5¢ for pedestrians. (Courtesy of Marjorie F. Mayes.)

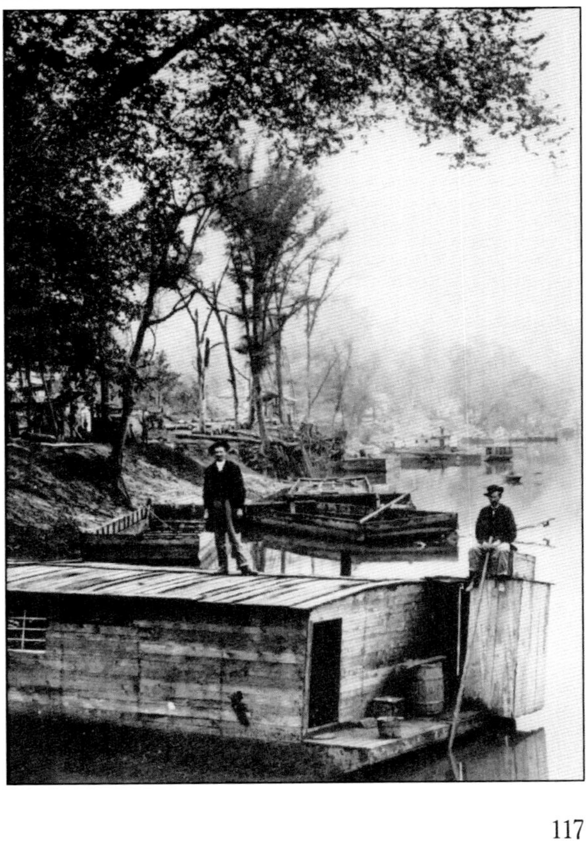

Following the discovery of oil in Burning Springs in the 1860s, houseboats became a popular source of shelter for oil field workers. This is one of many houseboats that lined the Little Kanawha River during the oil boom. These boats were often moored so closely that one could literally walk up and down the river on board the boats. (Courtesy of the Ludwig family.)

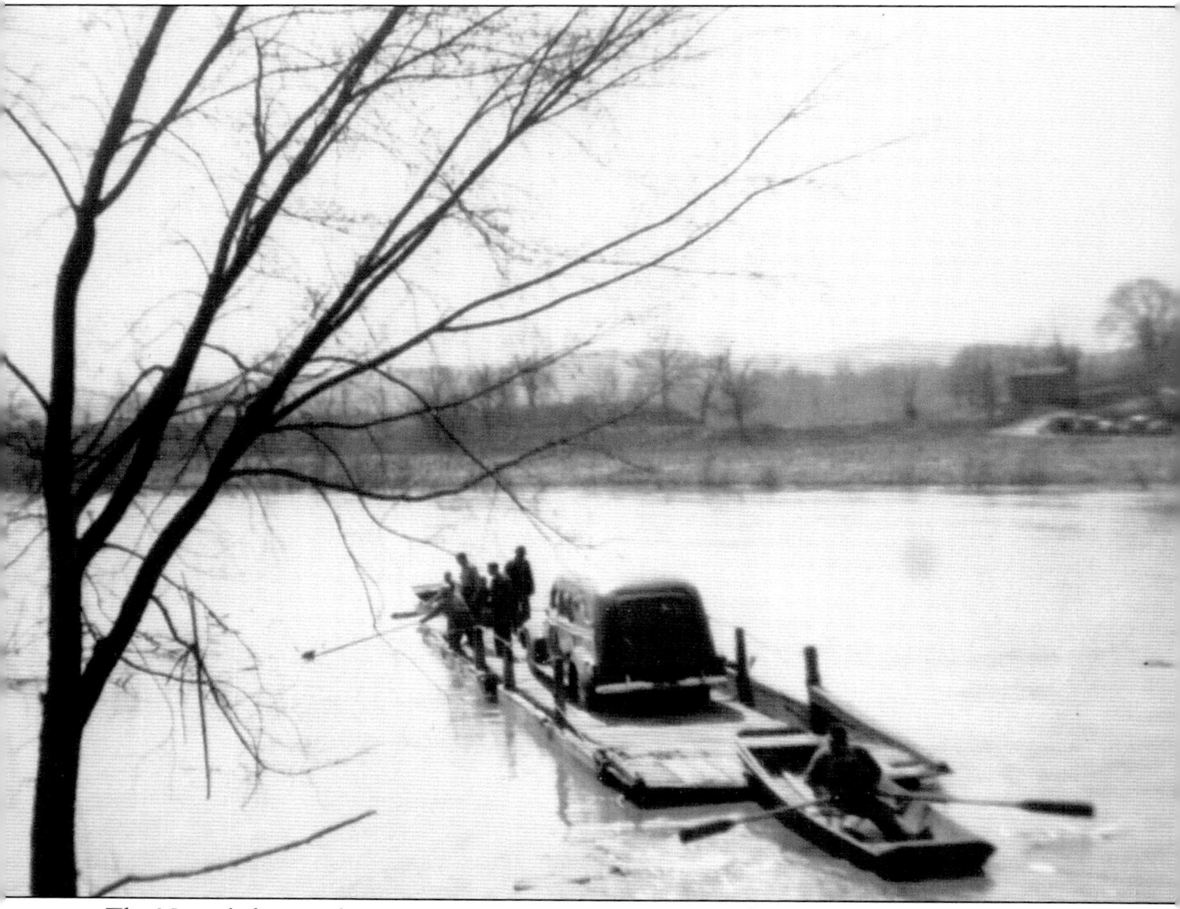

The Newark ferry is shown maneuvering its way upstream during the flood of 1948 in order to deliver the Franklin Funeral Home hearse to the dock on the other side of the river. The hearse was headed to the Fought Cemetery for the burial of esteemed Newark resident Theodoria Smith, who died March 25, 1948. (Courtesy of Marjorie F. Mayes.)

Eight

Fires and Floods

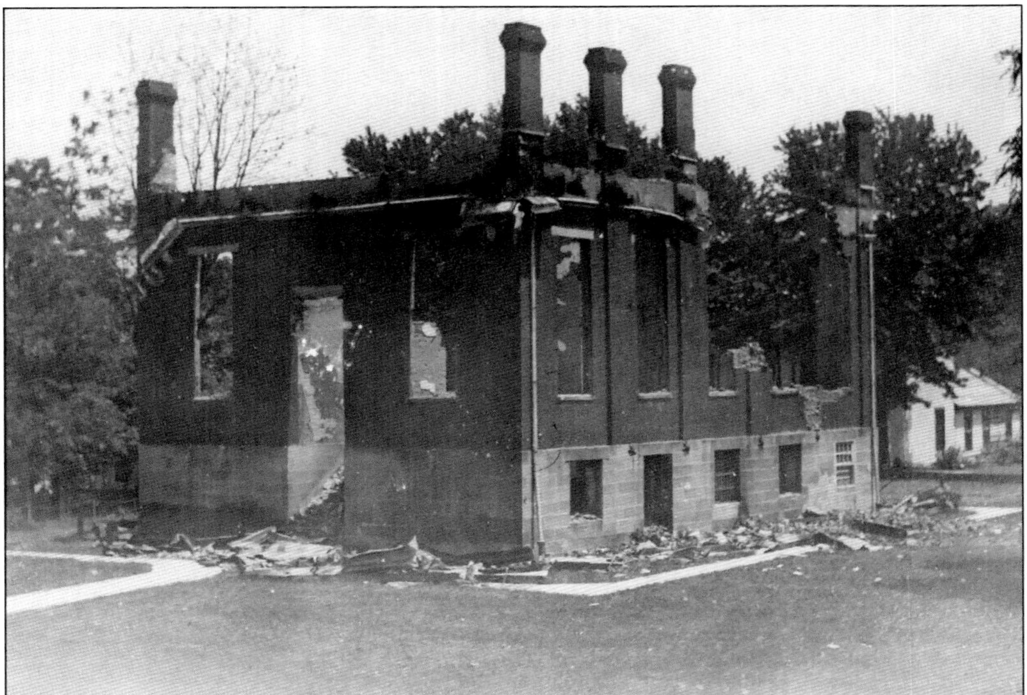

A fire destroyed the original Wirt County Courthouse in 1909. The fire originated in the courtroom when two prisoners attempted to escape by using a hot poker from a nearby stove to burn holes through the floor joists from their jail cell below. The straw matting that covered the courtroom floor above eventually ignited and created a fire that could not be put out. Some of the county's records were saved before the fire raged out of control. County court was convened in the grade school until a new courthouse was built in 1911. (Courtesy of the DAP.)

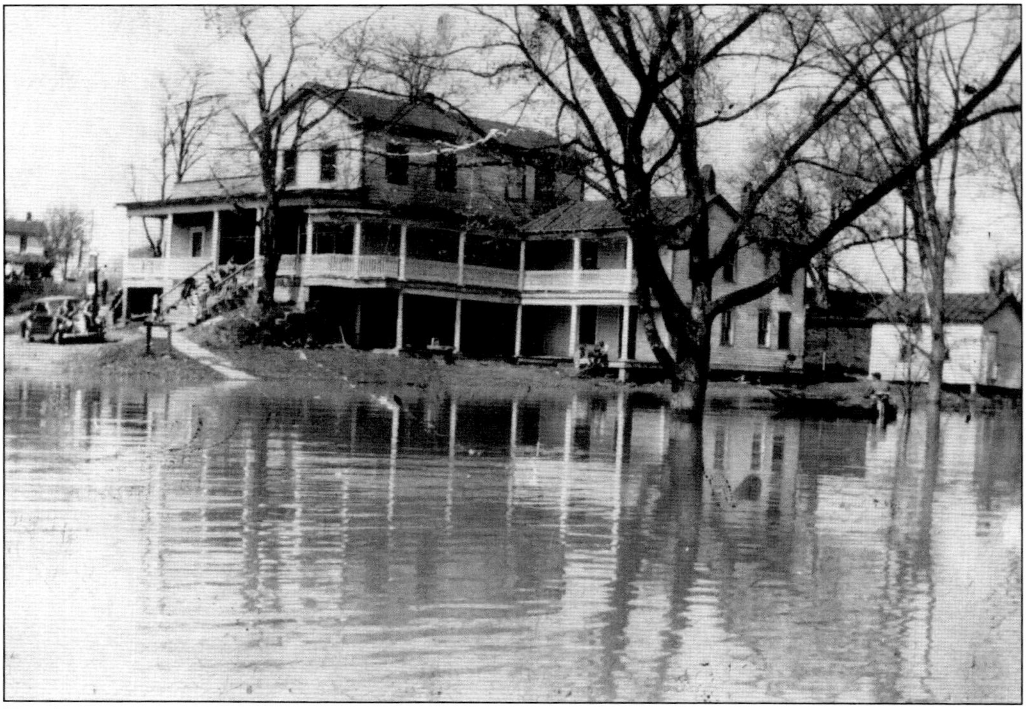

Fought's Store is pictured during the 1948 flood. (Courtesy of Marjorie F. Mayes.)

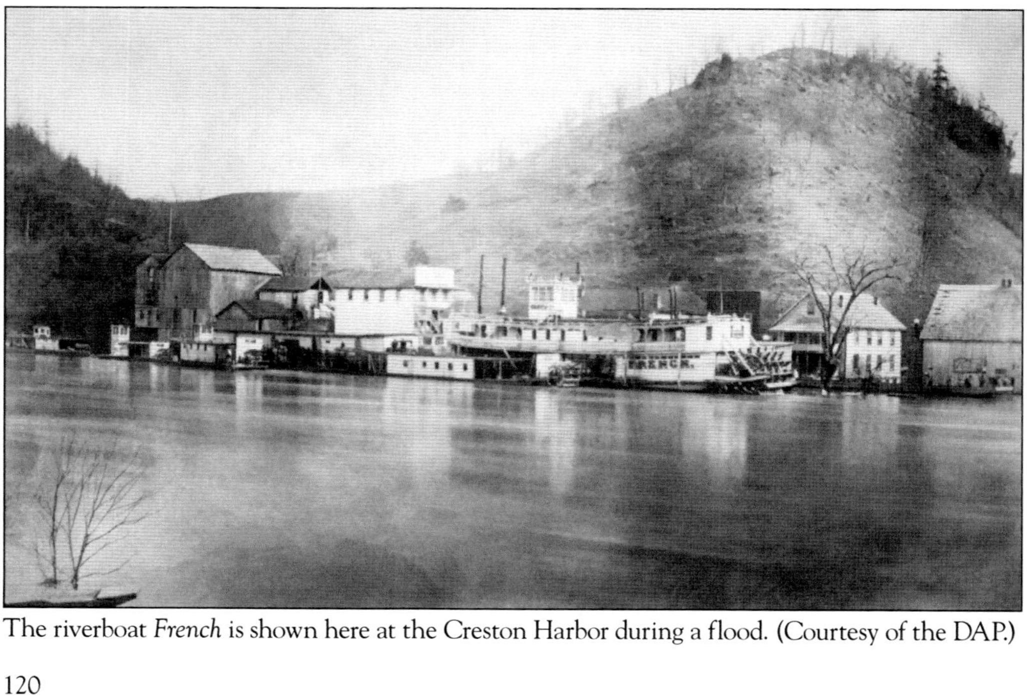

The riverboat *French* is shown here at the Creston Harbor during a flood. (Courtesy of the DAP.)

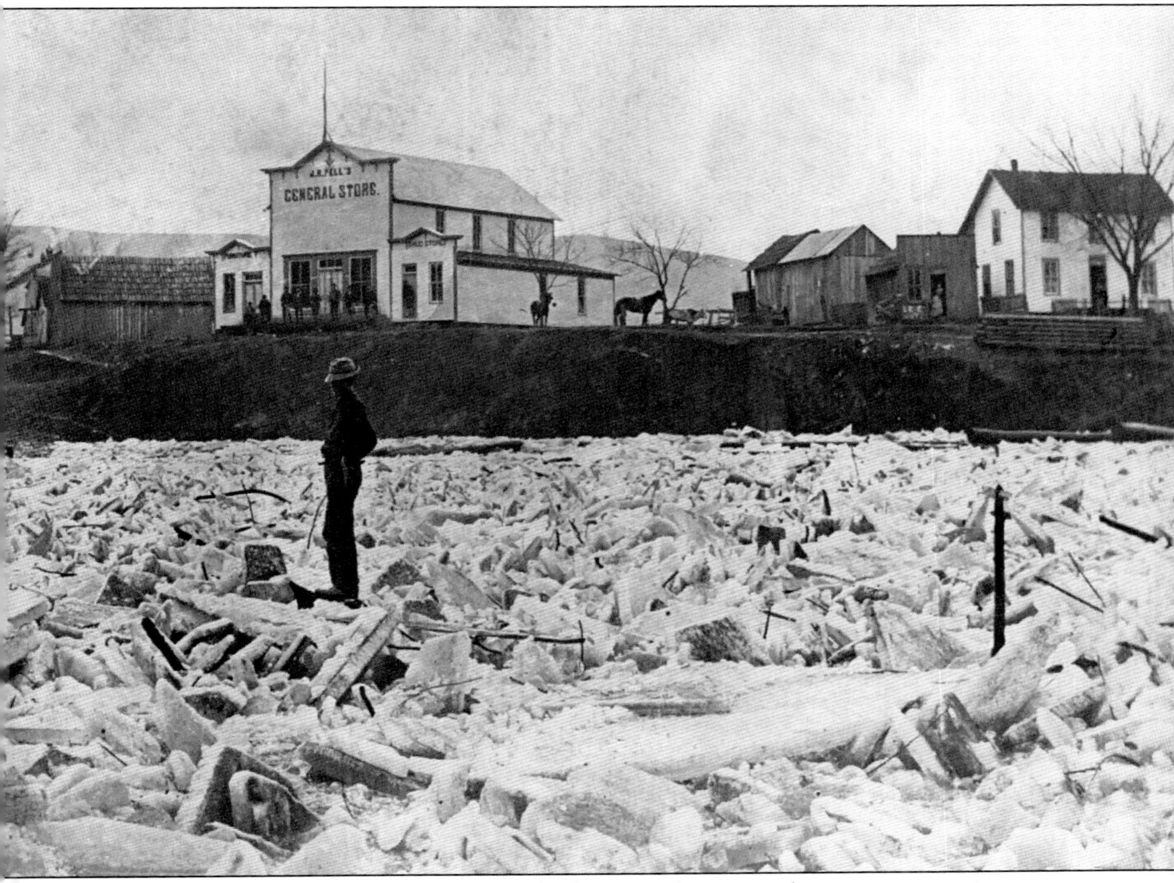

Patrons of J. R. Pell's General Store in Creston look on as a daring gentleman crosses an ice gorge in the river. (Courtesy of the DAP.)

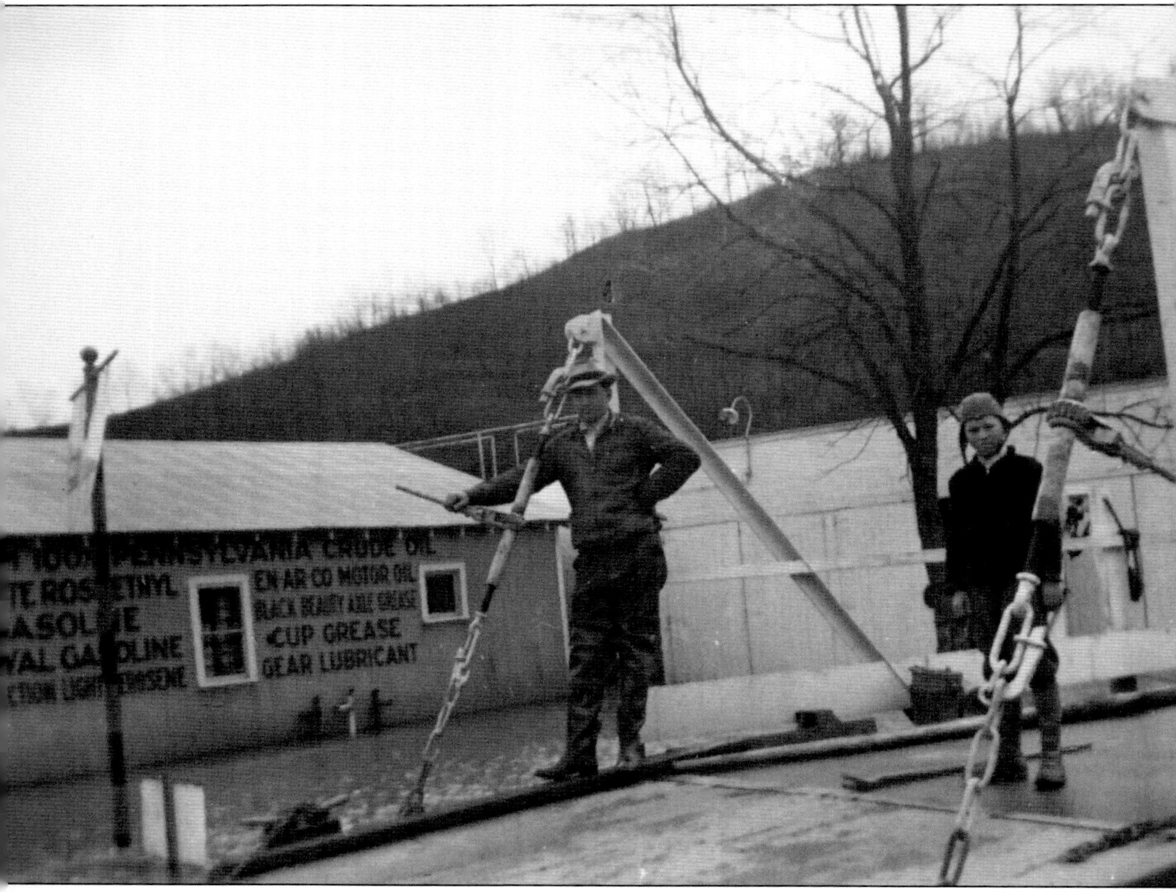

Ferryman Virgil Snider is navigating the ferryboat on the upper ferry located at the end of Washington Street in Elizabeth during the 1937 flood. (Courtesy of Annabelle Snider.)

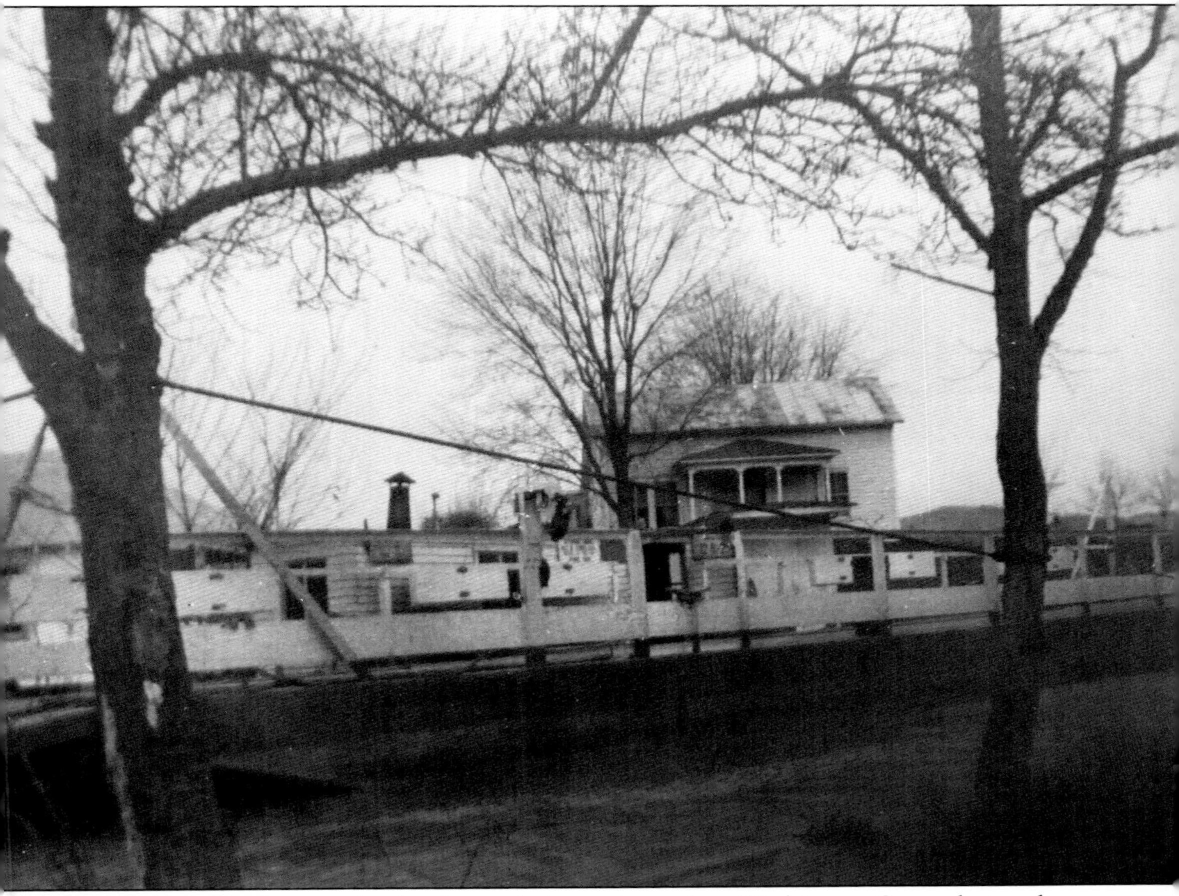

This ferryboat was photographed in front of a house located on Washington Street during the flood of 1937. It was one of five boats that owner Jake Huffman kept on hand to carry passengers across the Little Kanawha. (Courtesy of Annabelle Snider.)

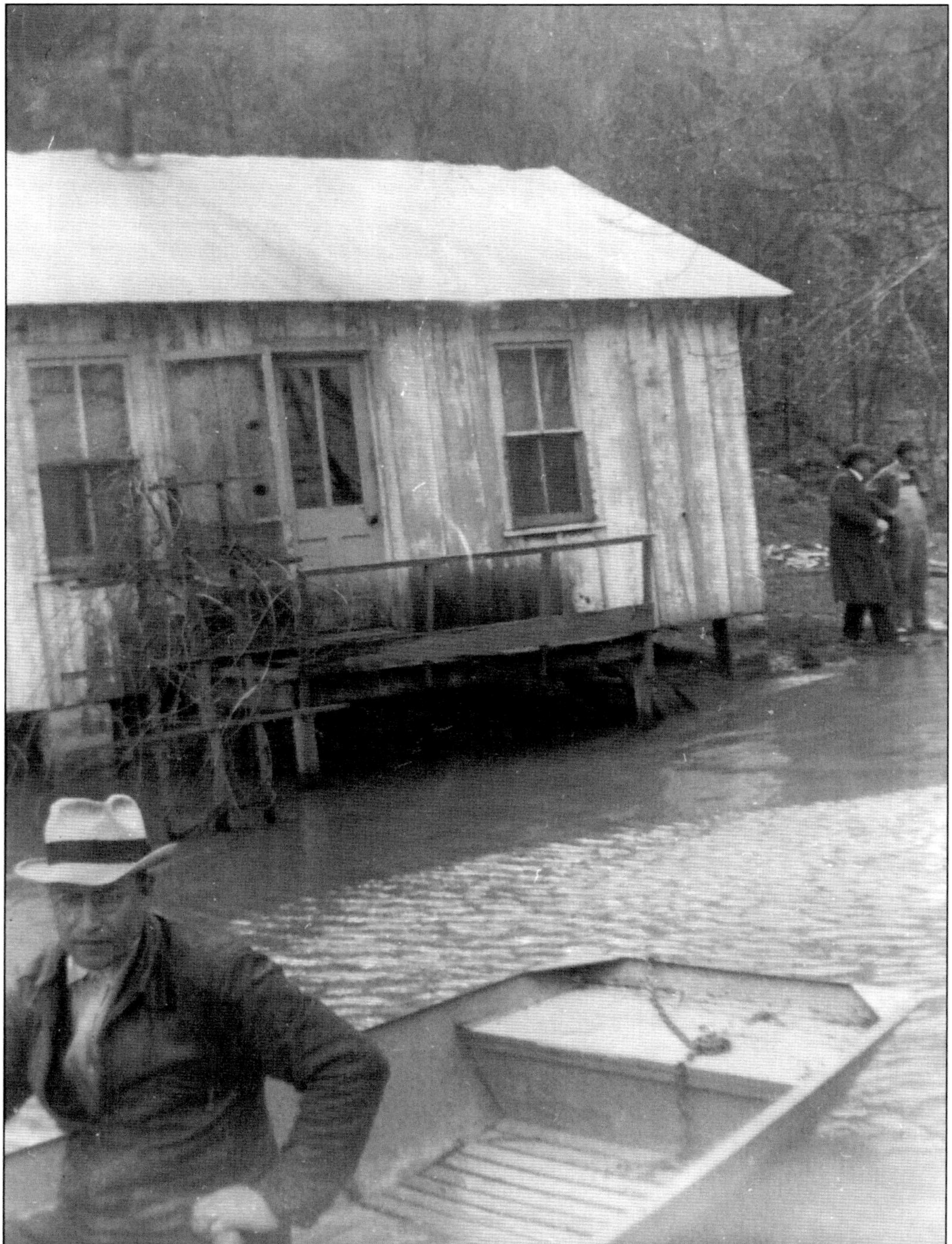

Virgil Snider boards a johnboat to assess the damages in Elizabeth during the flood of 1937. According to the Army Corps of Engineers, the floodwaters rose to 31.65 feet. (Courtesy of Annabelle Snider.)

Floodwaters cover State Route 14 near the old service station in Elizabeth. The station (right) was owned at one time by Jube Snyder and Everett Gibson and later by Roy Waggoner. (Courtesy of the DAP.)

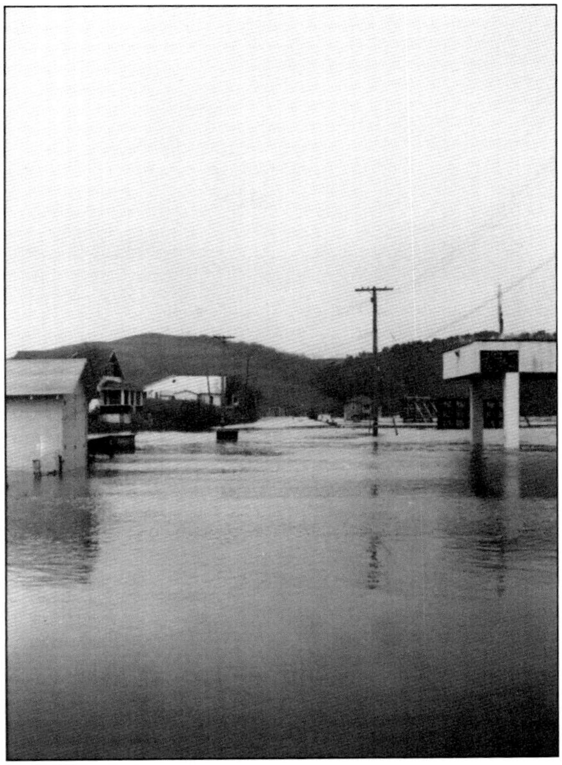

Clyde Hill's residence, below, stands on Mulberry Street in Elizabeth during the 1967 flood. (Courtesy of Sherry R. Smith.)

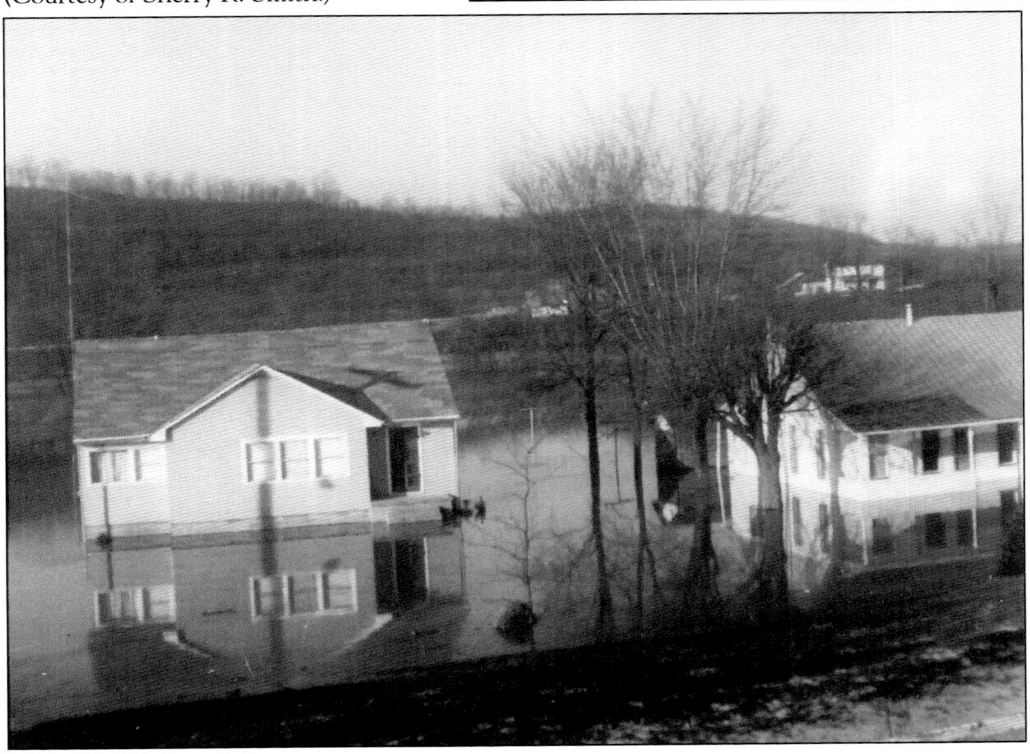

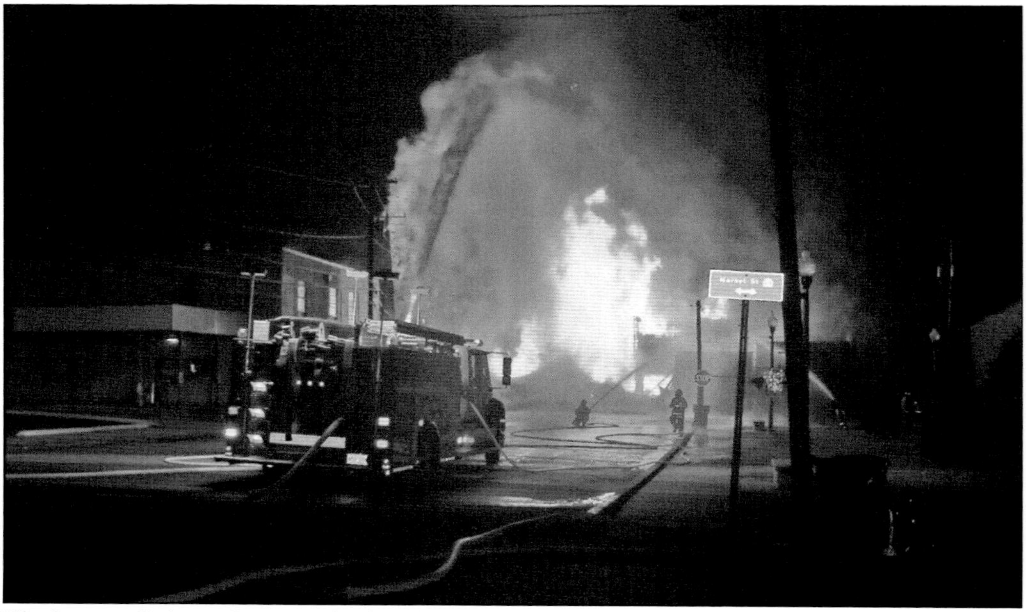

The historic Roberts Store in Elizabeth burned to the ground in an early morning fire on June 14, 2006. Firefighters from the Elizabeth-Wirt VFD were first on the scene, with several neighboring fire departments assisting. Arson was to blame for the fire.

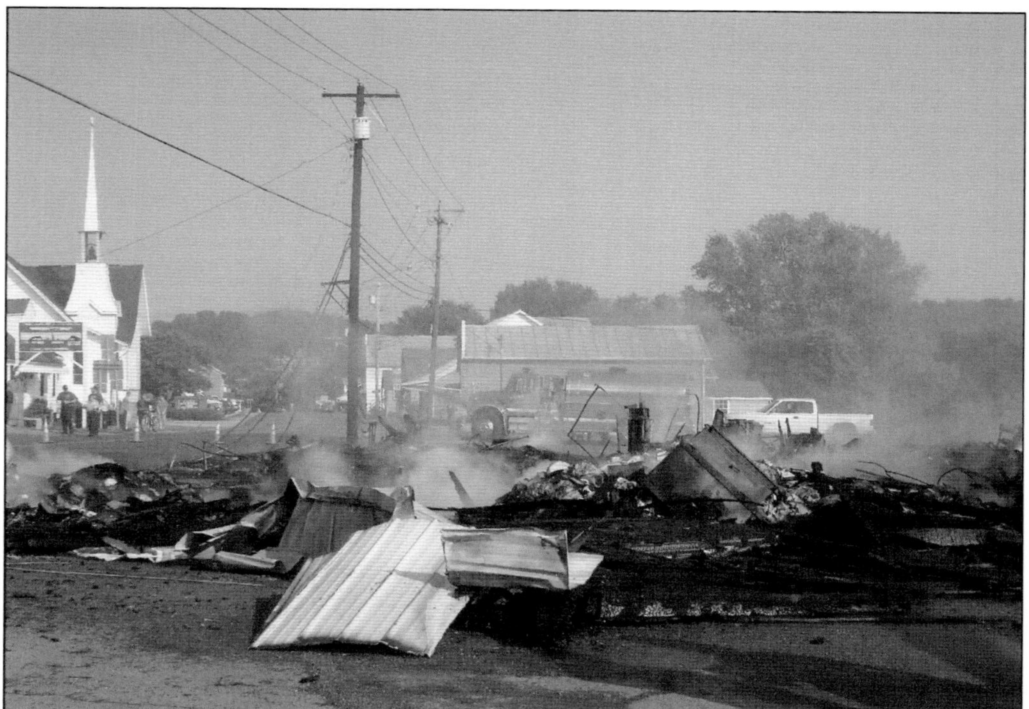

By mid-morning on June 14, 2006, this pile of rubble was all that was left of the 120-year-old Roberts Store in Elizabeth.

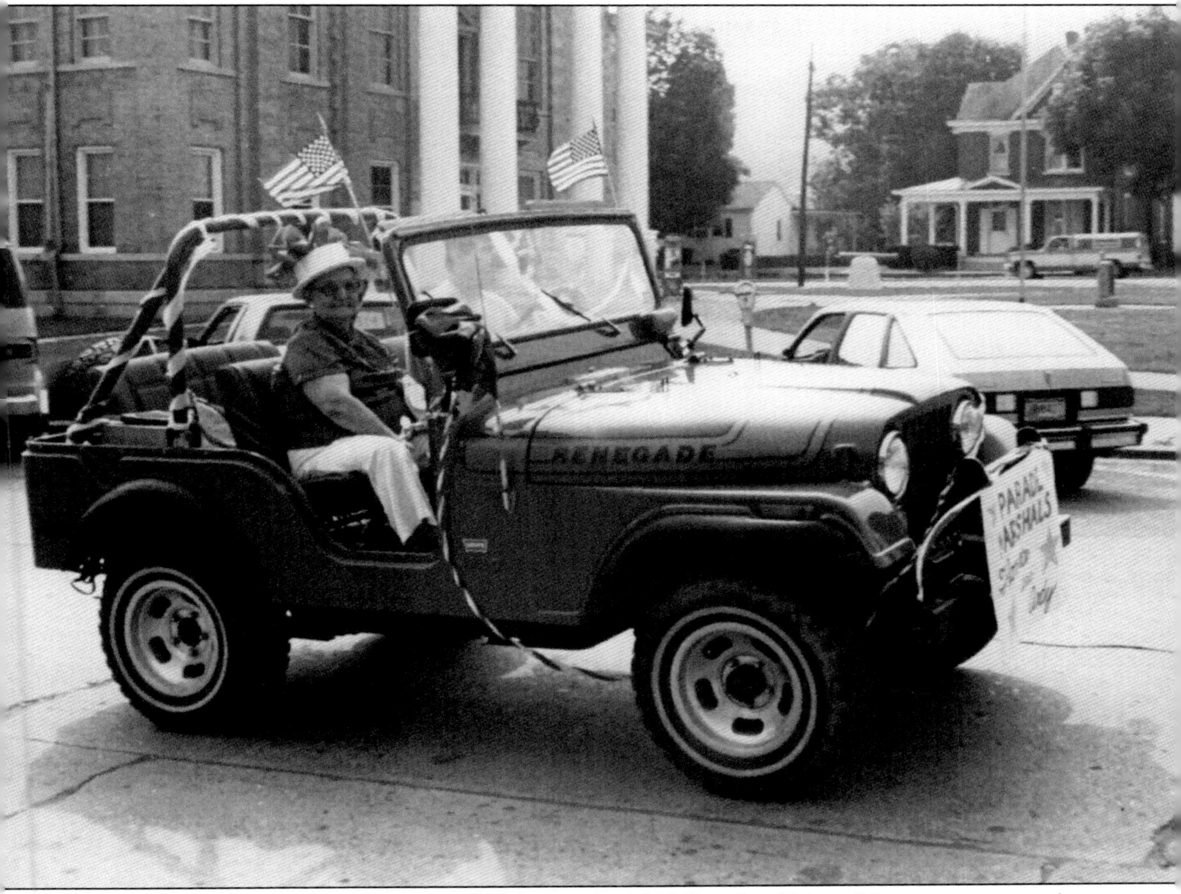

Florence Cline served as the parade marshal during the 1983 Fourth of July celebration sponsored by the Elizabeth-Wirt Volunteer Fire Department. Florence was honored as parade marshal for her countless hours spent in support of the fire department and the American Red Cross. (Courtesy of Basil Cline.)